The *Acts of Peter*, Gospel Literature, and the Ancient Novel

# The *Acts of Peter*, Gospel Literature, and the Ancient Novel

## Rewriting the Past

CHRISTINE M. THOMAS

OXFORD

UNIVERSITY PRESS

2003

# OXFORD
## UNIVERSITY PRESS

Oxford   New York
Auckland   Bangkok   Buenos Aires   Cape Town   Chennai
Dar es Salaam   Delhi   Hong Kong   Istanbul   Karachi   Kolkata
Kuala Lumpur   Madrid   Melbourne   Mexico City   Mumbai   Nairobi
São Paulo   Shanghai   Taipei   Tokyo   Toronto

Copyright © 2003 by Christine M. Thomas

Published by Oxford University Press, Inc.
198 Madison Avenue, New York, New York 10016

www.oup.com

Oxford is a registered trademark of Oxford University Press

Library of Congress Cataloging-in-Publication Data
Thomas, Christine M.
The Acts of Peter, Gospel literature, and the ancient novel :
rewriting the past / Christine M. Thomas.
p. cm.
Includes bibliographical references and index.
ISBN 0-19-512507-X
I. Acts of Peter—Language, style.   2. Classical fiction—History and criticism.   I. Title.
BS2880.P472T48 2003
229'.925—dc21       2002025821

1 3 5 7 9 8 6 4 2

Printed in the United States of America
on acid-free paper

*To my parents, in gratitude*

# Preface

When I first began working with the Apocryphal Acts of the Apostles, the second-century narratives of the exploits of the first followers of Jesus, I was stymied to see them frequently compared to the ancient novel in the secondary literature on this topic. For I had read Chariton, Achilles Tatius, and parts of Heliodoros, and these elegant products seemed worlds apart from the unsophisticated and clumsy Greek prose of the Apocryphal Acts. It was John Strugnell, one of my professors at Harvard, who said to me, "Perhaps you are comparing them to the wrong sort of novel." He suggested to me the Alexander romance as a better model, which became the point of departure for the present study.

Already the investigations of Virginia Burrus and Dennis MacDonald had demonstrated the utility of employing models from oral tradition to explain the odd compositional history of the Apocryphal Acts. My texts of the *Acts of Peter* did not fit neatly into this model, however: they were not the simple textual fixation of oral tradition. When one took into account the later editions of the *Acts of Peter* as a group, it became abundantly clear that the texts themselves were behaving in a fashion strikingly similar to oral tradition. The structure of the narrative from one edition to the next was fluid. The characters and motivations had been updated in each text to correspond to the present reality at the time of telling, a feature that is called "homeostatic organization" in the study of oral tradition. This surprised me greatly, since the later Roman Empire was not a "primary oral culture," but one infused with literature and literacy, as had been the Mediterranean world for centuries. In the course of further study, I became convinced that the key to understanding this phenomenon was the significance of the Apocryphal Acts as historical records. The successive "homeostatic" updating of the narrative tradition is a chosen strategy to maintain the relevance of a narrative tradition that is fundamentally historical. Correspondingly, as I continued my studies, the Apocryphal Acts began to look less and less fictional, although I would contend that they are still novelistic.

These features of fluidity and homeostasis are characteristic of many types of early Christian narrative, the other Apocryphal Acts and the gospels being the closest analogs to the *Acts of Peter*. Although the constraints of space have prevented me from drawing out the full implications of my findings for these related texts, this examination of the *Acts of Peter* should provide an illuminating case study for them. Moreover, students of the novel will find extended discussions on the relationship of the novel to history, and on the genre of the novel as such, which are important considerations for generic classification of early Christian literary works.

My list of debts is long. Most of the chapters were presented in one form or another in a series of conference papers from 1992 to 1994 held at the Society of Biblical Literature, for the Ancient Fiction and Early Christian and Jewish Narrative Group, and for the Intertextuality in Christian Apocrypha Seminar. It was my happiness to find that professional meetings do sometimes achieve their goal, for the discussion and individual comments after these presentations materially improved my work. In particular, I would like to thank Judith Perkins and Richard Pervo, both of whom have been generous and unstinting in their support and have given me the impetus of their own erudite interest in related questions; Dennis MacDonald, whose immense and learned creativity and spirit of respectful and productive controversy has been a gift to me and many others; and Robert Stoops, who has kindly allowed me to see his work in progress, who has never failed to offer me useful criticism, and from whose work on the *Acts of Peter* I have learned much.

This book is a substantial revision of my dissertation at Harvard University for the Committee on the Study of Religion. The writing of the initial draft was carried out in a sunlit office overlooking Mt. Auburn Street, a stone's throw from the hidden treasures of Widener Library, in the congenial atmosphere of the Society of Fellows. The support of this fellowship improved the quality of this work by offering the time for concentrated creative pursuits. My conversation partners at Harvard were many. It is my hope that the publication of this manuscript will not constitute the final chapter of these discussions with learned friends, whose faces I see before me as I write, but will instead constitute the renewed beginning of an ongoing conversation.

At the risk of leaving others unnamed, I would like to thank in particular Christopher Matthews, Bernadette Brooten, Allen Callahan, Georgia Frank, and Ellen Aitken for offering particularly illuminating comments on one or another chapter of this manuscript. Rebecca Lesses allowed me to see her work in progress and granted me hours of enlightening discussion on the topics of orality and performance. Helmut Koester and François Bovon together offered an expertise in early Christian literature that can hardly be rivaled and saved me from many an error, always with grace and kindness. Few experiences can match the probing intensity of the conversations I enjoyed with Albert Henrichs, many of which I still remember extensively. His native intellectual curiosity has afforded me constant encouragement in my work and has suggested productive lines of investigation. I was fortunate to have run alongside Larry Wills while he was engaged in a project on another type of novelistic literature, the Jewish novellas. He was not only generous, but completely unselfish in sharing with me his work in progress and in granting me long discussions of theoretical issues we were both pursuing at the time. A series of conversations in May and June 1992 were particularly crucial in determining the shape of this work. In the years after Harvard, I would also thank Thomas Drew-Bear, who faithfully read and commented on the articles that appeared as preliminary studies for this book and also gave the manuscript itself a careful reading late in its gestation. My husband Jorge Castillo helped me navigate the turbid waters of modern literary criticism, and my inability to master it completely results from my own obstinacy rather than any fault of instruction on his part.

*November 2001*                                                                        C.M.T.
*Santa Barbara, California*

# Contents

# Abbreviations

In the interest of making this work accessible to people outside the field of New Testament and Patristic studies, I have endeavored to keep abbreviations to a minimum. I have referred to biblical books and the Apostolic Fathers using the abbreviations typical in the *Journal of Biblical Literature*. Additional abbreviations include the following:

| | |
|---|---|
| AcAnd | Acts of Andrew |
| AcVer | Actus Vercellenses |
| AcPaul | Acts of Paul |
| AcPetMart | the Greek version of the martyrdom preserved in Codex Patmos 48 and Codex Vatopedi 79 |
| c. | century |
| l., ll. | line(s) |
| P. | Papyrus |
| Oxy. | Oxyrhynchus |

# Note on the Text and Symbols

Study of the *Acts of Peter* is hampered by the lack of widely available modern editions of its texts. The textual basis of this study may soon be outdated, for Gérard Poupon is preparing a new edition for the Corpus Christianorum series, as he has been for the entire time of the writing and revision of this book and the thesis on which it is based. For the *Actus Vercellenses*, I have used the edition of Richard Adalbert Lipsius, ed., *Acta Apostolorum Apocrypha* (Leipzig: Hermann Mendelssohn, 1891) volume 1. The edition of Léon Vouaux has certain advantages, but does not print the Latin of the martyrdom (*Les Actes de Pierre* [Paris: Letouzey et Ané, 1922]). Unlike Lipsius, however, I print the text as I reconstruct it, not the sometimes nonsensical readings of the Vercelli manuscript. I note the emendations consistently and offer the manuscript reading in brackets. The only exceptions are in the case of the symbols ‹ ›, when the letters between the carets indicate an emendation involving the mere insertion of letters, rather than their replacement; and the symbols { }, when these indicate my preference simply to drop the letters between the braces. In these cases, I do not note the manuscript reading, since it is obvious.

For the *Martyrdom of Peter* ascribed to Linus, I have also employed Lipsius's edition. G. Poupon has prepared a fine edition of this text with commentary, but it remains unpublished and is not widely available ("La Passion de S. Pierre Apôtre," Magister diss., Université de Genève, 1975).

Unless otherwise noted, translations from the Greek, Latin, and Coptic are mine. For the *Actus Vercellenses* and the Coptic fragment, I have benefited from the translations of Wilhelm Schneemelcher in idem, ed., *New Testament Apocrypha* (5th German ed., 1989, ed. R. McL. Wilson; Louisville, Ky: John Knox, 1992); and also from the translation of Robert F. Stoops, "Acts of Peter," in *New Testament Apocrypha* (Sonoma, Calif.: Polebridge, forthcoming), which he kindly allowed me to see in advance of publication.

In the short texual references "Lipsius, x.xx–xx," the first number refers to the page in the edition of Lipsius (volume one of the *Acta Apostolorum Apocrypha*), and the number after the decimal point to the line numbers on the page.

The *Acts of Peter*, Gospel Literature, and the Ancient Novel

# 1

## The Apocryphal Acts in a Literary World

### The Greek Novel and the Apocryphal Acts

The assertion that the Apocryphal Acts were most like the ancient Greek novel,[1] and shared their genre, purpose, and intended audience, has become common. The first problem with this designation, however, is that it raises more questions than it answers. The ancient novel, sometimes called the ancient romance,[2] like our modern counterpart, agglutinates with other genres, preventing easy classification.[3] Ancient novels incorporate letters, speeches, dramatic monologues, and topographical descriptions, such as those practiced in rhetorical instruction.[4] The plots of the romantic novels derive from New Comedy, and the interest in travel and in the local color of exotic places can be found already, in prose, in Herodotos, and in the περίοδος of Hekataios of Miletos;[5] the epic precursor is the *Odyssey*. Scholarly discussion still continues about the precise definition of the ancient novel and the delimitation of those works belonging to the category.[6] Particularly vexing are those novelistic texts that have closer affinities to history or biography.[7] Recourse to ancient literary theory brings little benefit, since the ancients neither had an exact analog to our modern concept, "novel,"[8] nor do the texts that we now consider ancient novels even enter their theoretical discussions.[9] The two references to them in ancient literature are nontechnical and disparaging.[10]

In order to make this generic designation more precise, it is necessary to investigate the shadowy realm between ancient fiction and ancient historiography. This is important not only for the Apocryphal Acts, but for ancient Christian literature in general. All of the Acts and the Gospels purport to be accounts of the past and usually focus on a single figure of profound importance for the history of the various Christian communities. Yet these accounts do not share the literary conventions of ancient historiography: their authors cite no sources, construct no consistent chronological framework, do not stress eyewitness observation, and give no explicit indications of their purpose in writing about the past—in fact, the authors do not come forward at all as self-conscious personas. Along with the other historiographers, however, they do attempt to present the logical course of a series of events and their causation; they also employ the literary technique, so common in ancient historiography, of scripting speeches to convey the overarching significance of the raw events and the motivations of the principal actors.

This comparison to historiography is simplistic, but it suggests that the appearance of such works as the Apocryphal Acts in the high Roman Empire was likely to raise questions about their proper classification. Their hybrid character, which integrated the techniques of novelistic composition into a narrative about the past, reflected a deeper questioning about the nature of fiction and history in their immediate literary context. As Glen Bowersock has argued in his Sather Lectures, now published under the title *Fiction as History*, the first two centuries of the Roman period witnessed an ongoing debate about the proper evaluation of prose accounts of the past and the nature of the truths that such works conveyed. Bowersock begins with the second-century discussions by Lucian and Celsus, and then cites the surprising number of imaginative reworkings of the *Iliad*, the Greek equivalent of sacred history, that appeared during the high empire: the Neronian-period account of Diktys the Cretan, the work of Dares the Phrygian,[11] and, in the early third century, the *Heroikos* of Philostratos. Whether fanciful or entertaining, these each attempted to give a revisionist history of Homer from a foreign perspective. Though they are considered "novelistic" writings, they focused on the events by which Greek identity was founded. They may even be considered "fiction," if this conveys the sense of an imaginative construction, rather than simply "what is not fact," that is, a story requiring suspension of disbelief.[12] Whether "fiction" or "novel," however, there is "truth" in these works to the extent that they recast the past in a form more relevant to their contemporary situation. The Apocryphal Acts may be doing the same.

The first sustained attempt to compare the Apocryphal Acts with the novel, Rosa Söder's 1932 study, depends largely on an analytical comparison of content. Söder examines five primary motifs shared among the Acts and the novels: travel, aretology, wonders, propaganda, and an erotic element.[13] Each of the Acts shows these characteristics in profusion. Söder acknowledges, however, that many of these features are widely distributed throughout all ancient literature. For this reason, she does not finally identify the Apocryphal Acts as novels. Although she finds ample similarities between the literary techniques employed in both, she determines that these "novelistic" features had their roots in historiography and epic; the Apocryphal Acts are not a mere continuation of the Greek novels.[14]

Söder attempts to strike a balance between two sides of a previous controversy. On the heels of Erwin Rohde's rediscovery of the Greek novel,[15] Ernst von Dobschütz wrote a brief article suggesting that the Apocryphal Acts were Christian novels in the literal sense: that Christians consciously used the genre of the novel as a literary model for their own propaganda.[16] Richard Reitzenstein's work,[17] in which he placed the Apocryphal Acts among the less literary aretological writings of antiquity, was a direct reaction to von Dobschütz's thesis. J. Flamion argued von Dobschütz's case at much greater length a few years later.[18] Söder's work can be seen as an attempt to mediate this debate by drawing in a broader spectrum of literature and treating it with greater nuance.

Reception of Söder has been fairly critical. Some of the reasons that Söder rejected the novels as forerunners of the Acts are weak, such as the presence in them of an aretological element absent in the novels—a feature Reitzenstein emphasized in his treatment of the Apocryphal Acts—and the "popular" style of the narratives in the Acts, which contrasts with the relatively educated and sometimes Atticizing language of the Sophistic novels. Eckhard Plümacher objects that aretalogy does not define genre, and that the surviving novels have varying degrees of literary sophistication. He then concludes that the similarities between the novels and the Acts can only be explained by a conscious use of the completely developed erotic novel as a literary model for the Apocryphal Acts.[19] Many critics have also objected that it is impossible to define a genre solely in terms of literary motifs, as Söder attempts to do.[20] How could an element such as "travel" be a generic characteristic?

Söder succeeded, however, in bringing into discussion a broader range of texts than previously considered,[21] pointing out promising issues for future research. After concluding that the elements common to the novels and the Acts are widely distributed throughout Greek literature,[22] she notes that the Acts show more affinities to works that, like the *Ninos* romance, describe the "affairs of great men."[23] Though it would have been a logical development to follow these leads, most scholars writing on this issue content themselves to criticize Söder's methodology, and continue to cite the novel as the nearest literary antecedent of the Apocryphal Acts.

## The Genre of the Apocryphal Acts in Recent Research

The ancient novel is not, however, the only literary model of the Apocryphal Acts to enter scholarly discussion. In recent years, several scholars have emphasized the affinity of the Apocryphal Acts with the canonical gospels. Wilhelm Schneemelcher and Knut Schäferdiek argue that these two corpora show close similarities in their compositional history.[24] François Bovon judges that, in addition to the novels, the canonical gospels are an important model for the Apocryphal Acts, more so than are Luke's canonical Acts of the Apostles.[25] Richard Pervo similarly considers the Gospel of Mark to be the nearest antecedent of the Acts[26] and considers the gospels to be "fictional biographies roughly analogous to the *Alexander-Romance*, the *Life of Aesop*, or Philostratus's novel about Apollonius of Tyana."[27] This is also not a conclusive solution, because the debate over the genre of the gospels is anything but settled. Yet the argument that the Apocryphal Acts are more like the Gospels than any other group of literary works signals a new direction in research on the Apocryphal Acts: the literary problems of these two corpora can only be solved in tandem.

Church historians working with the *Acts of Peter* argue that the milieu that produced them was ecclesiastical, not literary, and that Luke's Acts are the most appropriate model;[28] this is, of course, a circular argument, since one would still have to determine to which genre Luke's work appertained—a genre consisting of only one work does not exist.

The description of the Apocryphal Acts as a variant of the ancient novel, however, is the classification most often repeated, not only in specialized studies, but in introductions and handbooks of Christian literature. Individual approaches to the question admit nuance. Some classify the Apocryphal Acts simply as novels *tout court*.[29] Judith Perkins and, following her, Tibor Szepessy, consider the Apocryphal Acts to be a subset of the novel, an ideological novel or *roman à thèse*, though Szepessy ultimately decides that they are "un type spécial du récit chrétien."[30] With more specificity, Richard Pervo designates both the canonical and apocryphal Acts as Christian historical novels, since they are fictions about famous figures.[31] Others concede only that the ancient novels served as one model among others, or as one source of the literary features found in the Apocryphal Acts.[32] Niklas Holzberg recognizes the similarity of the Acts literature with the ancient novel, but characterizes the Christian texts as the beginning of the reception of the novel, not as novels themselves.[33]

The manner in which the novel has been used in scholarship on the Apocryphal Acts, however, has been unilluminating. The label "novel" is usually applied to works of Christian literature inconsistently, almost exclusively to those Acts of Apostles that were eventually relegated to an apocryphal existence outside the canon of the New Testament. With the exception of Pervo, scholars of the apocrypha either do not consider the genre of Luke's Acts as a related question, because they view the Apocryphal Acts as an independent phenomenon; or they assign the two works to different genres altogether, usually, as will be seen, solely on the basis of theological prejudice, or of judgments, which can neither be proved nor disproved, about the intentions of the works.[34] The canonical Acts of the Apostles develop the same topic as the Apocryphal Acts: the missionary activities of the first apostles after the death of Christ and the establishment of the first Christian communities. The lengths of the works are comparable,[35] and, though the Greek style differs from one to another, all the Acts exemplify a relatively unadorned *Koine*.[36] Yet the search for generic parallels has headed in opposite directions. The canonical Acts of the Apostles have repeatedly been compared to ancient historiography in the course of modern scholarship;[37] the debate was rather to what degree Luke's theological motivation limited his historical aims—was Luke a historian or theologian? As Richard Pervo has argued, research on Acts has turned a blind eye to the entertaining aspects of the narrative, the colorful, humorous, and fabulous elements that he catalogs in charming detail.[38] Such was never the fate of the Apocryphal Acts.[39] I have found no comparison of the Apocryphal Acts to historiography of any sort, a glaring omission in the case of works that claim to narrate the deeds of individuals that not only had real existence, but are among the most important figures in the early Christian community that preserved these works.

In the characterization of the Apocryphal Acts, their fictional quality and ability to entertain is often contrasted with "history." David Aune writes in a standard work on early Christian literature: "The implicit yet conscious intention of the apocryphal acts was both edification and entertainment . . . the author of canonical Acts presents his work as *history*, while it is clear that the authors of the apocryphal acts were basically writing fiction."[40] Harry Gamble writes with somewhat more nuance that the Acts of the Apostles show many of the generic trappings of historiography, though they edify, entertain, *and* inform. The Apocryphal Acts, the chief purpose of which was to edify and entertain (but not to inform?), had more in common with novelistic writing.[41]

Éric Junod, one of the editors of the *Acts of John* for the Corpus Christianorum series, attempts to distinguish "novelistic creation" from "ecclesiastical tradition" in the Apocryphal Acts. He recognizes a difference between historical fact that is true and ecclesiastical tradition that is thought to be true, and he focuses only on the latter, as a means of overcoming the dichotomy between fiction and historical truth. The only ecclesiastical traditions in the Apocryphal Acts attested in sources external to them concern the countries in which each apostle sojourned and the place and manner of death. Junod considers the rest of the narratives to be "free creations" of the authors.[42] The argument is necessarily circular, however, since Junod has assumed at the outset that the Apocryphal Acts are not themselves repositories of ecclesiastical tradition, but require the confirmation of sources with greater historical reliability to determine their traditional elements. From the beginning, the Acts are considered unreliable fiction.

Indeed, as suggested above, separating novelistic and entertaining texts from history in this class of literature is problematic; one wonders whether it is even desirable. Richard Pervo raises this question in his work on the canonical Acts. He argues, not that Luke's Acts have no historical purpose or merit, but that such exists alongside the more entertaining and humorous elements. His conclusions lead one to doubt whether ancient readers would have perceived a clear distinction between the Acts of the Apostles and the Apocryphal Acts. Further, if the existence of the Christian canon has blinded observers to the humorous and novelistic aspects of the canonical Acts, could it be that the Apocryphal Acts have serious theological and historical dimensions that have similarly been overlooked? Precisely these theological qualities led Ben Perry, a scholar of the ancient novel, to disown them as entertainment literature:

> In the case of the apocryphal Acts, . . . it ought to be clear to anyone that the principal purpose of the writers was to propagate the ideal of Christian asceticism, and not, as in the secular romances properly so called, simply to entertain the reader by a series of adventures of whatever kind.[43]

Despite Perry's optimism that this would be "clear to anyone," most scholars of Christian literature have argued the contrary, that the Apocryphal Acts were too frivolous to be anything but novels. As it has been used in scholarly discussion of the Apocryphal Acts, the term "novel" has chiefly been equated with "fiction" and employed to emphasize their entertaining and fabulous qualities, the colorful profusion of miracles and conflicts they narrate. "Novel" is thus defined by a tendentious reading of their content, and used as a label to distinguish the Apocryphal Acts from the canonical Acts.[44] Defining the genre of a work according to content alone leads to anomalies such as the one illustrated above, in which the scholars of Christian literature disown the Apocryphal Acts as serious writings on the grounds that they are too entertaining, and the classicist will not allow them within the pale of ancient novelistic literature because they are not entertaining enough.

These criticisms granted, it is not the purpose of this study to argue that the Apocryphal Acts are not, in some sense, novelistic—quite the opposite. Confusion in past research has resulted, not solely from the use of the novel as a generic model, but from the uneven application of this term to early Christian literature, from an unduly limited consideration of ancient novelistic literature, and from an inadequate range of criteria in comparing the two bodies of literature. Instead of using features such as the credibility of the narrative, or the (micro-)content of the text, its erotic, travel, or teratological elements, one must set the discussion on a more secure foundation by drawing further criteria into it, such as the treatment of sources, compositional procedures, fluidity or fixity of the texts, chronological orientation, and characterization; and by using these formal characteristics as points of comparison with other literature. If the Apocryphal Acts are "novelistic" in any sense, the comparison can also run in the other direction: consideration of these works can inform discussion of the ancient novel, as well.

## The Ancient Historical Novel

The five well-known *scriptores erotici*, consisting of Chariton (1st c. C.E.), Xenophon of Ephesos, Achilles Tatius, Longos (all 2d c. C.E.), and Heliodoros (4th c. C.E.), have dominated the study of the ancient novel. These erotic novels, or "ideal romances," are stories of young people who fall in love, are separated, and then reunited after countless voyages, shipwrecks, pirate attacks, sales into slavery, entombments alive, and attempted human sacrifices. The scantiness of the available data skews the perspective, however; many other novels are attested in addition to the five erotic novels, but most of them are either represented by mere fragments or by a sole surviving example. The fragments, however, testify to a far broader range of novelistic literature than the erotic, including even the comic and picaresque novels formerly thought to be the province only of Latin writers such as Petronius or Apuleius.[45]

The early development of the novel is a matter of speculation.[46] Few novelistic works have been preserved from the fourth century B.C.E. (Xenophon's *Cyropaedia*) to the first century C.E., precisely the period of literary history that would have most influenced Christian writers of the first and second centuries. The surviving novels and fragments, however, suggest that the Second Sophistic formed a significant divide even in the development of the erotic novel, quite apart from the other novelistic works then in currency. This is true not only on the level of language: Chariton writes a lovely but non-Atticizing Greek, and the *Ninos* fragments, though avoiding hiatus, have many *Koine* features;[47] the later novels[48] are examples of the Greek of the Second Sophistic.[49] On the level of literary form, as well, the pre-Sophistic novels show a much closer attachment to historiography than the later Sophistic and post-Sophistic products. It is true that even the Sophistic novels are "historical novels" in the sense that their settings are usually the distant past; most of them also make studied avoidance of references to Rome or her officials.[50] Only Achilles Tatius breaks the archaizing spell by placing his novel in the mouth of a first-person narrator, who approaches the author in a sanctuary as he gazes at a painting.[51] Even here, the references to "satraps," Persian officials, in the course of the story lead one to wonder whether this narrative, as well, was not meant to have taken place in the distant past.[52]

The pre-Sophistic erotic novels, however, preponderantly draw their dramatis personae from historiography proper. Chariton's Kallirhoe is the daughter of the Syracusan general Hermokrates, a figure mentioned several times in Thukydides.[53] The fragments of *Metiochos and Parthenope* suggest that it was set at the court of Polykrates of Samos, who is the father of the heroine; Metiochos is the son of the Athenian general Miltiades. The *Ninos* fragments refer to a legendary Assyrian king and a Babylonian princess, Semiramis.[54] Both Sesonchosis and Iamblichos's *Babyloniaka* have distinct historical settings. Moreover, many of the existing titles of the novels are formally identical to those used for ancient histories:[55] Xenophon's *Ephesiaka*, Heliodoros's *Aithiopika*, Iamblichos's *Babyloniaka*, the *Cypriaka*, Lollianos's *Phoinikika*, the *Lesbiaka*.[56] No less than three of the novelists call themselves "Xenophon," presumably an allusion to the historian of the *Anabasis* and author of the *Cyropaedia*.[57]

The Jewish novellas of the Hellenistic period show many affinities to the pre-Sophistic erotic novels. Greek Esther, Greek Daniel, and *Joseph and Aseneth* are all "historical novels" in the same sense; each is set in a distinct historical context, and the characters are either leading historical figures, or brush shoulders with them. They are also conversant to varying degrees with the same literary conventions known from the fragments and novels. But significantly, Esther and Daniel in their Greek versions predate even the fragmentary erotic novels; *Ninos* does not date before the first century B.C.E., and these two Jewish works must have been composed at the beginning of the same century.[58] It is tempting to believe that these Jewish novellas reflect the prevailing generic conventions of the erotic novel as it must have existed in the early first century B.C.E.: they are tales of romance and adventure based on historical figures, in a language far humbler than the Greek of the Second Sophistic.[59]

The Sophistic novels such as Achilles Tatius and Longos thus form the end point of the development of the genre of the erotic novel. Most likely they were, with the exception of Chariton, the only fully preserved examples because this most literary incarnation of the genre finally attracted the attention of the classes who would preserve them.[60] If this is the case, then the type of erotic novels in common circulation before the Second Sophistic—those that would have most influenced Christian literature in the first two centuries—may have been considerably less literary in their style and more closely related to historical figures and to the legends about them.

The historical decor of the pre-Sophistic erotic novels illustrates the literary pedigree of the ancient novel. The literary form of any novel, being an extended prose account, would have borne a striking formal resemblance to ancient historiography. Ben Perry has argued that, in classical literature, prose was primarily used for noncreative texts; texts that modern readers would class as "fictional" were written in verse.[61] These early erotic novels, then, are decked out in the external form of historiography. But these are not the only types of novels preserved from antiquity. Some novelistic works bear little resemblance to the erotic novel: biographies such as the Alexander romance, travel stories such as the *Wonders Beyond Thule*, comic novels such as the *Phoinikika*[62] and *The Ass*. Given the influence of the *formal* features of historiography upon this genre,[63] and the wide variety of novelistic works, the Sophistic erotic novel should not even be considered the center of the genre of the ancient novel.

All ancient novels, even the Sophistic novels, were "historical novels" in some sense, but the degree differed. For reasons both of chronology and of generic development, the more historicizing early erotic novels—such as Greek Esther or *Ninos*—or the less erotic historical novels such as the Alexander romance, may be more appropriate literary models for the Apocryphal Acts than the five surviving erotic novels. Like these earlier works, the Acts retell the stories of figures who were entirely real and historical to their readership, rather than the amorous affairs of average and otherwise obscure young people. In discussion of the generic classification of the Apocryphal Acts, the confusing dichotomies between ecclesiastical tradition and free invention, history and fiction, may have arisen in part because the Acts have been compared to the wrong type of novel. The use of the erotic novel of the Second Sophistic as the sole literary model for the Apocryphal Acts has tended toward their denigration as mere works of entertainment literature, rather than toward a consideration of them as literature meaningful to a community in constructing a vision of its past.

Thus the range and nature of literary works that might be considered "novels" in antiquity was broad; the treatment of the "historical" element in them varied; and the clear delineation between novel and history in antiquity was problematic because of their close literary relationship. This is a relevant factor in the evaluation of the Apocryphal Acts, not to mention other works of early Christian literature. Since the relationship between novel and history is more of a continuum than two sharply defined groups, works offering an account of the past could contain elements of both. "Novelistic" features should not disqualify a work from being a historical account. To distinguish rigorously between these two categories of literature is false.

## The *Acts of Peter* and Genre

The compositional history of the *Acts of Peter* provides relevant evidence for the overarching issues of its purpose, genre, and audience. The most striking physical characteristic of the *Acts of Peter* is the vexing multiformity of the text in the manuscript tradition. The search for the "original" version must be abandoned from the start. The *Acts of Peter* have a virtual existence as a collection of texts, the earlier versions serving as sources for the later, and the later existing as redactions of the former. The earliest source is a scrap of vellum in Greek preserved among the Oxyrhynchus Papyri, *P. Oxy.* 849, which contains some 28 lines. [64] Berlin Coptic Papyrus 8502 preserves an episode of the *Acts of Peter* that takes place in the first part of the narrative, in Jerusalem. [65] The most extensive version, the *Actus Vercellenses*, [66] do not preserve the work in their entirety. [67] They also do not preserve the original Greek, although the Latin translation is early, probably between 359 and 385 C.E.; [68] though flawed by occasional misunderstandings of the Greek, and displaying a tendency to abbreviate, it is otherwise slavishly faithful. [69] A further episode concerning a gardener's daughter, which Augustine knew in his version of the *Acts of Peter*, is present in the *Epistle of Titus*. [70] Greek texts of the martyrdom account, also attested in the Latin *Actus Vercellenses*, can be found in the ninth-century Codex Patmos 48, and in the tenth- or eleventh-century Codex Vatopedi 79. [71] Thus the earliest witnesses are a miscellany of excerpts and translations.

Later texts of the *Acts of Peter* are also valuable sources for the history of this narrative. Four later texts dating from the fourth to sixth centuries retell large parts of the *Acts of Peter*. The date of the Latin martyrdom account attributed to bishop Linus of Rome, [72] successor of Peter, is a point of controversy, though one is probably not far off dating it to the later fourth century. [73] It is a loose paraphrase of the Greek source text of the *Actus Vercellenses* containing numerous expansions, insertions, and paraphrases. At times, however, it is close enough to the Greek to correct the translation mistakes of *Vercellenses*. Pseudo-Hegesippos, a Latin translation of Josephus's *Jewish War* (*Hegesippus sive de bello Iudaico*), contains an episode closely related to both the *Actus Vercellenses* and the Pseudo-Linus text, and probably dates to around 370 C.E., since it was transmitted among the works of Ambrose of Milan. [74] The fifth-century *Acts of Nereus and Achilleus* refer to some of the events of the contest between Peter and Simon, which Marcellus recounts in a letter to two young Christians who have encountered some of his disciples. [75] The *Passion of Peter and Paul* attributed to Marcellus, a character from the *Acts of Peter*, diverges significantly from the preceding versions in its story, but overlaps in some of the minor narrative units, such as the arrest of Peter and the death of Simon Magos; it probably dates to the fifth or sixth century. [76] For the sake of convenience, the basic information about these versions is presented in tabular form in Appendix One.

With so many interlocking versions, to determine which of these is the "original" text, with all texts that come after it understood as redactions of it, and all that precede it as its sources, can only be done on the basis of some preliminary judgment. The decision to employ the *Actus Vercellenses* as a point of departure facilitates the study of the second century, a period of time as crucial for the formation of Christian literature as it is for the ancient novel. Though it is the earliest surviving version of any length, the *Actus Vercellenses* displays levels of redaction with variations among them analogous to the divergences among the later versions of the *Acts of Peter*. Reference is made to the entire collection of texts relating to the *Acts of Peter* with the phrase, "the narrative trajectory of the *Acts of Peter*." This refers not only to the existence of a collection of interrelated works, but to the fact that they develop in a certain direction from one version of the text to another.

The multiplicity of the versions, the entanglement of the sources, and the corruptions of the text that bedevil the textual critic have become grist for the mill in this study. It is simpler to consider the entire process of successive redaction a meaningful characteristic, rather than attempting to reduce what is complex by constructing an artificial text. Each successive version of the *Acts of Peter* is a reading of the former and can offer valuable information on the assessment of these texts by audiences much closer to the time of composition of the various versions than are we.[77]

The focus on the *Acts of Peter* as a single Apocryphal Act diverges from usual approaches to the Apocryphal Acts, which have been treated as a corpus in the history of research.[78] There are important similarities among them: each of these Acts can be assigned, at the latest, to the late second or early third centuries; relationships of dependence exist among some of them; and the five Acts were a corpus when the Manichaeans were reading and commenting upon them in the fourth century, and perhaps already in the third.[79] The advantage of the *Acts of Peter* over the *Acts of Paul, Andrew*, or *John* is that most of its remains are preserved in one continuous segment, the *Actus Vercellenses*, and not in a number of disparate fragments. Thus, it will be possible to investigate the process of composition for a more or less continuous segment.

Moreover, significant differences exist among the Apocryphal Acts, which are only coming into focus with closer attention to the individual texts. These differences require different methods for each text. Dennis MacDonald's work on the *Acts of Andrew* is an important counterweight to the present study.[80] The *Acts of Andrew* unquestionably represent the highest literary achievement among the earliest five Apocryphal Acts of the Apostles. Studies by David Warren and Evie Zachariades-Holmberg show that the Greek style is polished, employing a high ratio of participles in elegant periods, displaying a fairly consistent Atticizing style, and avoiding the more obvious features of early Byzantine Greek.[81] The author is aware of generic conventions, closing his narrative with an address to the reader that would be typical in a historical work.[82] MacDonald has cataloged an impressive array of intertextual allusions, mainly to Homer, but also to other canonical texts such as Plato. As he notes, if he is correct about even a portion of these allusions, one must grant that the author of the *Acts of Andrew* had in mind a serious literary project.[83]

For such a text, a literary study of the author's intention, and of the ideal reader that he or she constructs, is the proper approach. The *Acts of Peter*, on the other hand, although possessing a clean Greek and employing some facility with literary techniques, falls short of the aspirations of the *Acts of Andrew*. It shows a great love of participial constructions, but little ability to deploy them: the opening period of the Greek martyrdom account contains five genitive participles, in three genitive absolute constructions, with six different subjects, followed by a nominative circumstantial participle and two relative clauses, all dependent on the lowly verb εἶπεν ("he said").[84] In this sentence of eight printed lines, not a connective is to be found! The *Acts of Peter* also show no consciousness of the generic conventions of literary works.

This study is correspondingly less interested in proposing a literary genre for this work than in answering the historical question of how ancient readers would have classified it, and how they would have responded to its implicit claim to narrate events from the past. This is not immaterial for its generic classification but enters the discussion at a different point. Aristotelian definitions of genre are text-based, viewing a work as an inert object with features to classify. Structuralist approaches to genre are more interested in the act of reading than in literary works as passive objects to be described and classified. Structuralist study of genre takes into account the author and the reader as well, although it finds these roles encoded in the text as personas, as masks: the text itself constructs the *implied* reader and the *implied* author,[85] and literary communication takes place in the space between the two. From this perspective, genre can be viewed as a set of expectations on the part of the audience which are met, transformed, or perverted by authors; or as a contract between author and reader: the author signals her intent about the type of work she wishes to write at the outset and modifies this as the work progresses.[86]

Dennis MacDonald, for example, is working with a structuralist understanding of genre that also includes the important concept of an *ideal* reader, which is a construct of the text that points beyond it into the real world, explicating the competencies necessary for a reader to interpret the text correctly. Although the characteristics of the ideal reader of the *Acts of Andrew* become clear in MacDonald's study, he also notes that none of the real readers ever approached the reading that the author expected from his ideal reader.[87] No one in the history of its interpretation understood the Homeric allusions in the *Acts of Andrew*, although the early Christian readers were much closer to the ideal reader than is MacDonald: native speakers of Greek who lived in the world of early Christianity. No text can determine its reception. MacDonald argues that the best reading of a text is the one that most closely approximates the reading of the ideal reader projected by the text itself.[88] His argument is thus literary and aesthetic, rather than historical: his concern is what the text *means*, rather than what it *meant*. This study, on the other hand, is weighted decisively to the latter question, which is essentially a historical one. MacDonald's approach is indeed historically valuable in offering evidence of the type of literary work that was already possible in the late second century in the Christian church. But it also shows the limits of investigating only the generic definition and literary characteristics of a text, for the only readers to have understood the Acts of Andrew "properly" are the author himself and MacDonald.

The present study instead focuses on the reception of the text, thus placing its emphasis on the reader within the interpretive trio of text, author, and reader. The reception of a text is determined by the function it plays within its community of interpreters, that is, the reason it was preserved over a period of time with its specific focus. Reception also depends on the degree to which the readers share the conventions and background knowledge of the author. Even in antiquity, readers of the Apocryphal Acts would have appropriated them differently depending on their previous knowledge of the events and people described therein. One could thus posit multiple audience receptions of the Apocryphal Acts.[89]

At the heart of the study lie issues of relevance for the general world of early Christian texts. The Apocryphal Acts as a whole are extraordinarily valuable as a sort of "workshop" on the history of the transmission of Christian texts, as François Bovon has argued.[90] Traces of textual instability, or narrative fluidity, similar to that found in the Apocryphal Acts can also be detected in many of the texts now in the New Testament: the Gospels of Mark and John, as well as a few of the Pauline letters, may have undergone multiple editions; the Acts of the Apostles as they appear in Codex D also constitute a version of the work distinct from the majority text. Many of Jesus' miracle stories likewise exist in multiforms that are not necessarily the result of literary dependence. These cases are all controversial; indeed, the physical evidence is scantier and less univocal than exists for the Apocryphal Acts. Many of the sources of the works now in the New Testament have been obliterated, and a stable text of these works was also established relatively early in their history, much earlier than is the case for the Apocryphal Acts. The normative status that the works now in the New Testament soon achieved also cut short the stream of recensions and translations that is usual fate of the Apocryphal Acts. Thus, although the works now in the New Testament and the Apocryphal Acts may show great similarities in the history of their development, as they doubtless do in their style, literary devices, and subject matter, it is easier to follow and document the history of composition and transmission for the Apocryphal Acts.[91]

The *Acts of Peter* provide an illuminating example of a general characteristic of Christian narratives, one that is shared with many other works: the fluidity of the narrative. It is the purpose of this study to demonstrate that this fluidity depends on the function of these texts as narratives about the past, as histories. The successive redactions and reeditions are the product of a distinct type of historical consciousness, which is a conscious strategy for preserving a meaningful relationship between the narrative and the changing present.

# 2

---

## *Time and Revision*

### Literary Processes at Work in the *Acts of Peter*

Oral and Written Sources for the *Acts of Peter*

Both oral tradition and literary composition played a role in the development of the various texts in the trajectory of the *Acts of Peter*.[1] Moreover, oral and written sources cannot be dichotomized; they overlap in time. At no point was it suddenly decided that stories about Peter would henceforth cease to be told orally and that further development of the narrative would be committed only to writing. In the strict sense, this oral activity cannot be investigated, for any trace it left beyond the moment of its performance would either be in the memories of the audience, now long dead, or in writing, the substitute for memory.

Such a division between oral and written processes in the composition of texts is, however, too neat. It is simple to determine whether an author was using a written text when the verbal correspondence between the source text and the new composition is so high that it is necessary to postulate the presence of a written source text during the process of composition. For less exact degrees of "dependence," however, it is nearly impossible to distinguish whether an author was using an oral or written source. An author could use any source, written or oral, by means of an "oral" mnemonic. Citing a *written* text by memory, whether from a text read or heard, and citing an *orally circulating* tale would look the same, and perhaps, for the ancient world, have nearly the same import.[2]

It is thus easier, and perhaps more meaningful, to ask not whether two texts are literarily dependent on one another, but rather, whether one text is appropriating another by means of textually based procedures or by knowledge from memory. This still does not loose the Gordian knot, since use from memory can sometimes be extraordinarily accurate for smaller passages such as proverbs and apothegms, and thus determining whether text or memory is the source may be impossible in some cases; but to make the distinction between *textual process* and *memory*, rather than written source and oral source, might be closer to the conceptual framework of the authors and audiences of the ancient world. Albert Lord has suggested that, in societies with a lower degree of fixation on textuality, a written text can be treated as equivalent to an oral performance:

the oral poet feels free to use either one as an unfixed entity, a basis for a new performance from memory.[3] The critical difference in this case is not the use *of* writing, but the use *to which* writing is put. Writing does not invariably mean a desire to fix a text, nor is a written version always viewed as superseding all other possible performances or recastings of a narrative.[4] The question is not whether the source text for a document is written or oral, but the means by which the source is being appropriated.

Within the written sources that comprise the trajectory of the *Acts of Peter*, both of these means can be isolated. Literary activities, such as the excerpting, revision, and expansion of a source, have left their traces in the text. Additionally, traditions and narrative units cited from memory or used as a basis for new performances of the narrative have affected the shape of the texts in the *Acts of Peter* trajectory. These phenomena are two sides of the same coin, that is, they are *both* expressions of the nonfixity of the text and its perpetual revision and reapplication. They also cannot be clearly and easily separated in the history of transmission. The *methods* by which they can be detected differ, however, and that is why the two processes will be treated in separate chapters.

The literary processes at work in the *Acts of Peter*, the subject of this chapter, can be detected by standard source criticism, the handmaid of classical philology. Source criticism has become somewhat unpopular in recent years because of its tendency to generate elaborate theories about multiple sources and recensions, which sometimes obscure the meaning of the narrative rather than clarify it. I would plead with my readers for patience, however, because my use of source criticism actually intends the opposite of the usual aim of this method. The goal of text-critical investigations of manuscript transmission is usually the production of a single text, achieved by weighing the various manuscript witnesses against one another, in consideration of their relative age, accuracy, and the relationships of dependence among them. When it is clear that none of the available manuscripts is particularly close to the common source, source-critical investigation is meant to permit its reconstruction, or, at the least, the identification of those passages of the text that pertain to an older form of the text.

In the case of the *Acts of Peter*, however, a fixation with the search for an "original text" is not particularly meaningful. Instead, the very lack of anything resembling an "original text" is so striking a characteristic that it must form an important component of any literary or generic description of the work. It was the tendency of the *Acts of Peter* to resist fixed transmission from one manuscript to the next and to change rapidly, the better to accommodate the new historical circumstances in which the narrative was being reenacted. Source criticism is employed in this chapter because it is the appropriate tool for finding traces of the continuing processes of literary composition that formed the *Acts of Peter*. I hope in the following pages to identify clearly several of its component layers. I cannot, and do not attempt to "sift" every passage of the text to determine which part belongs to which layer. This is not possible, and tends to eclipse the skill of the authors in creating a harmonious narrative at each point in its history. More important is the general picture of a text that changed at various points in time. If the resultant picture seems complicated, this is only a demonstration of how common it was for the tradents of this tale to alter the text each time they wrote it. Investigation of the literary processes at work in the *Acts of Peter* is an initial entry into a stream of composition, redaction, translation, and adaptation that existed from the beginning of the narrative tradition and continued for centuries.

## Oral and Literate Models for the Composition of the Apocryphal Acts

Research on the development of the Apocryphal Acts has oscillated between a purely literary view of their origins and the hypothesis that orally circulating traditions played a role in their development. In the history of research, a direct relationship exists between the particular view of the history of the composition of the Apocryphal Acts and their generic evaluation. Scholars espousing the literary hypothesis tend to classify the Acts as novels or fictional works of some kind, and scholars holding to the oral hypothesis turn to folktales or gospel literature for their models. The admission of an oral component in the Apocryphal Acts, in fine, usually places it beyond the pale of strict generic classification and relegates it to the undefined sphere of *Kleinliteratur*.[5]

A proponent of the traditional oral hypothesis, Wilhelm Schneemelcher stresses the affinity of the Apocryphal Acts to the Gospels: in the case of both, he claims, individual units of oral tradition were committed to writing.[6] Form criticism, as employed in research on the Gospels, would then be the appropriate method. Schneemelcher suggests using the pronounced episodic style of the Apocryphal Acts as a guide to isolate the independent units out of which they were composed. The theological contradictions within individual Acts support this piecemeal model; the influence of variegated traditional materials may be what renders each of these Acts internally inconsistent in narrative style and theological perspective.[7] This hypothesis has gathered few adherents. Aside from Hans Conzelmann's article on an episode in the *Acts of Thomas*,[8] the only recent form-critical study is Robert Stoops's unpublished dissertation on vision reports and miracle stories in the *Acts of Peter*.[9]

The studies of Virginia Burrus and Dennis R. MacDonald represent a different approach to the question of the oral traditional sources of the Acts, informed more by recent cultural anthropological studies of orality rather than the various "criticisms" of standard German New Testament scholarship.[10] Both Burrus and MacDonald are primarily interested in the communities circulating the oral narratives that became the sources of the Apocryphal Acts.[11] Each of them assigns the storytelling function to women, making an implicit contrast between the illiterate common women and the literate male church hierarchy.[12] Though strongly sociocultural in their interest in the role of the Apocryphal Acts within their communities, these works also afford new insights on a literary level: instead of seeking parallels among the literary products of antiquity, both scholars turn to the themes and modes of transmission known from folklore. Burrus adapts a structuralist approach along the lines of Propp's classification of Russian folktales; MacDonald points out signs of "oral content" and "oral structure" that the Apocryphal Acts share with folklore.

Those who evaluate the Acts as literary compositions turn instead to source criticism. Some isolate liturgical materials in the *Acts of John* and *Peter*.[13] Éric Junod and Jean-Daniel Kaestli contrast the theology of the narrative sections of the *Acts of John* to that of the "preaching of John" (chaps. 87–105), a large independent unit assigned to these Acts.[14] In another study, Junod points out the shortcomings of source criticism, arguing that the *Acts of John* are too unified in vocabulary and style to permit the clear detection of source documents.[15]

Since the edition and study of the *Actus Vercellenses* by Richard Lipsius,[16] the *Acts of Peter* have undergone a variety of source-critical examinations, particularly early in this century by Carl Schmidt and J. Flamion.[17] The most recent treatment of the question is that of Gérard Poupon, who reviews the present state of the source-critical investigation and offers a new hypothesis on their levels of redaction.[18] After searching through the more recent manuscript discoveries for evidence of a text-form of the *Acts of Peter* earlier than the *Actus Vercellenses*, he concludes that the *Actus Vercellenses* remain the best source and proceeds to separate the latest layer of redaction from an earlier text form. Poupon views the problematic passages as traces of a consistent and thoroughgoing redaction, whereas Flamion takes this as evidence that the *Actus Vercellenses* were composite from the start.[19]

## The Earliest Manuscripts of the *Acts of Peter*

The *Actus Vercellenses*, the most significant witness to the *Acts of Peter*, are composed in Latin. The earliest surviving witnesses to the *Acts of Peter* are two fragments, both from around the fourth century,[20] the earlier in Greek, the later in Coptic. Both of them already represent some editorial activity upon the text. The Coptic is a translation of the original Greek in a tiny excerpt. The Greek fragment, though preserving the original language, is also an excerpt. In the corner of the codex fragment appear page numbers 167 and 168. According to the calculations of the editors, Grenfell and Hunt, the previous 166 pages of the codex would correspond to about 996 lines in the Lipsius edition. The *Actus Vercellenses* text of Lipsius up to the point at which it overlaps with the fragment occupies about 908 lines,[21] so the Greek codex held an excerpt of the *Acts of Peter* that began only a bit earlier in the narrative than the *Actus Vercellenses*,[22] which themselves only represent about two-thirds of the more complete version owned by the fourteenth-century church father Nikephoros.

The Greek fragment is vellum,[23] first published by Grenfell and Hunt in 1908 (*P. Oxy.* 849), comprising only twenty-eight short lines. The text spans chapters 25–26 of the Latin work,[24] which find Peter in the process of performing two resurrections, first of a young man, the emperor's favorite, and then of the only son of a poor widow; these feats form part of the contest against Simon Magos in the forum. The Greek text corresponds so closely to the Latin of the passage in the *Actus Vercellenses* that the text of the fragment must be nearly identical with that of the Greek version translated in the *Actus Vercellenses*.[25] The Latin of the *Actus Vercellenses* faithfully represents the word order of the Greek fragment and also translates idiomatic phrases literally:[26] for example, for ἡδέως ἔχει (ll. 16–17, Grenfell and Hunt), the *Actus Vercellenses* read *libenter habet* (Lipsius 73.22). The divergences are minor: twice the *Actus Vercellenses* add to the Greek text to indicate a location more specifically: ἐκεῖ (l. 10) is translated *ad Petrum* (Lipsius 73.19), resulting in greater clarity, and *in foro* is added to the translation of the Greek after *praefectus* (Lipsius 73.20). The Greek contains only one phrase not in the *Actus Vercellenses* translation (l. 6–7, ἄρα βούλει, μῆτερ). The fragment is chiefly of value as an early witness to the *Acts of Peter*, and as a guarantor of the general reliability of the Latin of the *Actus Vercellenses*.[27]

The Coptic fragment, first edited by Schmidt,[28] closes out the codex Papyrus Berolinensis 8502, discovered in 1896. The *Act of Peter*, as the text designates itself in a *subscriptio* (ⲧⲉⲡⲣⲁϫⲓⲥ ⲙⲡⲉⲧⲣⲟⲥ), occupies the pages following the *Gospel of Mary*, the *Apocryphon of John,* and the *Sophia of Jesus Christ,* copies of the latter two of which were also found among the Nag Hammadi codices discovered in 1945. The Coptic codex dates to the fourth to fifth century on the basis of the script and contains 144 pages (72 leaves); the first twelve pages (six leaves) of the manuscript are lost, as is the fourth leaf before the end of the codex. Since our story appears on the last fourteen pages of the codex, the missing leaf falls in the middle of the *Act of Peter.* In the *Act,* a crowd asks Peter why he does not heal his daughter, who is lying paralyzed near his house; Peter responds by first making her walk and then restoring her paralysis. To justify his surprising action, he narrates an incident from the past: when the daughter was ten years old, a certain Ptolemaios, enamored by her beauty, carried her off; at the prayers of her parents, she suddenly became paralyzed, and Ptolemaios returned the girl to her home unharmed.

As Andrea Molinari has recently demonstrated, the *subscriptio* that reads "Act of Peter" is not conclusive evidence that this fragment was excerpted from the *Acts of Peter* attested in the *Actus Vercellenses.*[29] Several other pieces of evidence, however, offer convincing proof that the excerpt belongs to the *Acts of Peter.* Augustine mentions that some Manichaeans read this episode in the apocrypha (*contra Adimantum* 17):

> in the apocrypha, they read as an important work the one that I have mentioned about the apostle Thomas, and [they read] that the daughter of Peter himself became paralyzed through the prayers of her father, and that the gardener's daughter died at the prayer of the same Peter. They reply that this was expedient for them, that the one should be crippled with paralysis and the other die, and they also do not deny that this was brought about by the prayers of the apostle.[30]

Augustine attributes this episode only to the "apocrypha," though it is clear that he means a written work (*opus legere*). Although it is true that the Latin word *apocrypha* as used in Augustine encompasses many more works than the Apocryphal Acts, it is highly likely, given the immediate context, that Augustine is referring to the Apocryphal Acts. After discussing God's loving vengeance in the episode of Ananias and Sapphira in Acts 5:1–11, Augustine recognizes that the Manichaeans reject the canonical Acts of the Apostles and proceeds to use examples from the apocryphal writings that they accept. The Apocryphal Acts are the obvious generic counterpart to the canonical Acts of the Apostles, and the use and acceptance of the five earliest Apocryphal Acts among the Manichaeans is well known.[31] Moreover, the work about Thomas mentioned in the same sentence is clearly the *Acts of Thomas.* Last, the redactional phrase, "this was expedient for them" (*hoc eis expediebat*) found in Augustine's account occurs twice in the Coptic papyrus (ⲡⲁⲉⲓ ⲣ̄ ⲛⲟⲩⲣⲉ ⲛⲁⲥ, see below), which increases the likelihood that the narrative of the gardener's daughter and that of Peter's daughter were found in the same text. For these reasons, it is likely that Augustine found the episodes concerning Peter's daughter and the gardener's daughter in the *Acts of Peter.*[32]

Some redactional features of the Coptic account also cohere with the *Actus Vercellenses.*[33] In the Coptic fragment, the episode begins on the first day of the week, when the crowd gathers around Peter: ⲥⲙ̄ ⲡⲟⲩⲁ ⲇⲉ [ⲙ̄]ⲡⲥⲁⲃⲃⲁⲧⲟⲛ ⲉⲧⲉ ⲧⲕⲩⲣⲓⲁⲕⲏ (*P. Berol.* 8502, p. 128, ll. 1–2).[34] As Schmidt notes, this temporal marker appears repeatedly in the Latin account:

*prima autem sabbatorum multitudine conueniente Petrum uidendi causa* (chap. 7; Lipsius 53.18-19)

*ueniente sabbato die alter te adducet in Iulio foro* (chap. 15; Lipsius 62.8)

*habebis autem agonem fidei ueniente sabbato* (chap. 16; Lipsius 62.23-24)

*in sabbato enim equidem*[35] *nolentem adducet eum dominus noster in Iulio foro* (chap. 18; Lipsius 65.30-31)

*Petrus autem constituerat die dominico i‹re a›d*[36] *Marcellum ut uideret uiduas* (chap. 29; Lipsius 79.4-5)

κυριακῆς οὔσης, ὁμιλοῦντος τοῦ Πέτρου τοῖς ἀδελφοῖς / *dominica autem dia, adloquente Petro fratribus* (chap. 30; Lipsius 79.16)

Three of these passages refer to the contest between Simon Magos and Peter, which seems to have been dated traditionally to fall on the Sabbath. The other occurrences are simple temporal markers that structure the narrative, just as one finds in the Coptic fragment. One may object that Christian meetings regularly took place on the Sabbath, and thus that the appearance of these phrases is hardly surprising,[37] but what is striking here is not the historical practice of meeting on the Sabbath, but the literary technique of structuring a narrative with this particular phrase.

Second, the Coptic *Act* and the Latin *Acts* both treat the miraculous with some reserve. The miracle that Peter performs on his daughter is temporary; the girl reverts to her former paralyzed state when Peter prays again. The point of the miracle is to show that God is neither powerless nor uncaring in cases in which a person is not restored to a healed state. Peter introduces his demonstration with the words, "Know, then, that God was not weak or unable to give his gift to my daughter" (p. 129, ll. 13-16),[38] and concludes by saying, "Know, then, O servant of Christ Jesus, that God watches over those who are his, and he prepares the thing that is good for each one. It is we who think he has forgotten us" (p. 139, l. 18-p. 140, l. 6).[39]

The *Actus Vercellenses* preserve a story with a similar reversal of a miracle. In chapter 21, a number of blind old widows[40] see wondrous visions of Christ, but, as in the Coptic story, they revert to their former blindness. Peter justifies this by saying, "If there is in you the faith which is in Christ, if it has been established in you, then see with your mind what you do not see with your eyes. . . . These eyes will again be closed, which see nothing but people and cattle and mute animals and stones and sticks; but not all eyes see Jesus Christ" (Lipsius 68.22-28).[41] The heavenly vision of Christ is more important than the restoration of earthly sight, which will eventually cease at death.[42] The conclusion of the story of Peter's daughter similarly emphasizes the beneficence of God even in the absence of miraculous healing. When his daughter returns to her paralysis, Peter responds, "This is beneficial for you and for me" (ⲡⲁⲓ ⲅⲁⲣ ⲡⲉ ⲧⲣ̄ ⲛⲟⲩⲣⲉ ⲛⲉ ⲛⲏⲙⲁⲉⲓ, P. Berol. 8502, p. 131, ll. 4-5; similarly, "This is beneficial for her and for me," ⲡⲁⲉⲓ ⲣ̄ ⲛⲟⲩⲣⲉ ⲛⲁⲥ ⲛⲏⲙⲁⲉⲓ, 131.13-14).

Third, as Schmidt notes, in the story of the widows, the eyes of the flesh are contrasted with those of the soul. This concept is repeated again in chapter 18 of the *Actus Vercellenses*. The congregation is instructed to pray to God, *etsi non uidetur istis oculis* ("even if he is not seen with these eyes," 65.33). In the Coptic account, Ptolemaios becomes blind from weeping over the loss of Peter's daughter. When he is healed, he is said to see both with the eyes of his flesh and with the eyes of his soul (ϵвολ ϩн ⲛ̄вⲁⲗ ⲛ̄ⲧⲉϥⲥⲁⲣ3 ⲁⲩⲱ ⲛ̄вⲁⲗ ⲛ̄ⲧⲉϥⲧⲩⲭⲏ, *P. Berol.* 8502, p. 138, ll. 8-10).[43]

Last, as Schmidt notes, Peter's daughter is paralyzed on one side of her body from her head to her toenails (ϵιв, *P. Berol.* 8502, p. 135, ll. 7-9), similarly to the manner in which Rufina is paralyzed in the *Actus Vercellenses* "on the right side from her head to the toenails (*ungues*) of her feet" (Lipsius 46.25). Molinari has demonstrated that, although accounts of half-paralysis are hardly unknown in ancient Greek medical literature, they are uncommon in Christian literature; he was not able to cite another, nor am I. Moreover, Molinari rightly points out that the Coptic ϵιв and the Latin *ungues*, which mean "hoof" or "claw," thus "toenail," are probably translating the Greek χηλή; Molinari was unable to find the combination of χηλή and κεφαλή, the Greek words behind the phrase "from head to foot," anywhere else in Greek literature.[44]

The episode concerning Peter's daughter takes place just outside of Peter's house, for, after distributing bread,[45] he goes into his house (ⲁϥвⲱⲕ ⲉ3ⲣⲁⲓ ⲉⲡⲉϥⲏⲉⲓ, *P. Berol.* 8502, p. 141, ll. 5-6). This episode, unknown in the Roman part of the *Acts of Peter* as preserved in the *Actus Vercellenses*, probably belongs to the lost part of the Acts that took place in Jerusalem. Internal references show that the version of the *Acts of Peter* employed in the *Actus Vercellenses* began with a face-off between Peter and Simon Magos in Judea (chaps. 5, 9, 17, and 23); in addition, a Syriac history of Peter which uses the *Acts of Peter* among its sources places the Eubula episode known from AcVer 17 explicitly in Jerusalem.[46] The *Actus Vercellenses* begin only with the continued confrontation of Peter and Simon in Rome. The Coptic episode then belongs to a longer version of the *Acts of Peter* predating the *Actus Vercellenses*, which provide only a truncation of them.

The discovery of this *Act of Peter* in a Coptic codex filled with Gnostic works known from Nag Hammadi seems, initially, to substantiate the claims of the orthodox that the Apocryphal Acts were employed largely among heretics, Gnostics in this case. No one has, however, explained satisfactorily the appearance of this excerpt in the codex. Schmidt is right, on one level, to say that the episode must have been chosen to finish out the quire, since it is the briefest text on the codex and appears last.[47] Among all of the texts available for this purpose, however, why choose this one? The Encratite ideals of the episode would cohere well enough with the sexual ethics of fourth-century Gnosticism (also pointed out by Schmidt), though this is not a specifically Gnostic feature. As Douglas Parrott has noted, the *Act* also capitalizes on a narrative link with the work preceding it in the codex, the *Sophia of Jesus Christ*: after Jesus finishes his revelation to the disciples, they begin to preach the "Gospel of God" (*P. Berol.* 8502, p. 127, ll. 5-9). The *Act of Peter* would then provide an example of this preaching. Parrott adds that the most compelling reason for including it may have been the rich allegorical possibilities of the text for a Gnostic reader: Ptolemaios, enraptured by the beauty of Peter's daughter, kidnaps the girl; struck with blindness as a result, he receives his sight again by means of a vision of Christ. This would be a human allegory of the fall of Sophia, whose erotic attraction to the beauty of the pleroma led to the creation of a physical world shrouded in the blindness of ignorance, which only the intervention of Christ could illuminate.[48] None of this resides in the surface level of the text, so conclusive proof is impossible. The excerpt, however, does show how the individual units of the *Acts of Peter* stood on their own and could be employed by Christians of a number of different theological directions. The *Actus Vercellenses*, the next version chronologically, are likewise an excerpt, but, in contrast, derive from a theological perspective that has little that can be labeled either heretical or Gnostic.

## The *Actus Vercellenses* as Redaction

The earliest manuscript witnesses of the *Acts of Peter* thus each testify to some manipulation of the text, in this case excerpting, in order to serve a purpose other than the simple narration of a tale. The next manuscript, the *Actus Vercellenses*, present a similar case. The text translated and printed in Schneemelcher's handbook as the "Acts of Peter," are not the original *Acts of Peter*, but a redaction of one version of them. As noted above, the *Actus Vercellenses* lack the first third of the narrative of the *Acts of Peter* as attested in the copy owned by Nikephoros, the fourteenth-century church father. The Coptic fragment, and back references in the narrative, also demonstrate that we have lost the original beginning of this version, which most probably took place in Judea. In this seventh-century codex, the *Actus Vercellenses* follow the Clementine *Recognitions* without any intervening title, and the text of the *Actus Vercellenses* itself contains an interpolation from that source (book 4, chapter 5 to chapter 10).[49] Schmidt first suggested that the motivation for the truncation of the first third of the *Actus Vercellenses* may have been to harmonize it with the *Recognitions*.[50] What the redactor of the *Actus Vercellenses* accomplishes is the suppression of all parts of the narrative taking place in Judea (with the exception of the "flashback" of the Eubula episode in chapter 17), and this harmonizes well with the *Recognitions*, which treat Peter's activity in the east. The Vercelli redactor would then be attempting to chronicle Peter's deeds, using one source for his activities in Syria and Palestine, and another for those in Rome. Additional support for Schmidt's hypothesis can be found in one of the Greek codices, Vatopedi 79; there, the martyrdom account itself has a superscript denoting its source as . . . ἐκ τῶν ἱστορικῶν Κλήμεντος Ῥώμης ἐπισκόπου. This most likely means that the manuscript source copied by this codex contained the martyrdom account as part of the *Recognitions*, just as the Vercelli Codex in fact does.

Manuscripts should always initially be taken at face value: the text of any manuscript is first and foremost a witness to the time at which the manuscript was copied, rather than to the time of any hypothetical compositional levels in the text it contains. It is nevertheless meaningful to distinguish, when possible, between the redaction or recension of the manuscript text and the source that the author may have used. The text of the *Actus Vercellenses* displays various discontinuities and inconsistencies—the usual grist of the source-critical mill—which not only suggest that the text was redacted at least once, but also fall into a pattern that expresses clear motivations for this redaction and the changes it introduced. The *Actus Vercellenses*, like the earlier two witnesses, thus present the *Acts of Peter* as a text in flux, a narrative subject to repeated interventions by its transmitters, a living story that was continually updated to accommodate new circumstances.

### Pauline Problems

The present redaction begins by narrating Paul's departure from Rome (chaps. 1–3), which sets the stage for Peter's arrival and his conflict with Simon Magos. Without wise apostolic guidance, Simon's arrival in the city and subsequent wonderworking cause the apostasy of nearly the entire Roman congregation (chap. 4). Christ then appears to Peter, directing him to leave Jerusalem and head for the capital (chap. 5).

As has long been recognized, the parts of the text mentioning Paul are those most suspect in the *Actus Vercellenses*. Crowded into the first three and last chapters of the work, the references to Paul are not well integrated into the text and cause a number of discontinuities. Chapters 1–3 narrate Paul's departure from Rome to Hispania. In these chapters, no mention at all is made of Peter, the central figure of the account; nor is the otherwise ubiquitous Marcellus, a prominent character in the rest of the narrative, listed among the members of the congregation who see Paul off in chapter 3. In fact, none of the individuals named in the first three chapters reappears in the subsequent narrative, with the exception of Paul, Nero (in the last chapter), and the presbyter Narkissos (chaps. 4, 6, 13, 14, 19).[51] Narkissos plays the role of host to Peter, and to the congregation, during the time that Simon Magos is enjoying the hospitality of Marcellus (chaps. 13–14); after Marcellus drives out Simon and purifies his house (chaps. 14, 19), he hosts the meetings of the congregation there (chaps. 19–22). Narkissos may have floated into chapter 3 from the subsequent narrative; although he is the only church official listed among the congregation who sees Paul off from Rome, he is named last of all:

> And a great crowd of women knelt down and pleadingly entreated the blessed Paul, and they kissed his feet and accompanied him to the harbor. But Dionysios and Balbus from Asia, who were Roman knights of high rank, and a senator named Demetrios kept close to Paul's right and said, "Paul, I would like to leave the city, if I were not a magistrate, so as not to part from you." And likewise, from the household of Caesar, Kleobios and Iphitus and Lysimachos and Aristeus, and two matrons, Berenike and Philostrate, with the presbyter Narkissos.[52]

Narkissos appears far behind all of the others of various ranks and stations, almost an afterthought.

Chapter 41, the final chapter of the *Actus Vercellenses*, also bears more relation to Paul than to Peter.[53] It narrates that Nero became angry with Agrippa, the prefect who had put Peter to death, because Nero had wished to punish him with extra severity. The cause of Nero's anger was that Peter had made disciples of some of Nero's servants. The appearance of Nero destroys the temporal framework of the *Actus Vercellenses*, which places Peter in Rome only twelve years after Christ's death (chap. 5),[54] thus making Peter's martyrdom under Nero (54–68 C.E.) impossible.[55] Aside from the chronological problem, nowhere else in the *Actus Vercellenses* is Nero tagged as the guilty party in Peter's death. It is the prefect Agrippa who plays the leading role, and who is also present at the contest between Peter and Simon (chaps. 23–28). In associating the martyrdom of Peter with Nero, chapter 41 of the *Actus Vercellenses* is in line with the tradition that Peter and Paul were both martyred under Nero.[56] This tradition, at odds with the rest of the *Actus Vercellenses*, also appears in the first chapter, in which the Christian congregation begs Paul not to stay away more than a year;[57] a voice from heaven responds to this request by predicting Paul's martyrdom under Nero: "there came a sound from heaven, and a loud voice that said, 'Paul, the servant of God, is chosen for service for the span of his life; but at the hands of Nero, that godless and wicked man, he will be perfected before your eyes.'"[58] Chapter 41 of the *Actus Vercellenses* sets the ecclesiastical record straight by ousting the lesser-known Agrippa in favor of Nero as the dominant figure in the martyrdom of Peter.

Stylistic considerations also suggest that chapters 1–3 and 40–41 were later additions. The Latin of the first three chapters of the *Actus Vercellenses* differs slightly from the Latin from chapters 5 to 36; the sentences are longer, less often paratactic, and the vocabulary is less repetitive than in the main section of the narrative. Since this is a translation, it reflects the continuous Greek text. The stylistic heterogeneity between chapters 1–3 and 40–41, and the rest of the narrative, is clearer in chapters 40–41, for which a Greek text is preserved. The ratio of circumstantial participles to the combined total of finite verbs and circumstantial participles runs at a consistent 35 to 40 percent for each individual chapter in the martyrdom account (chaps. 30–41), except at chapters 37–38, the discourse of Peter from the cross (20 to 21 percent), and at chapters 40 to 41 (45 to 46 percent). Chapters 40 to 41 thus have a Greek style that is significantly more hypotactic than the body of the martyrdom account.[59]

The Pauline presence in these *Acts of Peter* has left traces elsewhere in the body of the text, aside from the first and last chapters. The references to Paul are overwhelmingly more numerous in chapters 4 and 6, with four occurrences in each; chapters 10 and 23[60] carry one reference each. The fact alone that these occasional references cluster chiefly into the chapters nearest the hypothetical seam (end of chapter 3, beginning of chapter 4) would suggest that they are the work of the redactor who added the first three chapters and are meant to smooth the transition between the accounts of the activities of the two apostles in Rome.

Chapter 6 deserves some attention as the most amusing bit of Pauline-induced confusion. In it, the readers meet Ariston, the friend of the captain who brings Peter from Jerusalem to Puteoli; he seems to have no fixed residence. When the captain, Theon, and Peter land in Puteoli, Ariston meets Theon's important passenger. Ariston tells Peter why he is so pleased to meet him (chap. 6):[61]

> Ariston said that, since Paul had left for Spain, there had been no one of the brothers or sisters with whom he could refresh himself. Moreover, some Judean had forced his way into the city, Simon by name. "He disbanded the whole congregation on all sides with his magical incantations and wickedness, so that I also fled from Rome, in hopes that Peter would come."[62]

Ariston goes on to tell Peter that he had left Rome a mere two months ago and has been hiding in Puteoli since then. But only ten lines earlier, at the outset of the chapter, the readers were told that Ariston and Theon were old friends; Ariston was the man who ran the lodging house at which Theon usually stayed whenever, in the course of his long travels, he came to Puteoli:[63] "Theon . . . came to the lodging house where he usually stayed. . . . Now the man with whom he stayed was called Ariston; this man had always feared the Lord, and Theon entrusted himself to him on account of that name."[64]

This apparent case of mistaken identity results from narrative exigency. Ariston could have been left to spend his life happily in Puteoli had the redactor not wanted to make the account more vivid by offering an eyewitness account of mass apostasy at Rome. For that, she or he needed a recent refugee. The narrative does exploit the presence of Ariston: in addition to giving a report about Rome (cited above), he says he was expecting Peter's arrival, which he had seen in a vision. Paul had appeared to Ariston personally and commanded him to leave Rome; since then, for the previous two months, Ariston had gone down to the seashore every day to ask the sailors whether Peter had sailed with them. Ariston tearfully begs Peter to come to Rome without delay. The brief introduction of Ariston at the beginning of the chapter, in which he is presented as Theon's friend, is completely out of character with all that follows.

The interest in Paul behind these interpolations is partially motivated by the influence of the New Testament. Much of the information on Paul in the first three chapters is drawn from the Pauline epistles, particularly the letter to the Romans: the name Quartus (Rom 16:23), the reference to the household of Caesar (Phil 4:22), Paul's mission to Spain (Rom 15:28), and Timothy (Rom 16:21, and elsewhere). The Acts of the Apostles also played a role in the gestation of the first three chapters, for they leave Paul under arrest in Rome (28:30-31), and that is exactly where the *Actus Vercellenses* pick up the thread.[65] It is a result of his preaching at Rome that Paul is able to depart for Spain: Paul converts the wife of one of his guards; she converts her husband, and he lets Paul go free (chap. 1).

The manuscripts themselves testify to another characteristic of the redaction, the strong relationship between the martyrdoms of Peter and Paul. In the two manuscripts containing the Greek version of the martyrdom of Peter from the *Actus Vercellenses*, Patmos 48 and Vatopedi 79, the martyrdom of Paul follows immediately upon it. Likewise, the martyrdom of Paul usually called the Pseudo-Linus version, follows the Pseudo-Linus version of the martyrdom of Peter in many of the manuscripts.[66] The proximity of these two martyrdom accounts expresses the harmony between Peter and Paul so important to the self-conception of the early church. Although in the Pauline letters Peter and Paul differ sharply in their appropriation of Judaism and are the leaders of two different missions, one to the Gentiles and one to the Jews (Gal 2:9-10), the Acts of the Apostles presents them working in close cooperation. The first three chapters of the *Actus Vercellenses* continue this trajectory.

### The Apostate Marcellus

Gérard Poupon has argued that the *Actus Vercellenses* show further signs of redaction concerned, not with the figure of Paul, but with the character Marcellus. In the initial version of the *Acts of Peter*, this senator seems originally to have been a wealthy polytheist who first supported Christianity, was then deceived by Simon Magos, and was finally converted to the faith by Peter; however, in the *Actus Vercellenses*, he is already a Christian before the arrival of Simon Magus and becomes an apostate when he is deceived by the wonderworker.

In the early part of the narrative, as Poupon notes, Marcellus is never claimed by the congregation as a Christian, but as a benefactor. The major complaint of the Christians who apprise Peter of this situation in Rome is not that Marcellus has become apostate, but that his "compassion has been changed into blasphemy" (*misericordiam in blasfemia translatam [est]*; chap. 8; Lipsius 55.11-12). Marcellus laments the money that he spent on the welfare of the Christians and calls his erstwhile Christian clients "impostors" (*inpostores*; chap. 8; Lipsius 55.18). It is largely the withdrawal of financial support that the Christians cite; this is the salient result of his having been won over by Simon, not a changed confession of faith.[67]

In chapter 10, Marcellus is clearly presented as a Christian who apostatized. He calls himself a *labsus a domino* (Lipsius 58.9) and says that he was caused to stumble (*scandalizatus sum*; Lipsius 57.32). Peter makes reference to this in his response to Marcellus's speech of confession in the same chapter, in which he welcomes Marcellus into the community as a lost sheep—none of which really coheres with the initial description of affairs given by the Christian "brothers" in chapter 8. Peter makes no reference to financial affairs here at all. This sole chapter, chapter 10, is the only indication in the text that Marcellus had been a Christian before Peter came to Rome.

Chapter 10 is also one of the few in the *Actus Vercellenses* that mention Paul, so it is possible that the chapter as a whole was redacted by the person who added the first three chapters. Marcellus begs Peter, "do not punish my sins, if you have any true faith in the Christ whom you preach, if you remember his commandments, not to hate anyone, not to be angry with anyone, as I have learnt from Paul, your fellow-apostle. Do not call to mind my faults."[68] The reference to Paul is superficial.[69] The characterization of Marcellus as a lapsed Christian would cohere narratively with the addition of the first three chapters: had Paul been active in Rome before Peter, he could well have converted Marcellus. In chapter 3, among those Christians who wish Paul farewell are two knights, a senator, and two matrons. The conversion of a senator was not a remarkable event at this level of the text. In the earlier version, it would have been: Marcellus, in the earlier version, is merely a friendly polytheist at the outset of the story, and his conversion to Christianity (for the *first* time) in the (unredacted) chapter 10 would have been an unusual and highly significant event.

The figure of the wealthy polytheist benefactor appears elsewhere in the *Actus Vercellenses*. In chapter 30, Peter receives a large donation from the promiscuous Chryse, who is apparently not a Christian: she comes in response to a vision from "the one whom you say is God."[70] Peter must defend himself before members of the congregation who would shun a donation from such a source: "I do not know who this woman is with regard to her usual way of life."[71] Peter accepts her donation in good conscience.

Eubula in Judea, "a woman of quite some distinction in this world,"[72] forms a close parallel to Marcellus. In a flashback in chapter 17, Peter describes how he miraculously exposed Simon's theft of all of her gold, including a golden satyr,[73] from her house. This event apparently formed the climax of the lost Judean section of the narrative, because, once his guilt became evident, Simon fled Judea, never to return: "and he [Simon] saw a large crowd coming, and those men [his associates] bound in chains. He immediately understood, took flight, and has not been seen in Judea to the present day."[74]

Like Marcellus, Eubula's troubles began when she offered the hospitality of her home to Simon. The text is clear, however, that she did not actually convert to Christianity until Peter miraculously demonstrated Simon's true nature:[75] "And Eubula, after she had recovered all of her belongings, gave them for the support of the poor. And she believed in the Lord Jesus Christ, and, after being strengthened [in the faith], she despised and renounced this world, and kept giving alms to the widows and orphans, and clothed the poor, and, after a long time, she went to her rest."[76] Marcellus is Eubula's Roman counterpart. Deceived by Simon, he converts to Christianity when Peter miraculously disproves Simon's ruses. His conversion provides one of the climaxes of the Roman section of the narrative, just as that of Eubula was the resounding conclusion of the Judean portion.[77]

In addition to chapters 1–3, 4, 6, and 10,[78] the Greek version of the final episode concerning Simon, that is, his last flight over Rome, as preserved in Codex Vatopedi 79, offers additional evidence that both Paul's prior sojourn in Rome and the prior Christian status of Peter's audience are later redactional elements. Chapters 30 to 32 assume that Simon and Peter are battling chiefly for the unconverted crowds of Rome. Simon's final salvo is reserved for them (chap. 31):[79]

> After a few days, Simon promised *the crowd* that he would refute Peter decisively. . . .
> Through all this, Peter kept following him and unmasking him before the onlookers.
> Since he [Simon] was constantly disgraced and ridiculed by *the crowd of Romans*, and no
> one believed him since he did not achieve what he had promised to do, it came to such
> a point, he declared everything to them, "*Men of Rome*. . . . " (emphases added)

After this, Simon promises to fly up to God over the Sacred Way on the following day. The Latin translation has left out the references to the "crowds."[80]

While he is in midair, Peter, indeed, shows concern for those already converted to Christianity, which at this point in the narrative would also include Marcellus. He prays to Christ, "If you allow this fellow to do what he has attempted, all those who have put their faith in you shall now be caused to stumble, and the signs and wonders that you gave them through me will be discredited" (chap. 32).[81] The salient point, however, is that those who have believed in Peter are Peter's converts, not Paul's, and they do not in fact lapse. Even while Simon is flying in midair, "the faithful look to Peter."[82] Peter's prayers are effective, Simon falls to the ground, and not one of the converts disbelieves.

The Greek version of this passage also alludes to Simon's earlier attempt to fly through the air over Rome: "For when he [Simon] made his entrance in Rome, he amazed *the crowds* by flying. But Peter, the one who exposed him, was not yet in *Rome, which* he led astray to such an extent by his ruses, that they were amazed at him" (chap. 32; emphases added).[83] The Latin translator treated this passage by simply omitting it.[84]

This is very different from the account given in the first three chapters of the *Actus Vercellenses* of the situation in Rome prior to Peter's arrival. In chapters 31 and 32, no mention is made of Paul. Simon and Peter are battling for the crowds of Rome; the people whom Simon leads astray are not the Christians, but the city of Rome. The text assumes that, had Peter been there, not even the polytheist Romans would have been won over by Simon. The Greek at this point gives us a valuable insight into the state of the narrative before it reached the hands of the redactor. The issues are not apostasy and heresy, inner-Christian concerns, but rather the efficacy of Christianity in the competition of the religious marketplace, where the new religion has not yet achieved pride of place and where every Roman deceived by a rival miracle worker is a potential loss to Christianity.

The portrayal of Marcellus and the Christians as apostates coheres logically with the emphasis on Paul's prior activity in Rome. Peter is a relative latecomer, and, in this redaction, he does not convert polytheists as much as strengthen the existing Christian community against the onslaughts of deception. But it is more than this. Gérard Poupon also sees in the *Actus Vercellenses* a specific concern to support the viability of second penance for the sins of apostasy and adultery.[85] This would motivate the redactions that transform Marcellus from a polytheist into a lapsed Christian in chapter 10, and the addition of the account of Rufina the adulteress in chapter 2.[86] Because of the theological interest in second penance, Poupon dates these redactions and interpolations to the early third century and cites Hippolytos of Rome and Tertullian on this topic.[87]

Some modifications of this hypothesis are necessary. The redaction postulated by Poupon took place in Greek, not Latin and should be located in the eastern Empire, not the west. The mention of Paul in chapter 40 appears in the Greek, and not in the Latin, which seems to have omitted it.[88] We need not suspect theological motivations for this, since the Latin translation has the tendency to abbreviate throughout, but it does show that the Greek text of the martyrdom accounts, despite the later date of its manuscripts, is a witness to the original Greek text independent of the Latin translation. The interpolated Pauline material, then, was present in the continuous Greek text used by the Latin translation, as Graecisms in the Latin translation of the interpolated chapters 1–3 also suggest.[89] There is thus an unredacted continuous Greek text and a Greek redaction.[90]

Internal considerations show that not much temporal or geographical distance lies between the continuous Greek text and the Greek redaction; the redaction was carried out in a time and place not far removed from the context of the composition of its source. The first three chapters share redactional features with the rest of the *Actus Vercellenses*:[91] visions and prophecies, such as the voice from heaven that predicts Paul's martyrdom in chapter 1, are common throughout the rest of the narrative; Paul fasts to determine God's will, as elsewhere in the *Actus Vercellenses*; Paul offers a eucharist without wine, as elsewhere;[92] the *Strafwunder* that paralyzes Rufina in chapter 2 is similar to the episode concerning Peter's daughter, though the purpose differs radically.

Asia Minor is the most promising candidate for the provenance of the unredacted Greek text. Ficker observes, first, that the geographic data about Rome range from the vague to the inaccurate.[93] In favor of Asia Minor, he notes the otherwise inexplicable mention of the *hospitium Bithynorum*, in which live the only two lay Christians, elderly women, who have not been deceived by Simon (chap. 4; Lipsius 49.16). The figure Marcellus is most likely a provincial governor of Bithynia from the reign of Tiberius (see Chapter Three below). The *Acts of Peter* also bear a close textual relationship to the *Acts of Paul* (see below), which Tertullian attributes to a presbyter in Asia Minor (*de baptismo* 17).[94] Last, 1 Peter directs a letter to Pontos, Galatia, Cappadocia, Asia, and Bithynia. Bremmer, after noting other details that suggest the Greek world rather than Rome, suggests that Nicomedia might be the home of the continuous Greek text, since this city would have been the seat of Granius Marcellus and had a large Christian community by 170. The cities of southern Asia Minor that are probably the home of the *Acts of John* and *Acts of Paul* are not likely to be the place of origin of the *Acts of Peter*, since the phrase, "the first of the city," so common in that region, is absent from the latter text, though found throughout the *Acts of Paul* and *Acts of John*.[95]

In the Greek redaction, the interest in Asia Minor evident elsewhere in the narrative finds its echo in the knights from Asia, Dionysios and Balbus, mentioned in chapter 3 along with a senator named Demetrios (one assumes this is his cognomen). The Balbus mentioned here is probably Q. Iulius Balbus, proconsul of Asia in 100–1 or 101–2 C.E.,[96] thus a clear indication of Asian provenience. Moreover, the apostasy of entire congregations to heresy, such as occurs at Rome in chapters 1–3, is hardly uncommon in second-century Asia Minor, the age of Montanism, which erupted in nearby Phrygia; Marcion himself hailed from northern Asia Minor. Even the vague and improbable data concerning Roman geography have apparently been left to stand both in the Greek redaction and the Latin translation. The theological and geographic perspective of the continuous Greek text and of the Greek redaction is thus not tremendously different.

Dating the continuous Greek text and redaction is a complicated matter. One is on firmer ground with the Latin translation. Jan Bremmer has argued convincingly that the Latin text of the *Actus Vercellenses* must date between 359 and 385 C.E. The mention of the *curiosi*, an imperial secret police (chap. 11), would set the Latin translation after 359 C.E., for it was only after this date that these *agentes in rebus* reported directly to the emperor and became feared as spies, which is presupposed by the narrative.[97] On the other hand, since Priscillian shows knowledge of the Apocryphal Acts, the translation into Latin must have circulated before his death in 385 C.E.[98] Tamás Adamik argues that features of the Latin, such as the confusion between the dative and ablative cases, place it much later than this, in the seventh century.[99] The variants he notes are chiefly on the orthographic level: this indicates the orthography current at the time of copying, even if the manuscript is transmitting a substantially earlier base text. C. H. Turner dates the Latin to not later than the fourth century on the basis of its language and style,[100] which would concur with Bremmer's historical evidence. Poupon argues for a North African provenience of the *Actus Vercellenses* because of certain incoherencies in the Latin text resulting from the misunderstanding of the chrism, the superimposed chi-rho (CR) used as a *nomen sacrum* to indicate Christ (Χριστός). At several points, it is read as PX in Latin letters, thus P[A]X. The chrism was very frequent in North African manuscripts, but was abandoned very early. Poupon correspondingly argues that the *Actus Vercellenses* were translated into Latin by Manichaean missionaries before the end of the third century, though he is more certain of the geographic provenience than the date.[101]

The continuous Greek text is a second–century document. The *Acts of Paul* are dependent upon the continuous Greek text of the *Acts of Peter*,[102] so Tertullian's attestation of the *Acts of Paul* before 200 C.E. provides a solid *terminus ante quem*. But how much earlier than this are the *Acts of Peter*? Bremmer repeats Schmidt's argument that the conversion of the senatorial elite to Christianity cannot be attested before the reign of Septimius Severus and thus dates the *Acts of Peter* to the 180s or 190s;[103] yet the narration of senatorial conversions does not presuppose that they have taken place in reality, any more than the crypto-Christianity of Nicodemus or Joseph of Arimathea in the Gospel of John indicates the conversion of Jews. Liuwe H. Westra's investigation of the *regula fidei*, a second- to third-century credal formulation found in Christian authors from Justin to Origen, however, finds that the *Acts of Peter* offers a conservative form of this creed. No mention is made of the Holy Spirit, and the treatment of Christ is quite abbreviated. Westra notes that this form is earlier even than what is attested in Justin (d. 165 C.E.).[104] As shown below, the citation of Scriptural witnesses in the *Acts of Peter* also would suggest a date before Irenaeus (fl. 180). The *Acts of Peter* do not cite specific gospels, only words of the Lord, both apocryphal and canonical. No other text is claimed as authoritative save the Septuagint, although the text is familiar with the Acts of the Apostles and Pauline letters and makes use of their language, though not of their content. This would be consonant with a date between Justin and Irenaeus. On balance, the 170s are a reasonable date for the continuous Greek text.

The Greek redaction itself is an argument for this earlier date of the continuous Greek text. The chief concern, that of characterizing Peter and Paul as comartyrs, is a second-century issue reflected in other sources[105] and can account sufficiently for the redactional features. Moreover, Dionysios of Corinth sent a letter around 170 C.E. to the churches in Amasis and Pontos, encouraging them to receive reconverted Christians from among those who have backslidden into bad conduct or heresy.[106] If it is necessary to claim a specific interest in reclaiming the lapsed to account for the redaction—one assumes that such moral quandaries were widespread in early Christian communities—this witness, as well as the Montanist controversy of the 180s and 190s, are much closer geographically and temporally to the text than are Tertullian and Hippolytos of Rome, the authorities cited by Poupon for his third-century dating.

## The Written Sources of the Continuous Greek Text

The *Actus Vercellenses* betray more fundamental signs of written composition, which do not express concern about Paul's work in Rome and the reclamation of lapsed Christians. Unlike the redaction described above, these signs of composition in the *Actus Vercellenses* are not motivated by obvious theological factors. The compositional activity here appears to serve the purely narrative function of linking various written components of the narrative into a coherent whole.

The clearest indication of this literary activity is the prophecy of the speaking dog in chapter 12. The dog story is told in two halves, in chapters 9 and 12; between this appear several other miracles. In chapter 9, Peter comes to the house of the apostate Marcellus to confront Simon Magos, to whom Marcellus has extended his hospitality. The doorkeeper says to Peter that he was instructed by Simon to tell him that Simon was not in the house. Peter announces that he will do a miracle, unchains a dog, and commands it to beckon Simon to come out. When the dog enters the house and does so, Simon is stunned to silence. Marcellus then runs out of the house, repents of his error in allowing himself to be deceived by Simon, and watches Peter perform two miracles: an exorcism and the restoration of a shattered statue. In chapter 12, the scene shifts back to Marcellus's house. Simon tells the dog to inform Peter that he is not home. The dog excoriates Simon, runs out, reports their dialogue to Peter, prophesies about Peter's coming contest with Simon, and falls dead at Peter's feet.

The transition into this second half of the dog story, in which Simon instructs the dog to address Peter, is particularly rough. The end of chapter 11 and beginning of chapter 12 begin thus:

> and Marcellus was also exalted in spirit, because this was the first miracle done by his hands, and he therefore believed with all his heart in the name of Jesus Christ, the son of God, through whom all things impossible are possible. But Simon, inside, said this to the dog, "Tell Peter that I am not inside." And the dog answered him in the presence of Marcellus.[107]

This is a difficult transition. First, *intus* is an inspecific local designation; the *domus* was last mentioned at the beginning of the previous chapter, chapter 11. Moreover, chapter 11 ended outside the house, with Peter and Marcellus marveling at the restitution of the statue. The movement back toward the episode of Simon and the dog is unexpected and abrupt. And "in the presence of Marcellus" indicates that Marcellus is still in the house with Simon in chapter 12, whereas the readers know that he ran out of the house at the beginning of chapter 10, but have not been told that he reentered his house.[108] The redactor complicated an otherwise coherent story about Simon and the dog by interrupting it to have Marcellus run out of the house to address Peter and to witness two other miracles. The minor inconsistencies in the transition suggest that the dog story was split to include the other two episodes between its halves.

The author makes the theological concern of this literary activity evident at the end of the statue episode, cited above; Marcellus repents in front of Peter after the dog's first speech and is moved to a complete faith in Christ by the success of the miracle he performs. Marcellus's presence at Peter's side is crucial to both actions; to facilitate this, the author portrays him as running immediately out of the house to Peter after the dog's first speech and shows that his faith is confirmed by the last miracle with the statue.

The dog's speech in chapter 12 contains a detail that can be assigned to a level of redaction. After his encounter with Simon, the dog runs out to Peter:[109]

> And the dog reported what he had done with Simon. Moreover, the dog also said, "Messenger and apostle of the true God, Peter, you shall have a great contest against Simon, the enemy of Christ . . . and you shall convert many to the faith who were deceived by him. For this you will receive from God the wages for your labor." When the dog had said this, he fell before the feet of the apostle Peter and laid aside his spirit.

The account places two messages in the dog's mouth, one in indirect speech and one in direct speech. They are linked by a redactional formula, "and . . . also said" (*haec autem locutus est*). The two statements are unrelated: when the dog switches to direct speech, he does not mention any of the foregoing dealings with Simon Magos. Instead, this prophecy is connected to the entire scope of the *Actus Vercellenses*: not only does it mention the later contest between Peter and Simon, it alludes to the martyrdom of Peter in speaking of his "wages."

The prophecy of the dog, however, does not reflect the concerns of the Greek redaction: the concern is not for the lapsed Christians at Rome, their reconversion and forgiveness, but for (first-time) "converts to the faith" from among the Roman *populus* who have been deceived by Simon: "you shall convert many to the faith who were deceived by him." This is the concern of the continuous Greek text, and thus the dog's speech is an intervention into it. There are two distinct levels of written work: that of the editor who produced the Greek redaction from the continuous Greek text and that of the editor who knit together the continuous Greek text from prior written texts.

Source criticism cannot fully recover the earliest written sources. The continuous Greek text seems to have been pulled together out of at least three identifiable bodies of material: various miracle accounts, the contest, and the martyrdom. The martyrdom account proper (chaps. 37–41) shows a stylistic and philosophical heterogeneity from the rest of the *Acts of Peter* that suggests that it was an independent document later included in the continuous Greek text. In the discourse from the cross (chap. 38), Peter claims to be the type of the first man, who was born into the world upside down, and thus mistook the proper order of things because everything appeared to him reversed. This discourse shows philosophical similarity to other passages in the Apocryphal Acts. In the *Acts of*

*Andrew,* Andrew describes himself as Adam and his disciple Maximilla as Eve, with both of them correcting the error of the first fall from grace (*AcAnd* 5-7). The Hymn of the Pearl in the *Acts of Thomas* (chaps. 108-13) similarly describes the origin of evil in primal error and forgetfulness. Despite these similarities to the other Acts, however, the discourse in chapter 38 has no resonance with the rest of the *Acts of Peter*. Moreover, the style in chapters 37 and 38 stands apart from the Greek style of the rest of the Greek martyrdom account (chaps. 30-41 in the *AcVer*).[110]

The *catena* of miracles in chapters 10-13 are rife with signs of composition.[111] Oracles are inserted into a written text in an otiose fashion, with the sole purpose of linking the narrative units of the *Acts of Peter*. In the exorcism account in chapter 11, Peter addresses the demoniac twice in nearly the same words. He first address the man as, *quicumque es qui risisti* ("Whoever you are, that laughed," Lipsius 58.28-29); the man comes forward, prophesies that the dog will address Simon again and then run back to Peter and die. Peter then immediately says, *Et tu itaque, quicumque es daemon* ("You, too, then, whatever demon you may be," Lipsius 59.4-5), addressing now the demon in the man. The redactor apparently inserted the prophecy about the dog after Peter's address to him and then repeated the sentence from the source after the intervention. The prophecy reminds the reader of the continuation of the dog episode in chapter 12, separated by chapters 10 and 11, thus integrating the exorcism episode into the immediate context.

Many of the redactional additions, especially visions and prophecies, serve to link the three major sections of the narrative: the miracles, the public contest, and the martyrdom. As noted above, the dog's prophecy, a redactional addition, appears in the section describing Peter's miracles and alludes to the two later sections of the narrative, the contest and the martyrdom. The prophecy of the infant in chapter 15 performs a similar function. It summarizes the previous narrative, the talking-dog story, and predicts the exact time and location of the coming contest between Peter and Simon in the Forum Iulium: "'When a dog reproved you, you were not shaken. I, an infant, am compelled by God to speak, and you still do not blush! But even though you are unwilling, on the coming Sabbath, another will lead you to the Julian Forum, to prove what kind of person you are'" (chap. 15).[112] This prophetic speech fulfills the same functions as the two cited above: like the dog's prophecy, it knits together the various components of the *Actus Vercellenses* in Rome; like the prophecy of the exorcised man, it recapitulates and foreshadows the immediate course of events.

## The Intertext of the *Actus Vercellenses*

The *Acts of Peter* existed in an intertextual world and contain a tremendous number of quotations of and allusions to other surviving texts of Christian literature.[113] Exact determination of individual allusions is difficult, since the *Acts of Peter* employ a number of phrases that can be found in more than one early Christian text, and thus pertain to the general world of discourse in early Christian literature. Yet the sheer density of potential intertextual connections to the gospels, Pauline letters, Acts of the Apostles, and other early Christian works carry a combined weight of proof that no single instance affords; moreover, analysis of these intertextual references results in clear patterns of usage.[114]

## The New Testament

The relationship between the *Acts of Peter* and the works that were to become the New Testament canon should not be portrayed as a static series of interconnections at one point in time, but as a diachronic series of contacts, which altered in nature as the synoptic gospels, Pauline letters, and Acts of the Apostles moved closer to canonical status, and the *Acts of Peter* progressively moved toward the margins of Christian literature. Early in their history, no direct literary dependence existed between the *Acts of Peter* and other such texts. At the later end of the chronological spectrum, however, the redactor(s) of the *Acts of Peter* borrowed directly and explicitly from the works that had, by that time, become normative, such as the synoptic gospels and the Pauline epistles. Moreover, by the later second century, one of the redactors of the *Acts of Peter* consciously modeled it on the Acts of the Apostles.

Mapping the density of the allusions to early Christian writings over the various parts of the *Actus Vercellenses* confirms the redactional hypotheses set out in the previous sections of this chapter. In the first three chapters of the *Actus Vercellenses*, the density of intertextual allusions is high. Phrases and names from the Pauline, pseudo-Pauline, and pastoral letters abound, especially in Paul's speech in chapter 2 (see Appendix Two for specific references). Chapter 41 alludes to events narrated in full only in another apocryphal work, the *Martyrdom of Paul*.

In contrast to the first three and last chapters, long sections of the narrative of the *Actus Vercellenses* have very few intertextual references. Chapters 11-15, the brace of miracle stories, have no convincing references to any other text. Chapters 22-27, which narrate most of the contest between Peter and Simon, allude, with two exceptions,[115] only to the Hebrew Bible and to synoptic tradition; the Pauline epistles and the Acts of the Apostles do not figure here at all. Chapters 37-41, the crucifixion and address from the cross, cite only four logia of Jesus, three of which are extracanonical.

Intertextual allusions[116] are most dense in the speeches in the *Actus Vercellenses*, but individual speeches vary greatly in the selection of texts to which they refer. Chapter 7, Peter's first speech in Rome, alludes to Acts 4:10, 12;[117] it also cites stories known from the gospel narratives (especially Matthew and Luke) and contains verbal reminiscences of Ephesians 6 and possibly other Pauline and pseudo-Pauline epistles (see Appendix Two for explicit citations):

> Peter began to declaim at the top of his voice, "Men who are present here, who hope in Christ, who will suffer temptation for a little while, learn why it is that God sent his son into the world, and why he brought him forth through the Virgin Mary. Was it not to achieve some grace or means of salvation,[118] because he wanted to refute all the offenses and ignorance, and all the activities of the devil, his elements and powers by which he once prevailed, before our God shone forth in the world? Because in their many and varied weaknesses[119] they fell into death through ignorance, the almighty God, moved by his mercy, sent his son into the world. And he walked on the water, and I myself remain as his witness."[120]

Though no text is cited explicitly, the allusions are dense, and the effect is that Peter's speech sounds "biblical," in fact, rather "Pauline." Thematically, the speech belongs to a later level of the text, the Greek redaction, for in the part that immediately follows this citation, Peter attempts to console the lapsed Christians by telling them how Christ forgave him when his faith wavered, when he tried to walk on the water, and denied Jesus three times out of fear.[121] This last allusion is a reference to a specific gospel, for Peter describes how, after the third denial, Jesus "turned to me," a detail found only in Luke's gospel (22:61).

Speeches that belong to early compositional layers of the *Actus Vercellenses* do not contain allusions to other early Christian writings. The narratives of the contest (chaps. 23–28) and the martyrdom (chaps. 37–40) refer instead to *testimonia* from the Hebrew Bible (chaps. 23–24) and the words of Jesus (chaps. 37–38). Moreover, the use is by direct citation, with brief attributions, rather than by allusion. The intertextual references base the message of the text in the authoritative prophecies of God. In chapter 24, in their contest before the Roman public, Simon argues that Jesus cannot be divine, and Peter responds by citing prophetic scriptures:

> And he [Simon] turned to the public and said, "Men of Rome, is God born? Is he crucified?" . . . But Peter said, "May your words against Christ be cursed! Have you dared to say this when the prophet says about him, 'Who has declared his generation?' and another prophet says, 'And we saw him, and he possessed neither grace nor beauty.' And, 'In the last times, a boy is born of the Holy Spirit; his mother knows no man, and no one claims to be his father.' And again, it says, 'She has given birth and has not given birth.' And again, 'Is it a small thing for you to contend?[122] Behold, a virgin will conceive in her womb.' And another prophet says to honor the father, 'We have neither heard her voice, nor is a midwife come in.' Another prophet says, 'He was not born from a woman's womb, but has come down from a heavenly place' and 'A stone has been cut without hands and has struck down all the kingdoms,' and 'He has made the stone that the builders rejected into the head of the corner,' and he calls him a stone that is 'choice and precious.' And, again, the prophet says of him, 'And behold, I saw above the cloud one coming like the son of man.'"

Unlike Peter's speech in chapter 7, the use of texts in this case is explicit citation.[123] The point is not to make Peter's speech sound "Petrine" or "biblical," but to employ proof texts in an argument. The attributions are vague, usually a mere *alius profeta dicit*. The selection of prophecies, moreover, shows no awareness of canonical boundaries: alongside the favorite Christian prophecies from Isaiah (7:14; 53:2, 8), Psalm 118:2 (LXX 117), and Daniel (2:34 and 7:13), the use of some of which is attributed to Jesus in the Gospels,[124] one finds prophecies from the *Ascension of Isaiah* and from sources that no longer survive.

In passages such as these, which represent the level of the Greek source, the relevant texts seem to be the ones mentioned in the metatextual passage in chapter 13: Peter explains "the prophetic writings, and the things which Jesus did both in words and deeds."[125] The earliest levels of the *Acts of Peter* directly cite the prophetic writings and the words of Jesus and recount episodes from the gospel accounts. The later redactional levels, which also employ the epistles and the Acts, never explicitly cite them, but allude to them, using them as implicit models for the language and genre of the *Acts of Peter*.

This is illustrated by the most persistent set of allusions in the *Actus Vercellenses*, to Acts 2:46–47,[126] which appears four times. The text of Acts reads "Day by day, as they spent much time together in the temple, they broke bread at home and ate their food with glad and generous hearts, praising God and having the goodwill of all the people. And day by day the Lord added to their number those who were being saved." Without exception, the allusions to this verse appear in the summary passages of the *Actus Vercellenses*, which, as in Luke, are curt sentences that link longer narrative sequences. The phrase appears between Peter's speech and his first encounter with Simon in Marcellus's house (chap. 9). It appears in a summary passage narrating healings performed by Peter, separating the episode of Chryse from the story of Simon's attempt to fly over the city (chap. 31). The same allusion separates the end of the episodes concerning Simon from the beginning of the narrative about Peter's arrest and execution (chap. 33). The final usage, in chapter 41, concludes the entire narrative, leaving a lasting imprint of the ultimate meaning of the text: "And for the rest of the time, the brothers and sisters rejoiced in God with one accord and exulted him, glorifying the God and savior of our Lord Jesus Christ." A distinctly Lukan phrase from the Acts, then, performs a similar redactional task, that of joining self-contained narrative units and lending the events a more general significance.

These allusions did not result in the course of the translation into Latin, but pertain to the continuous Greek text. Allusions to the Acts of the Apostles in the Coptic fragment confirm this independently; as argued above, the fragment belongs to a part of the narrative not contained in the Latin *Actus Vercellenses* and is thus independent of the redactional work attested there. In the Coptic episode, Peter claims that he sold a plot of land and did not keep back the price, which is a reminiscence of the story of Ananias and Sapphira (Acts 5:1–11), thus an allusion, not a quotation. The summary descriptions of Peter's healings also allude to the Gospels (Matt 4:24; Mark 6:55 and parallels; Matt 11:5 and parallels).

The varying nature and density of allusions confirm the hypothesis above. The simplest form of intertextuality, citation of the Hebrew Bible or the words of Jesus, appears in the sources of the continuous Greek text. The collection of miracle stories (chaps. 11–15) are conspicuous for their lack of allusions or citations. The contest in the forum, which contains the speech recounting the testimonia, also shows signs of independent existence as a source. And the martyrdom account (chaps. 37–40), which cites the words of Jesus, presents a philosophical heterogeneity from the rest of the *Acts of Peter*, as mentioned above. Thus the passages of the *Actus Vercellenses* in which no reference is made to early Christian works are precisely those narrative units which may have been available already in written form before the composition of the continuous Greek text. The author who linked these narrative units to form the continuous story of Peter, possibly as early as the third quarter of the second century, made ample use of a phrase from the Acts of the Apostles (2:46–47) in the summary passages that united them. The final redactor of the *Actus Vercellenses*, probably a late-second-century figure who added chapters 1–3, and 41, and reworked chapters 7 and 10, merely intensified this trend of quarrying the synoptic gospels, Acts, and Pauline epistles for appropriately biblical language. The difference is one of degree; the intertextual relationship becomes denser and more explicit in the Greek redaction than in the continuous Greek text. But, if the suggested dating holds, early Christian works such as the Acts of the Apostles were influencing the vocabulary and discourse of the *Acts of Peter* trajectory already in the third quarter of the second century.[127]

In addition to the allusions and quotations, points of narrative overlap exist. The characterization of Paul is taken wholesale from the Acts of the Apostles: he is under guard at Rome (Acts 28:30), and he disputes with the Jews there (28:23–29; cf. *AcVer*

1), a motif missing elsewhere in the *Actus Vercellenses*.[128] Paul's role as the great former persecutor of the church can also be found in the Acts and the Pauline epistles: "I once was a persecutor, now I suffer persecution" (*AcVer* 2, which can refer to Acts 8:3; 9:1, 15–16, as well as Phil 3:6, Gal 1:13). The beginning of the *Actus Vercellenses* is more than a mere allusion, as well; it presents itself as the logical conclusion of the narrative in the Acts of the Apostles. There, Paul is last seen preaching freely under house arrest. In the *Actus Vercellenses*, he is able to leave for Spain only as a direct result of this preaching in Rome. These direct uses of early Christian texts as narrative models appear in chapters 1–3, which are late additions to the text.

The characterization of Peter, however, is weighted more toward the Gospels; at only one point does it overlap with Luke's Acts, that of Peter's encounter with Simon in Jerusalem. The *Actus Vercellenses* refer to the same episode narrated in Luke's Acts (chap. 8; AcVer 23):[129]

> For you see . . . that I chased him out of Judea because of the ruses that he inflicted on Eubula, a dignified and most decent woman, by employing his magical techniques. After he was driven from there by me, he came here, believing that he could lay low among you. And here he stands in front of you! Tell me, Simon, did you not fall at the feet of Paul and me in Jerusalem, when you saw the healings that were done by our hands, and did you not say, "I beg you, let me pay you as much as you want, so that I can lay on hands and work such miracles!"

This is a verbal allusion to Luke's Acts (8:19), although the author of *Actus Vercellenses* freely contradicts some narrative details of that account: the conflict with Simon is placed in Jerusalem, not Samaria; Paul is present (if one accepts this reading),[130] rather than John. The closest parallel between the two versions is the motif of the offer to buy a power associated with the laying on of hands. This is a distinct theological concern of Luke.[131]

Christopher Matthews has argued, in a methodologically sophisticated treatment of these similarities, that the *Acts of Peter* ultimately developed out of a narrative that was Luke's invention, the contest of Simon and Peter in Samaria. The story of the contest between Simon Magus and Peter in the *Acts of Peter* and the confrontation between the two in Acts 8 are structurally very similar and thus have some relationship;[132] they each share traditions about Simon that are very different from those known by Justin Martyr.[133] Matthews is also correct in outlining a series of intertextual contacts much more complex than the simple relationship of one-time literary dependence.[134] Because the *Acts of Peter* narrative continued to develop, it likely picked up direct influences from the—by then—more fixed account of the Acts of the Apostles. Simon is called the "Great Power of God," or the "Power of God," consistently throughout the *Actus Vercellenses* (*magnum virtutem Dei, Dei virtutem*, chap. 4, 8, 31). In Luke, he is similarly called at one point, "The Power of God which is called Great" (ἡ δύναμις τοῦ θεοῦ ἡ καλουμένη μεγάλη, Acts 8:10).[135] This may indeed be an instance of Lukan redaction entering into the *Actus Vercellenses*, as Matthews has argued.[136] Matthews also notes that the concern with the proper use of money is a Lukan redactional motif: but it is also a prominent motif in the *Acts of Peter*, one of the primary concerns of which is the proper use of wealth by the senatorial elite (cf. chaps. 8, 28, 30). This motif is rather a sign of the improving status of converts in both Luke's community and that of the *Acts of Peter*.

Yet the relationship is, I would argue, more complex than Matthews' reconstruction allows. The passage cited above is an allusion to Acts 8 in the *Acts of Peter*, and yet it refers to an episode in Jerusalem distinct from its present context, the contest in Rome between Simon Magus and Peter. There is no true narrative overlap with the Acts, since the Jerusalem tale is not narrated in this passage of the *Acts of Peter*. Because the allusion to the Jerusalem episode appears within the narration of the Roman contest in the *Acts of Peter*, the contest in Rome is not a clear elaboration of the episode in Acts 8. Moreover, the Acts 8 episode is not even the main conflict in Jerusalem between these two characters in the *Acts of Peter*. In Luke's Acts, Simon's offer of money to receive the power to bestow the Holy Spirit becomes the conclusion of his encounter with the apostles in Samaria. In the *Actus Vercellenses*, the final refutation of Simon in Jerusalem seems to have been the Eubula incident. This is narrated in full in chapter 17; after Peter exposes Simon's theft of Eubula's gold, he flees Judea without further confrontation with Peter. The episode with Simon about purchasing power would have thus taken place before the Eubula incident, if it was in fact narrated at all in the *Actus Vercellenses*.

There are thus *three* points of contact between the *Acts of Peter* and chapter eight of Acts: the allusion to purchasing power, the conflict with Simon in Jerusalem concerning Eubula, and the conflict with Simon in Rome. If Matthews is correct, all three would have developed from the juxtaposition of Simon Magos and Peter by Luke. Matthews argues that the traditions of missionary activity in Samaria and the conflict with Simon Magus were initially connected with Philip, who converted him (Acts 8:13). Luke then introduced Peter into the Samaritan account and brought him into conflict with Simon Magus there. In his view, Luke is then responsible for "introducing" Peter and Simon.[137] The main question is whether Luke invented the account of Peter's conflict with Simon Magus, or whether Luke opportunistically used an earlier tradition concerning Simon and Peter in Jerusalem, which he would have transposed to Samaria for two purposes: in order to overshadow the traditions about Philip and in order to make Peter (partially) responsible for one of the important advances of the Christian mission in Acts (1:8). Luke has an interest in Samaria, and in placing one of the major apostles there. But if the intent to supplant Philip is the dominant factor, then it would be more plausible to assume, as Matthews does, that Luke first replaced Philip with Peter in Samaria and that Samaria was then transferred to Jerusalem by the *Acts of Peter*, since the authors of the *Acts of Peter* in faraway northern Asia Minor had no concern for Samaria. Yet a geographical translocation of a preexisting conflict narrative from Jerusalem to Samaria is equally possible, given Lukan redactional concerns.[138] Moreover, the sheer multiformity of the traditions known to both the *Acts of Peter* and Luke suggests that the tradition antedates both. The *Acts of Peter* know a wealth of information about the conflict with Simon that is unknown in the Acts of the Apostles, such as the signature conflict in Rome. The account in Acts may very well be a brief, epitomized allusion to these traditions, employed for clear redactional purposes.

The intertextual nexus of the treatment of Paul in the *Actus Vercellenses* is very different from that of Peter. For reasons of the story alone, the treatment of Peter in the *Actus Vercellenses* overlaps narratively with Luke's Acts, yet there is no textual contact. The treatment of Paul does show textual dependence on a stylistic level, but the narrative of *Actus Vercellenses* 1–3 is a complement to Luke's Acts, not a direct overlap, because it narrates subsequent events. Luke's Acts play the same role in the characterization of

Paul that the Gospels do for the characterization of Peter. Although this is not evidence that *Actus Vercellenses* 1-3 are a later addition to the text, if one accepts this hypothesis on the grounds of the other data, it presents an interesting index of the time that has passed between the formation of the narratives about Peter in the sources of the continuous Greek text, and of those about Paul. The stories about Peter can, at points, overlap with and contradict the account in Acts; but the stories about Paul accept the Acts of the Apostles as a point of departure, and merely complete them.

The relationship between the *Acts of Peter* and other early Christian literature became more explicit, but less substantive over time. The only narrative overlap between the New Testament and the main body of the *Actus Vercellenses*, the encounters with Simon, do not show compelling evidence of literary dependence. The narratives seem to be products of independent development; they are multiforms.[139] Chapters 1-3, which may be later additions, do, however, show significant narrative congruence with the Acts of the Apostles. In this case, however, the *Actus Vercellenses* complement and supplement the account of Acts. They do not reproduce the same narrative content.

### The Acts of Paul

In addition to the synoptic gospels, the Acts, and the Pauline epistles, the *Acts of Paul* also have a significant intertextual relationship with the *Acts of Peter*. The problem of the dependence of the two is a vexed one; the *Acts of Paul* seem to have borrowed the *quo vadis* story from the *Actus Vercellenses* (chap. 35); but the *Actus Vercellenses* seems to depend on the *Acts of Paul* in chapter 41. Poupon suggested a solution that now should seem predictable: the *Acts of Paul* do depend on the *Actus Vercellenses*, but since chapter 41 is a later addition to the *Actus Vercellenses*, it is possible for that chapter to have borrowed from the *Acts of Paul*.[140]

In the *Martyrdom of Paul* (chap. 2), Nero decides to persecute the Christians because his servants Patroklos, Barsabbas Justus (of the flat feet), Urion the Cappadocian, and Festus the Galatian have converted; Patroklos was earlier raised from the dead by Paul himself. The *Actus Vercellenses* attributes the same activity to Peter (chap. 41): "for by making disciples of some of his servants Peter had caused them to leave him . . . for he sought to destroy all those brothers and sisters who had been made disciples by Peter."[141] The conversions play the same role in both texts; they anger Nero and become the indirect cause of the first persecution of Christians. They also appear at the same point in the narratives, that is, in the martyrdom accounts. The redactor of chapters 1-3 and 41 of the *Actus Vercellenses* is explicitly trying to tie the stories of the two apostles together by use of this allusion. And an allusion it is; no attempt is made here to narrate the entire story, only to allude, however inexactly, to something known from another source.

The use of the *quo vadis* story in the *Acts of Paul* is secondary to its use in the *Actus Vercellenses*. It is neither citation nor allusion, but rather the adaptation of a narrative unit. Carl Schmidt presented the Greek papyrus of the Hamburg *Staats- und Universitätsbibliothek* (PH) in his 1936 edition of the *Acts of Paul*.[142] Its publication solved a scholarly riddle; Origen (*Commentary on John*, 20:12) attributed the *quo vadis* scene to the *Acts of Paul*, but until PH, the *quo vadis* scene was known only as a component of the *Acts of Peter* preserved in the *Actus Vercellenses*.[143] In the Hamburg papyrus, however, the scene appears in the context of Paul's journey from Corinth to Italy. Jesus walks upon the water toward Paul, who is still on board. He wakes Paul, for it is night. Paul asks him why he is downcast; the Lord responds, "I am about to be crucified afresh." "God forbid!" responds Paul. Jesus then commands Paul to go to Rome and admonish the Christians and walks before the ship to show the way.[144] Schmidt recognized that Jesus' statement, "I am about to be crucified afresh," was singularly inappropriate as a foreshadowing of the martyrdom of Paul, who was to be beheaded. The martyrdom of Peter provides the more appropriate context.

The points of contact between the two acts, however, betray in only one detail the exactness one would expect from the use of a written source. Only the word of Jesus, ἄνωθεν μέλλω σταυροῦσθαι (*AcPaul*) or πάλιν σταυροῦμαι (*AcVer*), are closely similar. Paul does not even ask Jesus the crucial question, *quo vadis?* Peter meets Jesus on the road leading away from Rome, fleeing certain martyrdom. Paul is not in flight, but rather about to arrive in Rome; nor is he on land. The device used to bring Jesus in contact with Paul, walking on water, is familiar from Gospel tradition. Even the reaction of the apostles is diametrically opposite: Peter is overjoyed that he will follow his Lord in martyrdom. Paul, on the other hand, does not cheer up until he meets the Christians at Rome. This may be a simple redactional alteration: in the *Actus Vercellenses*, the appearance of the Lord turns the ever-irresolute Peter back to Rome and signifies the identification of the apostle with his Lord, over which he rejoices. In the *Acts of Paul*, however, Jesus' words may not apply specifically to Paul, but may rather foreshadow the general persecution of Christians under Nero described in chapter 11.[145]

Dennis MacDonald has used these same data to argue that the *quo vadis* scene in the *Acts of Peter* is secondary and dependent on its use in the *Acts of Paul*.[146] He aptly argues that the reference to crucifixion in Paul may be a general reference to Paul's martyrdom, since Paul does use the metaphor of crucifixion in his letters to express his identity with Christ. The *quo vadis* scene also appears in both narratives at the correct point, that is, just before the martyrdom account, so this also cannot be used as evidence for the priority of the *Acts of Peter*.[147] MacDonald then notes that it is precisely the "drastic improvement in apostolic intelligence and disposition in the *Acts of Peter*" that argues for its secondary character.[148] Unlike Paul, Peter immediately understands Jesus' symbolism and responds with joy; MacDonald views Peter's reaction to be a secondary improvement, one of the three criteria he employs to determine dependence. MacDonald also understands Peter's flight from the city to be a clumsy narrative device to make him able to meet Jesus going into the city. Yet Peter's cowardly flight from martyrdom is typical of his character as presented in the *Acts of Peter*.[149] Peter lost faith while walking on the water (chap. 10), he denied Christ, but yet he was forgiven his sins (chap. 7): "For if Satan overthrew me, whom the Lord held in such great honor, so that I denied the light of my hope . . . what do you expect, you who are new to the faith?" He is thus the patron saint of those with wavering faith, whether it be Marcellus the polytheist patron who is led astray from supporting the Christians or Marcellus the apostate Christian. Peter's character is consonant with his role in both redactional levels of the *Acts of Peter*. His flight from Rome is just the last in a series of lapses of faith from which he is graciously restored by Christ.[150] The *quo vadis* story thus adheres best narratively with the *Acts of Peter*, fulfilling the second of MacDonald's criteria, internal consistency.[151]

The *quo vadis* story appearing in the *Acts of Paul* is not a citation. Rather, the *Acts of Paul* borrowed the narrative unit from the *Acts of Peter* and recast it in a different manner. The relationship between the *Acts of Peter* and the *Acts of Paul* thus forms an analogy to that between the *Acts of Peter* and the Acts of the Apostles. The relationship between the two documents is not close enough to indicate an explicit allusion. The early point of contact is a substantive one; the *Acts of Paul* borrow the *quo vadis* story in filling out its own narrative. The second point of contact, in the martyrdom of the *Actus Vercellenses*, occurs during a later redaction of that text. At this point, the *Acts of Paul* were surely a written text, and the *Actus Vercellenses* do not borrow the story, but only allude to it as though it were generally known.

## Conclusion

The *Actus Vercellenses* is a neat, single manuscript that can be taken and held in one's hands. Yet, together with the other two brief manuscript witnesses, it attests that the *Acts of Peter* were markedly fluid. The Pauline interpolations in the *Actus Vercellenses* date to the late second century. The translation of the document into Latin occurred in the fourth century. The excision of the Jerusalem narrative probably took place in the sixth century, when the manuscript was copied. These stages of redaction do not only refer to periods of time, but to three distinct "authors" who changed the shape of the text decisively. And "before the text," one also finds traces of source documents. An author collated these sources, supplying more speeches, transitional and summary passages, and predictive passages that provided an overview of the entire narrative. This compositional activity resulting in the continuous Greek text took place prior to the late second-century Greek redaction, probably in the 170s. At this point, the author knew the Acts of the Apostles and occasionally used them as a stylistic model. The written sources of the continuous Greek text are earlier still and presumably possessed independent value as records of Peter's deeds; these sources, however, though aware of the gospel narratives, do not show the guiding influence of other early Christian literature either in literary style or narrative development.

Though all of the individuals who took part in this literary activity clearly treasured the story of Peter, none of them, apparently, felt constrained to retain the sources in precisely the form in which he or she received them. The transmission of the narrative is fluid. On the written level, the continuous reedition of the *Acts of Peter* in various written manifestations makes the recovery of the "original text" of any of the versions impossible from the standpoint of scholarly method. On the level of audience and reception, it is unclear what is to be considered the "real" *Acts of Peter*. Their multiformity, the nemesis of the scholar in search of *the* text, is a literary characteristic inseparable from the work itself.

# 3

## Fixity and Fluidity in the Narrative Trajectory
## of the Acts of Peter

### Texts in Trajectory

If fluidity is characteristic of the transmission of the *Actus Vercellenses*, what was it about this text—and texts like it—that attracted this degree of literary activity? The numerous changes in form and language point to the function of this text for its audience: they tell something about the reception of the text, how its ancient audiences approached and appropriated it. Even at the level of the *Actus Vercellenses*, there is a marked tendency to *alter* the text in the course of transmission, whether by translation or excerpting. The text is behaving similarly to oral tradition, with each manuscript representing a new "performance" of the work in another context. Yet this occurs on the level of a written text.

The *Acts of Peter* as presented in the *Actus Vercellenses* are only one text in a narrative trajectory of related Petrine texts dating from the fourth to the sixth centuries. This fluid, performative tendency is even more marked in the broader collection of Petrine texts related to the *Actus Vercellenses*. The earliest Latin texts are the account of Pseudo-Hegesippos attributed (probably falsely) to Ambrose of Milan (ca. 340–397 C.E.) and the martyrdom of Peter ascribed to the bishop Linus (mid-fourth century; hereafter "the Linus text"). In Greek and Latin, there are also the *Acts of Peter and Paul* ascribed to Marcellus (fifth to sixth century; hereafter "the Marcellus text") and the *Acts of Nereus and Achilleus* (Greek, fifth to sixth century; Latin, seventh century). The Old Church Slavonic translation of the *Acts of Peter* also contains one independent use of a story known from *Actus Vercellenses*, which will not be treated here because it otherwise follows the Marcellus text. Pseudo-Abdias likewise presents a version of part of the *Acts of Peter*, but, since it is a mechanical compilation of the sources already mentioned, it too will remain outside the limits of this study.[1]

The previous chapter demonstrated that, even at the earliest level of the *Acts of Peter* trajectory, we have not a simple text, but two excerpts, one of them a Coptic translation, the other a truncated and interpolated Latin translation of a Greek text, which itself had already undergone redaction and had earlier been compiled from written sources. A look forward, to the later versions of the *Acts of Peter*, shows the same processes to be at work: narrative recasting, insertions, translations, expansions, and excerpts.

These Petrine texts display almost complete narrative overlap: they all tell the tale of Peter's activity and martyrdom in Rome, using the same cast of characters: Peter, Simon, Marcellus, Agrippa, and Nero. Each Petrine text has its own history of related redactions and translations. The *Actus Vercellenses*, for example, have undergone a number of alterations and recastings on a textual level: the text itself was redacted, translated, excerpted, or expanded. These processes leave traces in the text that can be discerned with source-critical methods. The Linus text and the Marcellus text also show similar processes of redaction and translation among their manuscripts. The Marcellus text is available in at least two distinct recensions.

The redaction and translation of a single work, however, is a phenomenon distinct from the relationships among the various works of the *Acts of Peter* narrative trajectory, for example, the rather loose family relationship between the *Actus Vercellenses* and the Marcellus text. Among these various later versions, only the Linus text and the *Actus Vercellenses* show the same degree of close literary relationship as that existing between the sources and redactions of the *Actus Vercellenses* itself: the Linus text and the *Actus Vercellenses* are both translations of similar Greek texts. The other three later versions show a use of the earlier texts that is not primarily one of literary dependence or close literary manipulation. The *Actus Vercellenses*, the Linus text, and Pseudo-Hegesippos are close enough that scholars have advanced hypothetical relationships among them: the *Actus Vercellenses* as an abridgment of the Linus text,[2] Pseudo-Hegesippos as dependent on Linus, or Linus on Pseudo-Hegesippos.[3] Although it is presently generally accepted that Linus is an independent translation of a Greek text similar to that translated in the *Actus Vercellenses*, and that Pseudo-Hegesippos depends on Linus, the sheer number of learned articles shows that the relationship among them admits some ambiguity. *Nereus and Achilleus*, though more distantly related, retells some parts of the contest known from the *Actus Vercellenses*, and explicitly refers to an account written in Greek (!) by Linus (Achelis 14.4–6).[4]

The texts thus clearly know one another on some level, but do not show a direct literary relationship; something between textual dependence and completely free invention is at work here. Thus the methods in this chapter will differ from those of Chapter Two. Though the Petrine texts are written texts, one finds present among them the hallmarks of oral transmission, such as the presence of multiforms, the telescoping of chronology, and the fluidity of the text. Just as important as the fluidity of the text are those elements that remain fixed, or rather, the relationship between fluid and fixed. The logic that determines which aspects of the narrative were fixed and which fluid is the most important indicator of the reason these texts altered so much from one version to the next. The multifarious versions of these works and their lack of verbal overlap suggest that it was the general line of the story, rather than the specific text at any given point, which was the significant aspect of these works. The fluidity of the narrative allowed it to be continually reshaped. In this chapter, the nature and direction of these changes will be examined in detail. It is an attempt to write "the story of the stories" within the *Acts of Peter* trajectory.

The shape of the narrative imposes some limits on this investigation. Since most of the versions of the *Acts of Peter* preserve only the martyrdom account, this is the only narrative complex that can be examined at any length in all of the surviving versions. Also, the secondary characters show more radical, and therefore more instructive, development than do the primary figures, Peter and Simon. This stands to reason; if the major figures alter too much, the story would no longer be recognizably the same. The critical changes in the narrative are thus best illustrated in the characters of Marcellus, Nero, and Agrippa.

### Later versions of the *Acts of Peter*

Early Christian narratives about Peter are numerous.[5] In addition to the gospels—synoptic and other—the Acts of the Apostles, and the *Acts of Peter*, there is the Clementine literature, transmitted fully in two versions, the *Recognitions* and the *Homilies*, and the large number of sources from which they seem to have been drawn.[6] Moreover, a significant number of writings are attributed to the authority of Peter, although they form a corpus distinct from narratives *about* Peter.[7] With slight exceptions, as seen in the last chapter, the *Acts of Peter* trajectory relates events distinct from those known in the gospels and the Acts of the Apostles. The relationship between the *Acts of Peter* and the Clementine literature is closer, if only because their general topics overlap: both present an extended conflict between Simon Magos and Peter, who follows the former all over the Mediterranean basin, finally arriving in Rome for the ultimate contest. Despite this, the Clementine literature does not transmit any of the individual narrative units found in the *Acts of Peter*. Only the four Petrine texts enumerated above, the *Actus Vercellenses*, the Linus text, the Marcellus text, and Pseudo-Hegesippos offer direct narrative overlap.

### Linus

The Linus text[8] bears the closest relationship to the *Actus Vercellenses*. Despite a significant similarity in content between the Linus text and the *Actus Vercellenses*, the Latin wording of each document is radically different. Very little verbal overlap occurs; completely different Latin words are chosen to render the Greek source. The Linus text offers a more sophisticated and idiomatic Latin than the *Actus Vercellenses*, lacking the characteristic woodenness of the latter; it is also more pleonastic (see AcVer 36 and Linus 10 in Appendix Three). The Linus translation is more idiomatic and graceful than that of the *Actus Vercellenses*, which translates the text almost word for word. The tendency of the *Actus Vercellenses* to abbreviate, and of the Linus text to paraphrase, can also be seen in the episode in which Agrippa confronts his concubines about their recent change in sexual habits (see AcVer 33 and Linus 2 in Appendix Three). The Linus text is characteristically prolix; it adds the novelistic detail that Agrippa was driven to angry accusation by his insane love (*vehementissima amoris captus insania*) for his concubines.

The Linus text is later than the Latin translation edited in the *Actus Vercellenses*, in that it often adds trinitarian formulae and explicit language on the divine and human natures of Christ.[9] Yet not all that late; fifth- and sixth-century dates had been proposed on the grounds that the Linus text harmonizes Scriptural allusions with the Vulgate version of the Bible, but, on closer inspection, the passages show more affinity to the *Vetus Latina*, in the cases in which its translation is not identical to the Vulgate.[10] Surprisingly for a text with such orthodox language, Peter's speech about the mystery of the cross is repeated in the Linus text (*Linus* 13) in partial verbal overlap with the *Actus Vercellenses* (*AcVer* 38); this is one of the few cases in which close verbal similarity occurs.[11] In it, Peter claims that he wishes to be crucified upside-down as a symbol of the first man, who came into the world upside-down and thus reversed the relationship of the human race to the entire order of the creation, mistaking left for right, and evil for good. The appearance of this passage in the Linus text is remarkable because of its Gnostic overtones. Gérard Poupon has argued that the text should be dated prior to the decree of Gelasius (ca. 382–84 C.E.), which tagged as heretical any attempt to separate the martyrdoms of Peter and Paul, for the Linus text does not contain Paul's martyrdom. Whether this is sufficient grounds, the other considerations would suggest a mid- to late-fourth-century date.[12]

The content of the Linus text is very close to the story of the martyrdom in the *Actus Vercellenses*. Only two episodes appear that are not known in the *Actus Vercellenses*: while in prison, Peter converts his two guards, Processus and Martinianus, who are miraculously baptized when a font of water gushes forth from the rock wall of the prison; this is told as a flashback (*Linus* 5).[13] The second extra episode is a riot in the Roman Senate, as the senators complain that Peter has estranged their wives from them by preaching abstinence from sexual relations (*Linus* 3).

There are a few other significant differences from the *Actus Vercellenses* story. In the Greek martyrdom account (the *Actus Vercellenses* have a lacuna in chaps. 35–36), Peter is arrested by Agrippa (*AcPetMart* 7) only after he tries to flee Rome, encountering Christ on the way out of the city; this is the setting of the *quo vadis* dialogue (*AcPetMart* 6). In the Linus text, the martyrdom account begins with Peter already in prison, under arrest by Nero. The four concubines of Agrippa convert to chastity when they visit him there (*Linus* 2); in the *Actus Vercellenses*, this happens while Peter is still free (*AcVer* 33). In the Linus text, Peter's friends convince him to flee when he is already in prison, and he makes his flight from there (*Linus* 6). This jailbreak passes without comment, perhaps because Peter has already converted his two guards to Christianity. When Peter is again arrested, it is at the hands of Agrippa, the prefect (*Linus* 8), as in the *Actus Vercellenses*. Unlike the later martyrdom accounts, Nero still is not prominent in the story of the arrest and execution of Peter. On the whole, the completely different wording of the Linus text, and its numerous small expansions dotting every page, give the impression of a completely new telling of the story, although the content is mostly familiar from the *Actus Vercellenses*.

### Pseudo-Hegesippos

Pseudo-Hegesippos 3.2.1[14] recounts the martyrdoms of both Peter and Paul, but Paul seems to be a superficial addition to a text primarily concerned with Peter; he appears at the end of the passage in his own martyrdom account, but nowhere else in the text save the first line. This is another example of the "framing" technique seen in the Pauline interpolations in the *Actus Vercellenses*. The text appears as an episode in some manuscripts of a Latin rendering of Josephus. The account is quite brief, no more than a page or two, and gives the impression of an epitome. Little verbal overlap occurs with either the *Actus Vercellenses* or the Linus text. The story derives much from them, although it often appears in a form conflated with Eusebios' account of Peter (*Ecclesiasti-*

*cal History* 2.14–15). Peter has several encounters with Simon, but the only point of contact with the *Actus Vercellenses* is the contest over the resurrection of the youth in the forum (*AcVer* chap. 28; Ussani 184.26–185.17): Simon is able to make the youth's head move, but only Peter restores him to life. As in the *Actus Vercellenses*, Simon tries to take to the air over the city of Rome, only to break his leg, to die later in Aricia (the *Actus Vercellenses* have him die in Terracina, chap. 32; Ussani 185.22–186.2). Similar to the Linus text (and not the *Actus Vercellenses*), Peter is arrested twice; he flees after the first arrest and has the *quo vadis* dialogue with Christ (Ussani 186.18–26). Pseudo-Hegesippos departs from both texts, however, in excising the speech about the upside-down man, along with the stories about Roman matrons who converted to sexual absti-nence and thereafter refused sexual relations with their husbands. Peter's execution, attributed in the other two texts to Agrippa's anger over his changed relationship to his concubines, is wholly motivated in Pseudo-Hegesippos by Peter's implication in the death of Simon (Ussani 186.2–6), who had become a favorite of Nero; for it is at Peter's prayer that Simon falls out of the sky, as also in the *Actus Vercellenses*. Peter also pleads to be crucified upside down, but for a different reason: not to reveal the mystery of the cross and the first man, as in the *Actus Vercellenses* and the Linus text, but because he consid-ers himself unworthy to die in the same manner as Christ (Ussani 186.26–187.1). Pseudo-Hegesippos anticipates later texts in adding the martyrdom of Paul to the account and in emphasizing the importance of Nero's friendship with Simon as a motivation for Peter's execution.

## Marcellus

The Marcellus text was composed in Greek. The majority of the Greek manuscripts begin with the voyage of Paul to Rome from the east (from the island of Gaudomelete), which presupposes that Peter's activity in Rome took place before Paul ever arrived on the scene.[15] Chapters 1–3 of the *Actus Vercellenses*, which were probably a later addi-tion, assume the opposite: there Paul is not arriving in Rome, but leaving from there for Spain; his martyrdom, not recounted in the *Actus Vercellenses*, presumably happens after he returns to Rome from Spain. The Armenian and Old Slavonic versions of the Marcellus text follow the majority Greek text. One Greek manuscript, however, does not narrate Paul's voyage but begins at the point that he enters Rome; this text also varies a good deal from the other Greek witnesses in the martyrdom account proper. It is this Greek text from which the Latin version was translated and which was the pri-mary version in the West.[16]

The plot of this version bears only a loose resemblance to the *Actus Vercellenses*. Peter's conflicts with Simon are largely in the past; he narrates some of them to Paul when Paul arrives, but only in summary (*Marcellus* 4), and he performs some further healings, also narrated summarily (*Marcellus* 12). The major conflict with Simon is a public hearing before Nero, at which both Peter and Paul are present and in which the chief piece of evidence is a letter from Pilate attesting to Christ's miracles (*Marcellus* 15–31).

The narrative thereafter picks up the same thread as the *Actus Vercellenses* and Pseudo-Hegesippos, with modifications. Simon also attempts to fly in midair in the Marcellus text, but, as in Pseudo-Hegesippos, dies immediately, broken in four pieces, when the prayers of Peter ground him permanently (*Marcellus* 54-56); in the *Actus Vercellenses*, he merely falls and breaks a leg in three pieces, to crawl off in ignominy and die later at the hands of his doctor (*AcVer* 32). Peter and Paul are arrested immediately thereafter in the Marcellus text because of their fatal opposition to Simon.[17] The Marcellus text narrates Peter's death similarly to the *Actus Vercellenses*: Peter also pleads to be crucified upside down, for the same reason given in Pseudo-Hegesippos, because he is unworthy to die in the manner of Christ (*Marcellus* 60). The *quo vadis* dialogue also appears in the Marcellus text, but as a flashback narrated by Peter as he hangs dying (*Marcellus* 61). The narrative concludes with Paul's martyrdom.

### Nereus and Achilleus

The *Acts of Nereus and Achilleus*,[18] originally composed in Greek, are the most imaginative retelling of the *Acts of Peter*. Unlike all the other texts, they do not contain an account of the martyrdom of Peter, but only a narration of some of the encounters between Peter and Simon. Any verbal similarity to the *Actus Vercellenses*, the only text containing this part of the Peter saga, is absent. The frame of the story is artful: the young Christians Nereus and Achilleus, exiled to a remote island, encounter two disciples of Simon Magos. The young men forthwith write to Marcellus in Rome, asking for information about Simon. In the epistolary reply, Marcellus retells some of his favorite episodes (*Nereus* 12-17). These include a version of the same resurrection story retold in Pseudo-Hegesippos and in the *Actus Vercellenses*. In *Nereus and Achilleus*, Peter and Simon encounter the corpse, not in the forum, but as the funeral procession winds its way through the streets of Rome (*Nereus* 12; *Achelis* 11.19-12.21). The talking dog known from the *Actus Vercellenses* also appears in *Nereus and Achilleus*, although the story differs: the dog attacks Simon, who then retreats in shame for a year (*Nereus* 13; *Achelis* 12.18-13.21). Nereus and Achilleus hear a story similar to the account of Peter's daughter known from the Coptic papyrus, which was probably part of the Greek *Acts of Peter* translated by the *Actus Vercellenses*. But it presents considerable differences: in the Coptic fragment, the daughter remains paralyzed, and Peter tells the story of her abduction by a certain rich Ptolemaios to justify leaving her in that condition. In *Nereus and Achilleus*, the daughter does gradually recover from her paralysis and dies in response to her own prayers when a Roman, *comes* Flaccus,[19] proposes marriage to her (*Nereus* 15; *Achelis* 14.7-15.9).

The relationships among these various retellings of the deeds of Peter are not "textual." The closest verbal overlap exists between the *Actus Vercellenses* and the Linus text; even in this case, the Linus text uses its original freely, paraphrasing, recasting narratives, and adding phrases, sentences, and entire episodes. In all of the other cases, the relationship between the texts is even less direct.

For describing nontextual relationships of similarity or dependence, the distinction between *fabula* and *sjuzhet* developed by the Russian Formalists is useful.[20] The fabula is the most generic form of a narrative trajectory: it denotes the events in their logical and chronological sequence and includes the basic elements of the narrative, such as situation, location, characters. In the case of the *Acts of Peter*, the fabula would be the sum of individual narratives about Peter, arranged in logical sequence according to the external dictates of his life. For example, events in Jerusalem precede those in Rome;

the contest with Simon takes place before Peter's trial and execution, and the *quo vadis* story just before his arrest. A *sjuzhet*, or, as I will call it, *storyline*, is a particular rhetorical organization of a fabula that may readjust standard temporal or logical sequences.[21] The materials of the fabula may be restructured, for example, by the technique of flashback; similarly, the motivations of the characters may not be presented in logical fashion. The Marcellus text preserves a unique storyline when it presents the *quo vadis* narrative as a flashback told by Peter as he is dying on the cross. To these two categories, narratologists have added a third, *text*, the storyline told on one occasion by a particular narrative agent, whether oral performance or manuscript.[22] Richard Valantasis first applied these terms to the study of the Apocryphal Acts.[23] As he notes, much of the overlap between the various Apocryphal Acts is not at the *textual* level, but at the level of storyline, or even fabula.

In these Petrine texts, the relationship among even the closest of these documents is not textual. Even where the content of two versions is similar, the author of each work has chosen to transmit a new version of the relevant narrative units. The texts do share certain tendencies, such as the addition of Paul's arrival in Rome and his later martyrdom, and the excision of such dogmatically problematic speeches as Peter's disquisition on the upside-down man; yet each text makes use of the common narrative material uniquely. The Linus text and the *Actus Vercellenses* have the closest relationship and follow the same storyline, that is, the same arrangement of the material. Pseudo-Hegesippos also relates to these two texts chiefly on the level of storyline, sometimes shadowing one, sometimes the other more closely, though omitting much of both. In the other texts, even the storyline has been crafted differently. The Marcellus text plucks out only isolated episodes, and alters them vis-a-vis those known in the other versions; even the *quo vadis* story appears in Marcellus as a flashback. In *Nereus and Achilleus*, the arrangement of the episodes is so unique that it bears only a family resemblance to the other texts. However variegated, the collection of narrative units about Peter among all these texts does belong to the same fabula. The episodes all have their place in the same basic outline of the deeds of Peter: his miracles, contest with Simon, imprisonment, and execution.

The texts vary in the weight accorded to the different elements of the fabula. The martyrdom forms the center of interest in three of the four texts discussed, the exception being *Nereus and Achilleus*; but the conflict between Peter and Simon is also significant in two of them. It is the main content of the letter of Marcellus in the *Acts of Nereus and Achilleus*; but the conflict also forms a large part of the Marcellus text, in which Simon and Peter do not engage in a contest of miracles, but in a judicial hearing of the historical evidence about Christ's miracle-working activity.

## First-Century Figures and Their Fate in Second-Century Narrative

The tendency in scholarship has been to assume that the Apocryphal Acts have only the most marginal relationship to history proper, hence the repeated claims that they are some variety of ancient novel. Instead of taking these texts to be what they claim, accounts of first-century figures, scholars have instead sought externally attested "historical" data to confirm the supposedly unreliable information given in the Apocryphal

Acts. In the case of Peter, it is difficult to find testimony in the apostolic fathers and the second-century patristic writings for anything but the bare bones of the narrative: that Peter came to Rome, taught there, and was martyred there in the same period as Paul. Even the datum that he was martyred under Nero is first given by Tertullian, who already knew one of the Apocryphal Acts, the *Acts of Paul*.[24] Only from the third century onward do the church fathers know the characteristic detail that Peter was crucified upside down; since these attestations postdate at least one version of the *Acts of Peter*, it is possible that Origen, the first of them, learned this detail from the *Acts of Peter* rather than from an unknown source. In this case, the apocryphon may be the originator rather than the recipient of church tradition, which would turn the usual scheme on its head.

The *Actus Vercellenses*, though an early third-century document, contain five figures from the midfirst century: Peter, Simon Magos, Nero, Agrippa, and Marcellus. About the historicity of the first three characters there need be little question; the conflict between Peter and Simon, the very fabric of the narrative, provides the dramatic date, and Nero, as discussed at length below, appears as a chronological index. Agrippa and Marcellus, however, are figures with less pedigree. Both of them persist throughout the narrative trajectory, even when changes in the storyline render their dramatic roles increasingly otiose. No corroborating sources have yet turned up to illuminate the character of Agrippa conclusively. Marcellus is attested briefly in Tacitus's *Annals*, which place him squarely in the first century. The mere fact that externally attested first-century individuals appear as protagonists in the pages of the *Acts of Peter* is sufficient to show that these narratives were not fictions completely divorced from historical memory. The narrative refers to something in the external world: the foundational period of the Christian community, and the deeds of one of its most famous early leaders. These texts have their points of departure in individuals and events already known to their audiences.

Marcellus, despite playing a secondary dramatic role in the narrative trajectory of the *Acts of Peter*, is a major figure in one of the texts, the *Actus Vercellenses*. He is given more script than is even Simon; aside from Peter, only Marcellus addresses us with extended speeches and challenges us with theological content. Like a shadow of Peter, Marcellus also works a miracle (*AcVer* 11) and sees a vision at a crucial point in the text, just before the major contest between Peter and Simon in the forum (*AcVer* 22). His apostasy from the Christian faith, as presented in the *Actus Vercellenses*, is described as a parallel to Peter's pattern of alternating faith and unbelief.[25] In his speech of repentance in chapter 10, Marcellus alludes to Peter's attempt to follow Jesus in walking on the water, known only from the Gospel of Matthew 14:28–31: "This Simon called you unfaithful, Peter, since you lost faith upon the water. . . . Therefore if you lost faith, you whom he laid his hands, whom he also chose, with whom he worked miracles, then since I have this assurance, I repent and resort to your prayers. Lift up my soul."[26] Marcellus reasons that those who have fallen from the faith should receive mercy if they repent, if even Peter, who was chosen by Jesus, lost faith on more than one occasion. He presents Peter as an example of God's mercy to those with wavering faith. Peter employs this example from his own life earlier in the narrative (chap. 7). The issue of God's forgiveness is an important concern in the *Actus Vercellenses*, and the additions exploit the parallelism between Marcellus and Peter to illustrate it.

Marcellus is a rich senator of noble family. When, in a vision, Marcellus hears Peter commanding him to kill an "evil-looking woman" (*mulierem quendam turpissimam*, *AcVer*

22; Lipsius 70.12-13)[27] who represents the power of Simon,[28] Marcellus cries that he is of a good family and has never so much as killed a sparrow. His class allegiance is significant in providing a basis for his benefactions. When Peter first arrives, the report of the brothers in Rome primarily concerns Marcellus (AcVer 8): once a supporter of widows, orphans, and travelers, he has been won over by Simon, who is now enjoying the hospitality of his house. Marcellus now regrets all the money that he devoted to the Christians: "I have spent so much money for such a long time, vainly believing I was giving my money to attract the attention of God" (AcVer 8).[29] When travelers arrive at his door, he beats them with a club and has them driven away. The Christians at Rome place the blame for their own lack of faith on Marcellus: "if he had not been won over, we in turn should not have deserted the holy faith" (AcVer 8).[30] The narrative emphasizes Marcellus's class-based responsibility both to provide financial support and to demonstrate leadership in issues of faith. His repentence is one of the climaxes of the narrative.

Gerhard Ficker first pointed out that Marcellus, patron of the Christian community, was most probably the Marcus Granius Marcellus mentioned in Tacitus' *Annals*.[31] Erstwhile governor of Bithynia during the reign of Tiberius, he was brought up on charges of embezzlement and treason (1.74):[32]

> Shortly afterwards Marcus Granius Marcellus, governor of Bithynia, was accused of treason by his own *quaestor*, Caepio Crispinus with the support of Romanius Hispo. . . . He [Hispo] alleged that Marcellus had told scandalous stories about Tiberius. The charge was damning. . . . Hispo added that Marcellus had placed his own statue above those of the Caesars, and that he had cut off the head of Augustus on one statue and replaced it with that of Tiberius. . . . Tiberius . . . voted for acquittal on the treason counts. Charges of embezzlement were referred to the proper court.[33]

The associate of Marcellus accuses Marcellus to Tiberius on two charges, embezzlement and treason. The emperor, after an angry public outburst in the Senate, decides to drop the charge of treason and prosecute Marcellus for embezzlement.

The only features of the life of Granius Marcellus mentioned in the *Annals* are thus his alleged treason and embezzlement. Precisely these two issues come up in the treatment of Marcellus in the *Actus Vercellenses*, although in altered guise. The charge of embezzlement noted in Tacitus is reflected in the small dialogue between Marcellus and the emperor recorded in chapter eight of the *Actus Vercellenses*:[34]

> To him [Marcellus] the emperor said, "I am keeping you out of every office, lest you rob the provinces and give the money to the Christians." Marcellus answered him, "Indeed, all the things that I have are yours." The emperor said to him, "They would be mine, if you guarded over them for me, but now they are not, because you give them to whomever you please, to I know not what wretches."[35]

The points of overlap between this and the account in Tacitus are the characters of Marcellus and the emperor, the charge of embezzlement, the emperor's prosecution of Marcellus, and the abrupt end of Marcellus's official career (*cursus honorum*). Charges of embezzlement and subsequent dismissal from office, however, are common in Roman history,[36] so this is not an airtight proof of the identity of the characters in the two accounts.

The statue episode is more peculiar and memorable in both narratives, and thus more compelling evidence. After Peter arrives at the house of Marcellus, at which Simon

Magos is residing,[37] the apostle exorcises a demon from a man in the crowd (*AcVer* 11). As the man writhes on the floor, he knocks over and shatters a statue "of Caesar."[38] Marcellus is terrified; he fears unsalutary rumors: "If one of the *curiosi* [39] informs Caesar, he will punish us severely" (*AcVer* 11).[40] Common to this account and the one in Tacitus is Marcellus's responsibility for the mutilation of an imperial cult statue, the presence of an informer, real or imagined, and the fear of punishment. These elements, as well as the character Marcellus, come from the same fabula. Despite the divergences, the outcome is the same: as in Tacitus, nothing results from the threat of an informant. In the *Actus Vercellenses*, the episode is rendered harmless by divine intervention: Peter instructs Marcellus to take water and sprinkle it over the statue in the name of Christ, and the statue is miraculously restored.

Nothing approaches verbal overlap between these two accounts; the relationship is not purely textual. Even the stories differ markedly; the motivations for the actions diverge, with the *Actus Vercellenses* giving a distinctly Christian cast to the events. The charge of embezzlement is not the grave crime in the *Actus Vercellenses* that it is in Tacitus. Marcellus's offense against Rome, for which he was accused in the Roman courts, is transmogrified into a virtue by the Christians because it worked to their benefit. The incident of the statue is likewise whitewashed: it is no longer Marcellus's fault; through miraculous means, the statue is restored and no harm comes to him. Though the storyline differs markedly, enough overlap exists on the level of the fabula to recognize that the character and basic series of events remain the same in both accounts.

The chronology is the decisive piece of evidence demonstrating that the relationship between Tacitus and the *Acts of Peter* cannot be direct. It is not impossible that a provincial governor from the reign of Tiberius (d. 37 C.E.) would eventually become a benefactor of the Christians. Strict chronology, however, shows that Christianity could not have motivated Marcellus's actions while he was in office from 14–15 C.E., through he may have been a benefactor of Christians later.[41] Chronological telescoping such as this is a hallmark of oral tradition.[42] Although it is impossible to reconstruct the first-century sources of the *Actus Vercellenses*, or to determine whether they were written or oral, it is clear that the traditions behind them date back to the first century, since it is unlikely that a character such as Marcellus would first be introduced into the narrative in the second century. These traditions, though, were treated with fluidity rather than exactitude.

The *Actus Vercellenses* present Marcellus as already a Christian when Peter comes to Rome, but as has been argued in Chapter Two, it seems that, in the unredacted version, Marcellus was merely a polytheist patron of the Christians. A similar illustrious aristocratic figure from Asia Minor appears in the *Acts of Paul*, the "queen Tryphaina" who takes in the Christian convert and missionary Thekla, providing her with money and protection (*AcPaul* 27–28). Tryphaina converts to Christianity in the course of the narrative, learning to pray to the "God of Thekla" (*AcPaul* 30) and being instructed in the "word of God" by Thekla herself (*AcPaul* 39).

First-century testimony about Tryphaina shows the same curious mixture of recognizable overlap and essential narrative independence as one finds in the development of the character of Marcellus in the *Actus Vercellenses*. Christian motivations are again assigned to an unlikely character. The *Acts of Paul* call Tryphaina a kinswoman of Caesar, and so she was. A distant relative of the Claudians, she made her home in Kyzikos, not

Pisidian Antioch, where the *Acts of Paul* place her.[43] She is known to have been a queen of Pontos; she was a priestess of Livia, popular for the many benefactions she gave to the city.[44] This case is a direct parallel to that of Marcellus. Both he and Tryphaina are genuine first-century Roman aristocrats with connections to Asia Minor. The Christian narratives present both as senatorial-class polytheist benefactors of the Christians, who convert upon seeing the miraculous works done at the hands of the apostles and their disciples. The Balbus mentioned in chapter 3 of the *Actus Vercellenses* is another senatorial figure with an Asian pedigree, most likely Q. Iulius Balbus, the proconsul of Asia in 100–1 or 101–2 C.E.;[45] he is a later figure, then, than either Marcellus or Tryphaina, which is not surprising if chapters 1–3 of the Actus Vercellenses are a later addition to the text. A turn-of-the-century figure is here telescoped with two mid-first-century figures, since the addition would have been made later.

For Simon Magos, the only first-century source is the Acts of the Apostles. The relationship between Acts and the *Actus Vercellenses*, as seen in Chapter Two, is on the level of the fabula: Peter and Simon appear in both narratives, and Simon asks for the power to lay on hands, but little else agrees directly. This shared episode, set either in Judea or Samaria, would necessarily fall at different points in the respective narratives, and thus has no overlap on the level of storyline: it is the concluding episode of the Samaritan segment of the Acts of the Apostles, but not of the Judean section of the *Actus Vercellenses*, which ends with the Eubula narrative. The contradictions between the two texts—the disagreement about where the episode took place, what was at stake, and who else was present—show that the narratives developed independently.

Other early datable testimonies to Simon Magos are no earlier than the late second century (Clement of Alexandria, Tertullian), with the exception of Justin Martyr and Celsus as transmitted by Origen, who are earlier. Justin places Simon's appearance at Rome, and the erection of a statue in his honor, during the reign of Claudius (*Apology* 1.26, 56). The *Actus Vercellenses* also recall the statue in chapter 10. Marcellus claims that he himself set it up: "for he swayed me so far that I set up a statue of him with the inscription, 'To Simon, the young god.'"[46] The inscription disagrees with Justin's reading, ΣΙΜΩΝΙ ΔΕΩ ΣΑΓΚΤΩ=*Simoni deo sancto* (*Apology* 1.26), but Justin's account is also not without its problems. In 1574, a statue base was found on the island in the Tiber, the location given by Justin, with the inscription *Semoni sanco deo Fidio sacrum*, a dedication to a Sabine divinity by Sextus Pompeius Mussianus.[47] Thus Justin likely misunderstood an inscription that had nothing to do with Simon.

The Claudian date attested by Justin agrees, not with the dramatic date of the *Actus Vercellenses* as they have survived, which describe Peter's death under Nero, but with the unredacted Greek text, before the addition of the first three chapters and the other interpolations concerning Paul. Peter's travel to Rome is dated to twelve years after the death of Christ (*AcVer* 5), resulting in a Claudian date. This datum contradicts the Greek redaction behind the *Actus Vercellenses*, but the agreement with Justin's account gives additional support to the hypothesis that the original date given in the continuous Greek text was Claudian, rather than Neronian. Justin's information proves that the account of Simon's appearance in Rome under Claudius was in common currency among Christians in the midsecond century, and apparently also informed the *Actus Vercellenses*. Justin's account is independent, however: it shows no influence of the continuous Greek text, or even its sources, since he knows nothing of the contest in the forum between

Simon and Peter, the centerpiece of the *Actus Vercellenses* narrative—as good an indication as any that the *Acts of Peter* did not originate in Rome.[48] Hippolytos is the first to mention that Peter opposed Simon in Rome (*Refutatio* 6.15); since his work was composed after 222 C.E., Hippolytos may be drawing this information from the *Acts of Peter* themselves, as Origen seems to do at about the same period.

As in the case of Marcellus, then, the *Acts of Peter* narrative trajectory coheres with earlier texts and traditions in its presentation of some basic data about a first-century figure: given the information in Justin Martyr, Simon Magos appears in the right city, at the right time (accepting the Claudian date as original), and, as the Acts of the Apostles show, against the right antagonist. Marcellus and Tryphaina in the *Acts of Paul* similarly crop up in approximately the correct geographic and temporal setting. The Christian narratives also correctly recall the basic identities of the figures: Tryphaina as kinswoman of Caesar and Marcellus as a senator and provincial governor. Yet, especially in the case of Marcellus, the motivations of the characters have been Christianized. Simple addition and subtraction shows that Marcellus could not have diverted provincial funds to the Christians. More fundamentally, the conversion of the senatorial elite to Christianity would not have been verisimilar in the first century, even to the Christians themselves; in the second century, this would be possible. Moreover, patronage by a senator of Christian provincials in Asia Minor would seem more likely than what is actually presented: patronage of provincial Christians in Rome. On the whole, the similarities between the *Actus Vercellenses* and Tacitus, Justin or Luke's Acts do not inhere in the literary use of one by the other, but in the larger fund of stories, the *fabulae*, known about these individuals. Each text focuses on the elements of the fabulae that suit its purpose, and in a manner that often freely contradicts the first-century versions. These individuals appear in the Apocryphal Acts, not primarily because they stem from a source text, but because they are figures significant to first-century Christians *in Asia Minor*.

## The Importance of Being Nero: Chronology and Historicization

Given the train of the narrative, the most surprising aspect of Nero's presentation in the *Actus Vercellenses* is that he appears at all. His character is superfluous on a narrative level, since Peter's arrest and crucifixion is carried out by the prefect Agrippa, whose four concubines Peter has succeeded in converting to lives of abstention from sexual intercourse. The appearance of Nero creates a discontinuity in the chronological framework of the *Actus Vercellenses*. As noted, the first introduction of Peter states that he travels to Rome only after remaining in Jerusalem for twelve years after Christ's death (*AcVer* 5). This tradition is attested in the *Kerygma Petrou*[49] and was also known to Apollonios, an anti-Montanist writer from Asia Minor whose work dates to shortly after 207 C.E.,[50] another hint that the continuous Greek text was composed in Asia Minor in the second century. According to the twelve-year tradition, Peter would have reached Rome in the early part of the reign of Claudius (41–54 C.E.), almost ten years before Nero's accession. As noted, this would cohere well with the traditions about Simon, whom Justin believes to have reached Rome during the reign of Claudius,[51] but not with Peter's alleged martyrdom under Nero. Despite the later tradition of Peter's twenty-five year episcopate over the Roman church, itself an attempt to harmonize the Claudian and Neronian dates, the *Actus Vercellenses* never indicate that Peter spent a period of several years in Rome. Most of the episodes are portrayed as taking place within days of one another, and the text assumes that Paul will return to Rome within a year.[52]

Within the text, Nero appears as an afterthought. He is mentioned only twice. In the first chapter, which has been argued above to be a later addition to the *Actus Vercellenses*, his name appears as a mere chronological marker for the date of Paul's martyrdom: "Paul will be made perfect at the hands of Nero, that godless and unjust man" (*AcVer* 1). Nero appears for the next and final time in the last chapter of the *Actus Vercellenses*. In it, we learn that Nero was eager to kill Peter, and would have done it, save that Agrippa did it first (*AcPetMart* 12; *AcVer* 41): "When Nero later found out that Peter had departed from life, he found fault with Agrippa the prefect, because he had not been put to death under his jurisdiction. For he had wanted vengeance to be wreaked on him more thoroughly and by means of a more extraordinary punishment."[53] This seems bizarre, since Nero is given no particular motivation for animosity toward Peter anywhere in the story. Why his hatred should surpass that of Agrippa is not a question that can be answered from within the story of the *Actus Vercellenses* itself. The reason for the anomalous characterization of Nero in the *Actus Vercellenses* is the result of the confluence of conflicting traditions about Peter's arrest and martyrdom (Agrippa vs. Nero), telescoped chronology, and the desire to fix a crucial event in the history of the early church within the larger canvas of world history.

The tradition that both Peter and Paul were martyred by Nero himself was unanimous by the fourth century, as Eusebios attests (*Ecclesiastical History* 2.25.5). Tertullian is the first to claim that Nero executed Peter.[54] Only two texts in the *Acts of Peter* trajectory, however, explicitly assign the responsibility for the death of Peter to Nero: Pseudo-Hegesippos, a late-fourth-century narrative, and the Marcellus text, from the fifth or sixth century. In both of them, Nero sentences Peter and Paul because he finds them guilty of the death of Simon Magos. *The Acts of Nereus and Achilleus*, likewise a fifth-century text, may also ultimately lay the blame on Nero, although the text is very condensed here: "After this, the Lord appeared to the apostle Peter in a vision, and said, 'Nero and Simon, since they are full of demons, are turning their efforts against you'" (*Nereus* 14).[55] This prophecy indicates a general attack upon Peter by Simon and Nero, but since *Nereus* does not narrate the actual arrest or martyrdom, it is impossible to tell exactly how the author believed this to have taken place. The Greek martyrdom account, the *Actus Vercellenses*, and the Linus text, three closely related texts, all assign the blame for Peter's death to the prefect Agrippa.

All of the versions of the *Acts of Peter* are unanimous in placing Peter's death in the period of Nero's reign. The entire trajectory of the *Acts of Peter*, however, demonstrates an insecure alternation between the prefect Agrippa and the emperor Nero as the guilty party in Peter's death. As has been shown, in the *Actus Vercellenses*, Nero finds out only later that Agrippa has crucified Peter and becomes angry because he wanted to torture him more cruelly. The Linus text also reproduces the same storyline, but characteristically has a fuller version of it. In it, Nero not only is angry because Agrippa carried out the execution without his consent, but also because Nero wished to vent his personal enmity toward Peter: he holds Peter responsible for depriving him of his friend, Simon.[56] Pseudo-Hegesippos similarly has Nero censure Peter for murdering someone "necessary to the state" (*necessarium reipublicae,* Ussani 186.4–5). By portraying Agrippa as acting beyond the range of his authority, these texts subtly undercut Agrippa's ultimate responsibility for Peter's death and emphasize the authority of Nero.

The Linus text further increases Nero's role by beginning with Peter already in prison, under arrest by Nero for causes unspecified. The action does not begin, however, until the four concubines of the prefect Agrippa visit Peter in prison and are convinced by him to stop having sexual relations with Agrippa. It is at this point that Peter's two guards, Processus and Martinianus, convince Peter to try to escape. They argue that Nero has forgotten about him, and that, at any rate, they can count on some votes in Peter's favor from the Senate, but that he does stand under imminent danger from Agrippa: "'Sir, leave for whatever location you wish, because we believe that the emperor has forgotten about you. But this most unjust Agrippa, because of his love of his concubines, and all aflame with the intemperance of his lust, is moving quickly to put you to death'" (*Linus* 5).[57] Peter succeeds in escaping but turns back when he meets Christ on the way out of the city (the *quo vadis* story). Agrippa then arrests him and executes him.

The presence of Agrippa in all of these narratives (only *Nereus and Achilleus* and Pseudo-Hegesippos fail to mention him) is clearly not motivated by any attempt to exonerate Nero. From the *Actus Vercellenses* onward, all of the texts make only vituperative reference to this emperor most hated by the Christians:

- *perditionis caput scilicet antichristus Nero, consummata iniquitas* ("the font of destruction, that is, the antichrist Nero, perfect injustice," *Linus* 2; Lipsius 2.12–13)
- Πονηρὸς δὲ ὁ Νέρων (*Nereus* 14, Achelis 13.20)
- ὑπηρέτης γάρ ἐστι τοῦ πατρὸς αὐτοῦ τοῦ σατανᾶ ("He is an assistant of his father, Satan," *Marcellus* 61; Lipsius 170.13–14)

It is rather the strength of the traditions about Agrippa that leads to this somewhat confused account of Peter's martyrdom. All of the texts in the *Acts of Peter* trajectory conform to the standard Christian portrait of Nero.

In assigning ever greater responsibility to Nero, the texts are coming into agreement with the Christian topos that Nero was the first of the emperors to persecute the Christians. The church fathers eventually separated the Roman emperors into the few vile emperors who persecuted the Christians and the rest, who, by Eusebios's time, were argued to have been, on the whole, useful in keeping the general order and in protecting the Christians from the Jews. Eusebios, for example, calls Domitian the successor of Nero in his hostility to God (*Ecclesiastical History* 3.17). He also cites Clement of Alexandria as claiming in an apologetic writing that the only emperors who were persuaded by evil men to persecute the Christians were Nero and Domitian (*Ecclesiastical History* 4.26.9). Tertullian also claims that Nero was the first to persecute the Christians (*Apology* 5). It is a short step from claiming that Nero was the first of the emperors to persecute the Christians, and that Peter was martyred during Nero's reign in Rome, to claiming that Nero himself killed Peter. The development of the *Acts of Peter* trajectory illustrates this taking place on a narrative level.

When the writers of the *Actus Vercellenses,* the Linus text, and the Marcellus text sat down to their work, they knew the traditions about Agrippa, but reached beyond these to the character of Nero, a figure more significant in the history of Christian persecution. They struck a delicate balance between the traditions about both. Nero provides some advantage in giving the events of the narratives a more distinct location in space and time than the shadowy Agrippa. Though preserved, this character moves off center stage in favor of the figure who refers to a universal chronological index employed by all historians of the Roman empire, from Tacitus to Luke to Eusebios: the reigns of the emperors.

The chronological inconsistency in the *Actus Vercellenses* shows how persistent was the tradition that Peter came to Rome during the reign of Claudius. The *Actus Vercellenses* respect this tradition by recognizing that some time elapses between the martyrdoms of Peter and Paul. It does this, however, by compressing, into a sole year, the interval of a decade required by strict chronology. The *Acts of Nereus and Achilleus*, the Marcellus text, and Pseudo-Hegesippos dispense with this reference to the intervening year between the martyrdoms of Peter and Paul, and simply portray them as having been martyred at the same time, a further telescoping.

From the *Actus Vercellenses* onward, then, considerable effort is devoted to smoothing out the chronological problems inherent in the conflicting traditions and to grounding the events vis-a-vis world political history. These impulses are historiographic; a similar tendency can be detected in the increasing attention to providing full and accurate details about Roman government and the governing classes. In the *Actus Vercellenses*, the most we learn about Marcellus is that he is of senatorial class.[58] The Linus text not only notes his aristocracy, but provides him with a genealogy; he becomes the son of Marcus, the prefect.[59] In *Nereus and Achilleus*, which refers its readers to the Linus text (*Nereus* 14; Achelis 14), Marcellus is also the son of Marcus, who is there specified as Μάρκου τοῦ τῆς πόλεως Ῥώμης ἐπάρχου (=*praefectus urbis; Nereus* 10; Achelis 9), a detail that must have been taken from the Linus text. Similarly, the Linus text describes Agrippa himself more exactly as *praefectus urbis*, and correctly recognizes that this official is accompanied by lictors. It also describes senatorial-class men as *viri clarissimi* and votes in the Roman senate as *sententiae*.

In addition to becoming progressively more careful in describing such details as Roman offices and titles, the judicial procedures surrounding Peter's trial and sentencing receive greater attention. The Linus text is careful to show that Agrippa does not decide to apprehend Peter without the support of the Senate and that Peter receives a hearing before sentencing. The Marcellus text grants Peter and Paul a lengthy hearing before Nero on what are essentially civil charges; they are only executed when considered guilty of a capital crime, and even then, a distinction is made between a charge of murder (Peter) and of accessory to murder (Paul). These details are unique to each text, so they may be seen as a form of embellishment, meant to heighten the verisimilitude of the narrative. In addition, they show progressively greater familiarity with Roman government and jurisprudence. Yet the direction in which these embellishments tend is not toward more colorful or dramatic description, better characterization, or more entertaining or fantastic narratives. Rather the opposite: the details concern sober points of political and judicial procedure, usually seen as the appropriate topic of historical discourse. The added materials attempt to give the impression of a more accurate historical account of their events.

"I Can't Place the Face, but the Name Is Familiar":
The Persistence of Named Individuals in the Narrative

The persistence of named secondary characters among the versions of the *Acts of Peter* is striking, especially since characters continue to appear in later versions even when their role has been written out of the script. The prefect Agrippa, for example, is the party responsible for the death of Peter in the *Actus Vercellenses*. Agrippa finds that his four concubines inexplicably begin to refrain from having sexual relations with him. After having them followed, he realizes that it is Peter who has been instructing them in this new behavior. He then threatens to kill both his concubines and Peter. When Albinus, an upper class[60] associate of Agrippa, also encounters the same behavior from his wife Xanthippe, he appeals to Agrippa in his office of prefect[61] to take some legal course of action against Peter, before Albinus does so himself. When Agrippa tells Albinus that he has experienced the same hardship, Albinus exclaims, "'What are you waiting for, Agrippa? Let's find him, and execute him as a public nuisance, so that we may have our wives, and that we may avenge those men who do not have the authority to execute him, whose wives he has also separated from them'" (*AcPetMart* 5 =*AcVer* 34).[62]

The Linus text narrates the same storyline, but tells of the collusion between Albinus and Agrippa in indirect discourse: "Thus it came about that . . . it was decided that, acting together with Agrippa, he would capture Peter in a trap just like a bird, and that he would kill him as a mischief-maker" (*Linus* 3).[63] Agrippa is encouraged, not only by Albinus, but also by the Roman Senate. During one of their sessions, a senator rises to complain about Peter's teaching and its effects, and the rest of the senators respond with an enthusiastic uproar (*Linus* 3).

In both versions, Agrippa then arrests Peter and puts him to death. The Linus text gives Peter a brief hearing before the execution (*Linus* 8); the Greek martyrdom account merely specifies that Peter was sentenced to crucifixion on the grounds of atheism (αἰτίᾳ ἀθεότητος, *AcPetMart* 7; Lipsius 90.3), the same charge given in the Linus text (*accusatio superstitionis*, *Linus* 8; Lipsius 10.10–11).[64]

In the Marcellus text, Agrippa wanes before the figure of Nero. Indeed, both the *Actus Vercellenses* and the Linus text recognize Nero's importance by introducing him into the narrative after the death of Peter. Nero hears that Agrippa executed Peter, and is angry because he wanted to punish Peter more severely; death by crucifixion upside down apparently did not exhaust the possibilities available to Nero's imagination (*AcVer* 41; *Linus* 17). The Marcellus text, however, blames Nero alone for the deaths of both Peter and Paul. The two apostles become victims of Simon's friendship with Nero. Peter and Paul first attract attention by criticizing Simon, who is enjoying widespread popularity and the approving audience of Nero himself because of his protean ability to appear in a number of forms, human and animal (*Marcellus* 14). Angered by their public defamation, Simon succeeds in having the two apostles brought before Nero (*Marcellus* 15–16). Much of the text records an inconclusive preliminary trial. Simon finally offers to demonstrate that he is the son of God by flying up to heaven from the top of a tall tower (*Marcellus* 50). While Simon is in mid-air, Peter abjures the "angels of Satan" who are carrying him into the air to release him in the name of Jesus. Simon correspondingly feels the force of gravity and breaks into four pieces when he hits the ground

(*Marcellus* 56). Nero asks Peter who allowed him to do such a terrible thing (*Marcellus* 57).[65] When Peter answers that it was Simon's own blasphemy that caused the unfortunate accident, Nero decides to destroy Peter.

Although the Marcellus text assigns to Nero the ultimate responsibility for the death of Peter, Agrippa the prefect still plays a role. When Nero wants to torment both with iron nettles,[66] Agrippa intervenes, "'Most blessed emperor, what you have commanded is not fitting for these men, since Paul seems innocent compared to Peter . . . It is just to cut off Paul's head, and to hang Peter on a cross, since he is the cause of the murder'" (*Marcellus* 58).[67] Agrippa has no other role in Peter's death. Earlier the readers learn that Livia, "Nero's wife,"[68] and Agrippina, the wife of "Agrippa the prefect" both convert and leave their husbands' sides (*Marcellus* 10).[69] But the conversion of Agrippa's wife is not the reason for Peter's arrest in this text.

Pseudo-Hegesippos is more radical than the Marcellus text in recognizing the obsolescence of the figure of Agrippa by not naming him at all; as in the Marcellus text, the cause of Peter's death is Nero's friendship with Simon (Ussani 186.3–6).[70] This text, however, is much shorter than the Marcellus text and characteristically contains fewer details.

Agrippa, a named Roman official, persists throughout the various narratives with the exception of Pseudo-Hegesippos,[71] even when the plot of the narrative itself renders his part unnecessary. None of these texts, however, communicates much background information on the figure of Agrippa. The Linus text transmits his official title, that of *praefectus urbis* (*Linus* 8; Lipsius 9.10). The *Actus Vercellenses* introduce him before the martyrdom, during the contest between Simon Magos and Peter in the *Forum Iulium*.[72] He exercises his office by maintaining civic order: he gives his permission to Peter and Simon to begin their contest there and announces the contest to the populace (*AcVer* 25). Later, he suggests that Peter and his jubilant followers go elsewhere when the successful outcome of the contest threatens to degenerate into disorderliness (*AcVer* 29).

Characteristically, the *Actus Vercellenses* also assign a miraculous episode to Agrippa. At the outset of the contest, he offers one of his foundlings (*alumnus*, *AcVer* chap. 25; Lipsius 72.23) as a sort of magician's assistant to Simon and Peter: Simon is to kill him by speaking a word and Peter to resurrect him. Simon slays the lad with dispatch, but Peter is interrupted by two widows who want their only sons raised. After some intervening episodes, the prefect grows impatient and wishes to know what will become of the boy, who also happens to be a favorite of the emperor himself (*AcVer* 26):

> "What do you say, Peter? Look, the boy lies dead, upon whom even the emperor's favor rests, and I have not spared him. At any rate, I had many other young men; but, because I had trusted you and your Lord, whom you preach, whether indeed you are right and true, therefore, I was willing to let him die."[73]

Peter directs Agrippa to perform the miracle himself, telling him to help the boy up with his right hand. This is a characteristic touch of the *Actus Vercellenses*. Peter earlier instructs the Roman senator Marcellus in the performance of another miracle, the restoration of a broken imperial statue; Marcellus himself mends the statue by sprinkling it with water (*AcVer* 11). The *Actus Vercellenses* express great interest in the conversion to and support of Christianity by the senatorial aristocracy.

We do not, however, find out from any of the texts in the *Acts of Peter* trajectory what we would most like to know: who is Agrippa, and why does he appear so persistently as a significant figure in the martyrdom of Peter? The name itself tells us little, since it is a common Roman cognomen. The son-in-law of Augustus, Marcus Vipsanius Agrippa, bore the name, and one could come up with many examples of such individuals during the first century. None of them, however, is known as a prefect in the first century.

Another Agrippa is attested elsewhere in Christian traditions related to Peter. Both of the Herods who ruled as "kings"[74] of Judea in the midfirst century were known in the Roman sources by the cognomen Agrippa (I and II, the grandson and great-grandson of Herod the Great);[75] modern Roman historians at times refer to both as "King Herod Agrippa,"[76] to minimize confusion with other Herods (Herod the Great, and Herod Antipas, the uncle of Agrippa I). Eusebios claims that Agrippa killed James, son of Zebedee, the brother of John, and imprisoned Peter in Jerusalem, during the reign of Claudius (*Ecclesiastical History* 2.9.4); the Agrippa in question is Herod Agrippa I, who became king over Philip's tetrarchy in 37 C.E., and reigned as king over all Palestine (41-44 C.E.) during the early part of Claudius's rule. Eusebios then paraphrases the arrest of Peter as narrated in the "divine scripture." He is referring to the Acts of the Apostles in this passage, since, a few sentences earlier, he quotes Acts 12:1-2 in describing the execution of James, son of Zebedee (*Ecclesiastical History* 2.9.1).

The account in the Acts of the Apostles tells us nothing about any Agrippa, but narrates how "Herod the King" ('Ηρῴδης ὁ βασιλεύς, 12:1) arrested Peter after the execution of James: "When he saw that this pleased the Jews, he decided to arrest Peter, too—it was the time of Unleavened Bread—and when he laid hold of him, he put him in the custody of four squads of four soldiers, to guard him, since he wanted to arraign him before the people after Pesach" (12:2-4).[77] Herod intends to bring Peter to trial (12:4), but is foiled when an angel awakens Peter, his chains drop off, and he walks free. Peter goes to report this to the other Christians and then quickly leaves the city, as indeed one would suppose a man under warrant would (v. 17): καὶ ἐξελθὼν ἐπορεύθη εἰς ἕτερον τόπον. In v. 19, we learn that Peter has left Judea for Caesarea. We never hear from him again in Acts, except when he stands to make a brief speech during the council of Jerusalem in chapter 15; this is a narrative discontinuity, since the readers do not learn when it was that he traveled back to Jerusalem. As in the case of Paul, in the final chapter of Acts, Luke also refrains from completing the story of Peter, never indicating the manner of his death.

Aside from the possible contact between the names "Herod" and "Agrippa" in the one person of Agrippa I, other points of overlap exist between these two stories. The tradition attested by Eusebios that the arrest in Acts took place under the reign of Claudius would set the dramatic date of Luke's story at about the same time as Peter's arrest in the *Actus Vercellenses*, if this is taken to have happened twelve years after Christ's death. The arrest takes place at the end of Peter's active role in each narrative, and it is clear from both narratives that Agrippa, or Herod, threatens the apostle with death. Although Peter escapes in Luke's Acts, Herod's motive in arresting Peter is to please the Jews as he had by the execution of James. Last, one should note the persistence of one detail both in Luke's Acts and in the *Acts of Peter* trajectory: Peter's arrest or custody by four soldiers, or four groups of soldiers, is repeated throughout. Luke's Acts, as quoted above, give the number as four groups of four (12:4); the Linus text mentions four lictors (*apparitores*) and ten further men (*Linus* 8; Lipsius 9.8); the Greek martyrdom account mentions four soldiers (*AcPetMart* 7).[78] This is an otiose narrative detail: the numeral four is not integral to tales of arrest, although the presence of soldiers is requisite.

The *Acts of Peter* also show elsewhere a vague knowledge of some of the other events in the life of "Agrippa." In the Greek martyrdom account, Nero forbids Agrippa to come into his presence for a period of time, in anger over the execution of Peter (*AcPetMart* 12, absent in the *AcVer*). In the Linus text, Nero arrests Agrippa, who, through the intervention of some friends, is allowed to return to his home as a private individual, after being divested of his office.[79] Josephus presents King Agrippa I as experiencing the same two difficulties: Tiberius forbade him to enter his presence after the death of Drusus, since the sight of his son's friends saddened him (*Jewish Antiquities* 18.6.1§146). Some time later, after Agrippa had run into financial trouble and fled from his creditors, Tiberius similarly barred him from audiences with him until he repaid (*Jewish Antiquities* 18.6.4§164). Toward the end of his reign, Tiberius also imprisoned Agrippa for paying court to Caligula rather than to his grandson Tiberius, the son of Drusus (*Jewish Antiquities* 18.6.6§187-91).[80] As in the case of Marcellus, Christian memory in the *Acts of Peter* recalls the two or three major events in the life of a historical figure: Agrippa's arrest of early Christian leaders and his difficulties with and imprisonment by the Roman emperor—though the texts of the *Acts of Peter* anachronistically represent him as Nero rather than Tiberius. These events, again, are retold in terms of their significance to the Christian community: Agrippa is punished for executing Peter.

The stories of the two imprisonments, in the Acts of the Apostles and in the *Acts of Peter*, are thus multiforms, related versions of the same story. The evidence is too slim to make any judgments about the historical basis of either of these stories;[81] strict history is not the concern of this study in any case. The most that can be said is that these two versions of the arrest of Peter show remarkable similarities; the basic story is that Peter was arrested under threat of death by a certain Agrippa. The fact that one of the multiforms takes place in Jerusalem, and one at Rome, should not be surprising. Precisely the same point of disagreement exists between the stories of Simon in Luke's Acts and the *Actus Vercellenses*, there between Judea and Samaria. More serious variances exist elsewhere among the Apocryphal Acts. The *quo vadis* story, an account memorable enough to find its way into twentieth-century cinema, is even assigned to separate individuals, by the *Actus Vercellenses* to Peter (*AcVer* 35) and by the *Acts of Paul* to Paul (PH p. 7).

The Albinus who encourages Agrippa to take action against Peter may also be a historical figure who has taken on a new life. In the *Actus Vercellenses*, a certain senator Albinus has a beautiful wife, Xanthippe, who also decides to follow Peter's teaching (*AcVer* 34). Carl Erbes suggests that this Albinus may be the successor of Festus, who, according to Josephus, came to Judea around 62 C.E., after the death of James, the brother of Jesus. This is the Lucceius Albinus mentioned in Tacitus, who was later proconsular governor in Mauritania Caesarea and Tingitania.[82] It was precisely in the four-month interregnum between Festus and Albinus that the high priest Ananus had James, the brother of Jesus, killed, according to Josephus. Albinus heard that Ananus had taken advantage of his absence in executing James and threatened to take vengeance upon him. King Agrippa II (ruled 50-94 C.E.) similarly deposed Ananus from the high priesthood for overstepping his authority and replaced him (*Jewish Antiquities* 20.9.1§197–203). Josephus's account shows a further similarity to the *Acts of Peter* texts in presenting the executor of a Christian leader as overstepping his bounds and being punished by his superiors. In the *Acts of Peter*, this is shifted up the social scale: instead of wreaking vengeance on a subordinate such as Ananus for acting beyond his authority, Albinus and Agrippa are themselves reprimanded for the same cause by the emperor.[83]

Multiforms such as these result from oral circulation, or from a usage of texts that views them as resources for retelling the story in another performance. If texts of the *Acts of Peter* ultimately drew on circulating stories, this would explain the persistence of Agrippa in the trajectory of the *Acts of Peter*. The tradition persists because it is early. The tradition was so widespread that even in the fifth or sixth century, when the most "ecclesiastical" version of Peter's martyrdom was written, the "Marcellus text," Agrippa is still present at the arrest and trial. The *Actus Vercellenses* thus were not created ex nihilo, but rest on a fund of circulating tales.

Marcellus suffers a fate similar to Agrippa in the later versions of the *Acts of Peter*. His role is greatly reduced in the Linus text and the Marcellus text. Neither of these preserves the portion of the narrative prior to the martyrdom account, in which Marcellus's deception by Simon and conversion at the hands of Peter figure so prominently. Both of these texts do, however, retain the other function he carries in the narrative complex, that of the patron who provides for Peter's burial, also known from the *Actus Vercellenses*. In the Marcellus text, this role is particularly residual, since some mysterious men arrive from Jerusalem suddenly to take the body of Peter and bury it in the Vatican; they do this "along with Marcellus" (ἅμα Μαρκέλλῳ, *Marcellus* 63; Lipsius 172.11).

Although Marcellus's role is all but written out in the storyline of these later versions, the character persists in a manner more fundamental; he takes on the function of witness and guarantor of the reliability of the *Acts of Peter*. Several Latin manuscripts of the Marcellus text append a *subscriptio* that reads, *ego marcellus discipulus domini mei Petri quae vidi, scripsi* ("I, Marcellus, a disciple of my Lord Peter, wrote what I saw").[84] This does not depend on the information found in the Linus text, or the Marcellus text, in which Marcellus is merely the person who takes Peter down from the cross and entombs him in his own family plot; it refers to the narrative complex beyond these texts, to the fabula of the *Acts of Peter*, in which Marcellus is the most significant witness of Peter's contests against Simon, even though these are not transmitted in the texts that present the martyrdom only. Although the storyline of the later versions offers no space for Marcellus, the character nevertheless persists at a metatextual level with the same degree of centrality that he possessed earlier in the narrative trajectory.

## The Elasticity of Secondary Characters

Though having a basis in the history of the first century, and though stubbornly retained throughout the Petrine texts, figures such as Marcellus and Agrippa show considerable elasticity as characters in the Apocryphal Acts. In the case of Marcellus, and his counterpart Tryphaina in the *Acts of Paul*, high-born polytheists of the first century become Christians in the second-century texts. Yet not second-century Christians—their conversion is retrojected into the first century, to the earliest days of the Christian mission. Peter's friends and disciples are senators and provincial officials, acting, as has been seen, out of wholly Christian motivations. In the Greek redaction of the *Actus Vercellenses*, however, Marcellus's conversion is unimportant. He is a Christian from the beginning of the text. Rather than a pagan benefactor who has imperiled the church by suddenly reneging on his support, he becomes the paradigmatic Christian *lapsus* at Rome.

The rehabilitation of Marcellus from pagan to Christian does not end with the *Actus Vercellenses*. In Linus, Marcellus is briefly introduced as a preeminent citizen who turned away from the pestilential teaching of Simon to follow Peter faithfully, an allusion to the contest from the broader *fabula* of the *Acts of Peter* not reproduced in the Linus text: "It [the plot against Peter] nevertheless became known to Marcellus, son of Marcus the prefect, who devoted himself to the apostle faithfully and usefully in all things, after turning away from the pestilential teaching of Simon Magos" (*Linus* 3).[85] Marcellus here finds out about the plot to execute Peter. When the Roman senators break out in a riot because of Peter, Marcellus tries to convince him to flee for his life (*Linus* 3–4). More significantly, Marcellus appears in the Linus text as a Christian witness, a role he retains later in the trajectory, as seen above. When Peter appears to Marcellus after Peter's death, he also commissions Marcellus (*Linus* 16): "You, then, since you have learned from me, go, preach the kingdom of God."

The Marcellus text does not contain this dialogue between Peter and Marcellus and only introduces the character of Marcellus after the martyrdom, again as a former follower of Simon Magos who left him to follow Peter and comes to bury his master: "And they, along with Marcellus, a man of high rank who had been faithful to Peter after he left Simon, took up his body" (*Marcellus* 63).[86] Though the figure of Marcellus all but moves out of the text, ironically the entire account of Peter's martyrdom is laid to his credit.

In the *Acts of Nereus and Achilleus*, Marcellus's career as a Christian author takes a new twist. Domitilla, the aristocratic protagonist of the Acts, is exiled to the island of Pontia with her two eunuchs,[87] Nereus and Achilleus, because she turned down the marriage proposal of Aurelian, the son of a consul. The three Christians find that the entire island has been won over by two disciples of Simon Magos, Furis and Priscus (*Nereus* 10). The gallant Nereus and Achilleus, after initial conversations with the islanders, suggest that they consult Marcellus, as a former follower of Simon, and convince the population to abide by the judgment that Marcellus will offer in letter form. Marcellus's fame is emphasized in the text and is one of the reasons that the followers of Simon Magos are willing to accept his judgment. At mention of his name, they respond, "And who is there who doesn't know him? . . . Whoever wouldn't believe the testimony of such an eminent personage would be quite a fool" (Achelis 9.30–10.3).[88] Marcellus, once contacted, sends a letter from Rome (*Nereus* 12–17). Contrary to all expectation, he unmasks Simon as an impostor, recounting the resurrection story which, in the *Actus Vercellenses*, takes place in the Forum (*Nereus* 28); in *Nereus and Achilleus*, it is simply called, "the place in which Simon contended with Peter" (Achelis 11.18).[89] Simon and Peter face a corpse: Simon makes the corpse move, but only Peter can really bring it to life. Unfortunately, we never learn whether the epistolary testimony wins over the island of Pontia because the author goes on to record another letter and loses the thread of the narrative.

Peter's daughter, known from the Coptic fragment, undergoes a similarly elastic development in the *Acts of Nereus and Achilleus*. As in the Coptic fragment, she becomes paralyzed at the prayers of her parents, but in the later version, she gradually recovers, only to be wooed by a certain *comes* Flaccus. She asks him to give her three days to consider his offer of marriage and, fasting and praying all the while, manages to die within that span of time (*Nereus* 15). In *Nereus and Achilleus*, Peter's daughter receives a name, Petronilla (Achelis 14.7–8), identifying her with a homonymous early Roman saint; in this account, the episode takes place in Rome rather than Jerusalem. The local history of Rome adds color to the character: the church of Petronilla was built around 390 C.E. The text of *Nereus and Achilleus* mentions this church, offering a *terminus post quem*.[90] Petronilla appears in a late fourth to early fifth-century painting in a fourth-century *cubiculum* in that church. Tradition identifies a sarcophagus of a certain Aurelia Petronilla as belonging to her.[91] The cognomen *Petro* is attested among the Flavians, and Achelis follows de Rossi in suspecting that this saint was a relative of the Flavian imperial family, who became identified with the daughter of Peter because of the similarity of their names.

The elasticity of these characters is not without bounds. Both in the case of Marcellus and in that of Petronilla, the characters do not lose their essential dramatic function or identity. Their rapprochement with Christianity, however, does become closer and more detailed as the narrative trajectory develops. Marcellus moves from beneficent polytheist to Christian convert to witness and guarantor of tradition, and Peter's daughter becomes an early Roman Christian saint.

## Renegotiating the Past

Despite the fluidity and change among the texts of the *Acts of Peter*, many aspects of the narrative remain constant.[92] Although the characterization and motivations of characters show great elasticity from one version to another, named figures persist throughout the trajectory, even when their roles are no longer a dramatic necessity. This is more apparent in the case of the secondary figures. Although Simon and Peter may be drawn slightly differently from one text to the next, it is impossible to alter these figures substantially, or omit them, without changing the story itself. Marcellus and Agrippa, and even Nero to some degree, do change guise but still persist through all the versions, even though they are not central to the plot.

One aspect of fixity is thus the persistence of named characters from one version of the narrative to another, even in the absence of direct literary dependence among the texts. The fluidity of the narrative line is evident in another narrative feature, in the motivations of the characters and the causation of events. The arrest and execution of Peter is a striking example: though the entire purpose of the narrative trajectory is to narrate the martyrdom of Peter, none of the versions agrees on the reasons for which the Roman government executed Peter. This is because the nature of the primary conflict changes with each version, although the parties involved in the conflict remain the same: the apostle Peter against the Roman ruling classes. The changes in the conflict result in the various minor plot adjustments that require the roles of the secondary characters to be rewritten.

The driving forces behind the alterations in the narrative are the inevitable historical changes resulting from the passage of time, as they are experienced by the audience of these narratives. The manner in which the primary conflict is portrayed clearly reflects the manner in which the relationship between the Christians and the Roman ruling classes was transformed over time. In the earliest two of these texts, the *Actus Vercellenses* and the Linus text, Peter is arrested as a result of his preaching of sexual abstinence. He converts a number of prominent women to the faith and convinces them that their new creed requires them to cease having sexual relations with their husbands. The basic conflict is between sexually abstinent female converts to Christianity and their polytheist husbands. Before Albinus approaches Agrippa, the Greek martyrdom account, as well as the Latin *Actus Vercellenses*, describe the situation in Rome: "And many other women, when they became enamored with the teaching of purity, were separating from their husbands, and men were leaving the beds of their own wives. . . . So when there was a huge clamor in Rome . . ." (AcPetMart 5; AcVer 34).[93]

This conflict is a commonplace in Christian narratives of the late second century in Asia Minor, further confirming the geographical and chronological location of the continuous Greek text. The *Acts of Paul and Thekla* (chaps. 11–15) and the *Acts of John* (chap. 63) both contain such episodes. Tertullian claims that the governor of Cappadocia, Claudius Lucius Herminianus, nearly instigated a persecution of the Christians there when his wife converted to their faith (*ad Scapulam* 3). In his second apology (chap. 2), Justin Martyr tells of a related episode at Rome, which he considers to be veracious: a married woman converts to Christianity and, after becoming dissatisfied with her husband's intemperate lifestyle, presents him with a bill of divorce. He accuses her before the Roman court of being a Christian, but she succeeds, through appeal to the emperor himself, in being granted a stay of the legal proceedings. The husband then proceeds to bring her Christian teacher, one Ptolemaios, to court, who is duly arrested, imprisoned, and punished by the *praefectus urbis* Q. Lollius Urbicus, who held this office between 146 and 160 (?) c.e.[94]

The *Actus Vercellenses* reflect a situation causing widespread concern in second-century Asia Minor, in which the lines of conflict are drawn along gender and class distinctions, and negative legal fallout results from unequal conversion between the genders. The Christians were perceived to have achieved an unequal success among the upper classes: more women were converting than were men.[95] And they were not merely rich widows, but the wives of men who were powerful enough to have access to the Roman courts. Perhaps the number of actual court cases resulting from conflict between husband and wife were few, but the fear of them was great. The audience of the *Actus Vercellenses* lived in an age in which they had clearly attracted the attention of the Roman government and the elite of the provinces. They viewed themselves as potential victims, like Peter, of a capricious system of justice over which they had no direct control and in which they were unfortunately outclassed by their morally inferior accusers. The *Actus Vercellenses* do not suggest any modification of the teaching of sexual abstinence and present their upper-class women converts as heroes of the faith.[96] Instead, the text targets precisely that class whose aggression is endangering the young Christian community, male Roman citizens, men of the same class as Marcellus, and appeals to them to become patrons of the movement. This is the preferred solution to the conflict.[97]

The Linus text, perhaps one hundred and fifty years later, also presents the same conflict as the root of the opposition to Peter. The teaching of continence has extended into a higher social class than that envisaged by the *Actus Vercellenses*. Albinus is here described as *Caesaris amicissimus*. The Roman Senate has become the locus of resistance to the Christian movement. Although Agrippa, and his senator friend Albinus, are the responsible parties for the arrest and execution of Peter, neither of them is impelled to action until a riot ensues in the Roman senate (*Linus* 3):[98] "One of the senators took the floor in the senate meeting and said, 'I am bringing to the attention of your excellencies, noble men, that, to the perversion of the eternal city, Peter is turning marriages into divorces, and is separating our wives from us, and is introducing to us we know not what new and unheard-of law.'" The conflict has become more pointed and has shifted to a juxtaposition of Christian teaching to the entire system of Roman values: the Roman senatorial males are described as considering Christian doctrine to be a more general assault on traditional Roman values, "a perversion of the eternal city," and Peter's teaching is given the status of a law. The Linus text is also less sympathetic to senatorial men: the role of the paradigmatic Marcellus is greatly reduced, and Agrippa and Albinus appear in a less favorable light. Although both of them are portrayed, as in the *Actus Vercellenses*, as lovingly pleading with their concubines or wives to desist from the continent life, the final verdict on Agrippa is that he is ridden with libido as with a disease: *morbo incontinentiae suae*, "because of his disease of lack of self-control" (*Linus* 8; Lipsius 10.10).

The Linus text was most likely written in the mid to late fourth century, during which time the Senate at Rome was the seat of polytheist resistance in general. The Linus text still presents sexual abstinence as primarily an activity of upper-class women—one thinks of the female friends of the circle of Jerome—but the reaction is more widespread and general than the dissatisfaction of an individual husband with his wife. The Linus text is searching for an audience that sees the Christian teaching of continence as a fundamental and necessary challenge to the old order, truly a "new law." Although the senators eventually triumph over Peter, they are on the wrong side.

The latest version, the Marcellus text, explains Peter's fate very differently. The ultimate cause of Peter's demise is Nero's friendship with Simon, rather than Peter's preaching of sexual abstinence. The motif of their friendship also appears in the Linus text, though it does not motivate the execution, since Agrippa is still the responsible party in that text. In the *Acts of Nereus and Achilleus*, Pseudo-Hegesippos, and the Marcellus text, Nero orders Peter's execution. *Nereus* envisages a close personal friendship that leads to a combined attack on Peter and Paul by Nero and Simon: "Later, [Simon] was found in the company of Nero the emperor. Since Nero was evil, he attached himself to an evil friend with his own friendship" (*Nereus* 12).[99] This is similar to the account in the Marcellus text. When Simon offers to demonstrate that he is the son of God by flying up to heaven from the top of a tall tower, he is grounded by Peter's prayers (*Marcellus* 56). Nero puts both Peter and Paul to death for murdering his friend. Pseudo-Hegesippos follows this same storyline: Nero has Peter killed when he finds that it is he who has deprived him of a friend who provided him with useful powers and who was "necessary to the state." At the beginning of that text, the readers learn that Nero has become dependent on Simon, who promises to provide him with military and political victory, longevity, and health by means of theurgy.[100]

By the time the Marcellus text was written in the fifth or sixth century, the problem of the continent Roman matron and her dissatisfied husband had lost its teeth. Peter is said to have converted Livia [sic], the wife of Nero, to continence, but this otherwise passes without comment. It can no longer be sufficient reason for the martyrdom of Peter. The same is the case in Pseudo-Hegesippos, which does not mention the teaching of sexual abstinence at all. The main threat to Christianity is located in the imperial court itself, where the emperor is capable of being duped and deceived by a theurgist such as Simon Magos. The larger society is not an independent locus of opposition to the new faith; its fate depends rather on imperial politics. Such a conception would not have been possible before the official acceptance of Christianity as the state religion. Imperial power and the Roman system of government is placed in a more positive light. The two apostles are only executed after due legal inquiry and sentencing. To the author(s) and audience of this text, it seems impossible to imagine that an emperor would oppose Christianity, unless he were deceived by an evil man.

The narrative elements that remain constant in each of these three versions are more substantial than the points of difference. Each is a story of Peter, a founding figure of a religious cult, early Christianity. In each version, Peter comes into conflict with an official of the Roman government. This was significant for the various tradents of these versions; in its first few centuries, Christianity defined itself in opposition to the Roman government or in heated engagement with it.

These examples also show the basic fluidity of the plot line. The items that are subject to change from one version of the narrative to the next are precisely those that one would assume responsible historiography would want to settle once for all: the causation of the events and the motivations of the characters. As we have seen, the five narratives do not even agree on the motivation for arresting Peter in the first place. It seems that the narratives are more interested in preserving the name of the man who arrested Peter than in the reason Peter first attracted the hostile attention of Rome, an issue that we would assume to be as important to the early Christians as it is to us. In these tales of the trial and execution of Peter, aspects of the narration such as causation and motivation alter to reflect the social concerns of the age in which they were composed. In each case, the text reflects the particular points of conflict that the Christians were experiencing with the polytheist culture of their time.

## Multiforms

As the narrative of the *Acts of Peter* passed through various versions, recensions, and translations, the repetition of the story lead to multiple attestations of individual narrative units, such as the *quo vadis* episode or the story of Simon's flight from the tower. These attestations are not mere copies from one document to another, but recastings. In this sense, they might be called multiforms, that is, components of a set of individual performances of the same narrative.

Numerous parallel narratives exist within the *Actus Vercellenses*. They are not doublets in the sense that one finds in the synoptic Gospels, in which appear, for example, the feeding of the five thousand (Mark 6:33-44) alongside the feeding of the four thousand (Mark 8:1–9). More often, the same dramatic role is played by a different charac-ter, or the same series of events happens to a different figure.

Such multiforms also exist between the *Acts of Peter* and other narrative trajectories, such as the *quo vadis* episode, which appears both there and in the *Acts of Paul*. Simon Magos and his attempt to buy the power to lay on hands also appears in the Acts of the Apostles. Neither of these cases, each treated in Chapter Two above, shows close literal dependency, but rather transmits the details of the account in a markedly different fashion.

The changes evident in these multiforms are different in nature from the changes in conflict and motivation charted in the preceding section. None of the episodes that appears in multiform is integral to the narrative in the same sense as is the central conflict be-tween the Christians and the Roman ruling classes. The episode of the resurrected young man, for example, although an important component of the contest between Simon and Peter in the forum, is not completely determined by the storyline; it does not mat-ter if there are one or three young men whom Peter resurrects, or whether they are the sons of poor or wealthy mothers. The episodes appearing in multiform thus are not necessary components of the narrative on the level of its storyline. This characteristic explains the otherwise bewildering fact that the same role in these multiforms can be played by completely different characters in different versions of the story. The father of the paralyzed daughter can be either Peter or the gardner. Since these episodes are not central plot components, it does not really matter who plays their roles.

On the other hand, these episodes represented by multiforms clearly belong to the fabula of the *Acts of Peter* in the same way as do the persistent minor characters dis-cussed above. These episodes retain stubbornly their attachment to the entire complex of narratives associated with Peter. Like the persistent minor characters of Agrippa or Marcellus, they form part of the fabric out of which any given storyline can be com-posed. The persistent characters and the recurring episodes of the *Acts of Peter* thus perform the same function, and have a similar elasticity. The nature of the elasticity is differently expressed, however, in these two classes of narrative building blocks. Because the persistent characters are more integrally attached to the plot line, they retain their names and personas, instead of becoming rather anonymous plot elements such as one finds in the multiforms that follow. The persistent characters are defined by *role*: Agrippa is the individual bearing responsibility for the arrest of Peter. These episodes in multi-form, however, are determined by the *action* they represent: an episode such as Simon's flight over the city demonstrates his ability to trick the populace of Rome, and it finds its place at those points in the plot that require such an action.

## The Arrest of Peter

In the *Actus Vercellenses*, Peter's arrest is doubly motivated. First, Agrippa becomes angry because his four concubines have declined to have sexual relations with him (AcVer 33). As the text tells it, however, he is not moved to take action until the same situation arises between Albinus, the "friend of Caesar"[101] and his "especially beautiful" wife Xanthippe (*AcPetMart* 5). The text describes his reaction in much the same terms as Agrippa: "He was filled with fury and passionate love for Xanthippe, and was amazed that she would not even sleep in the same bed with him. He was raging like a wild beast in his desire to lay his hands on Peter" (*AcPetMart* 5; *AcVer* 34).[102] This is essentially the same story as Agrippa's; only the names have changed. The text is conscious of the multiform and makes narrative sense of it by including the conversation between Agrippa and Albinus, in which the latter appeals to the prefect to exercise the duties of his office and execute Peter.

This is not the only multiform of the story; Virginia Burrus catalogs seven of them among the Apocryphal Acts and the additional account in Justin Martyr.[103] All of these stories have the same storyline, with the exception that they are played out by different characters. What seems important, both in Peter's case and in the case of the other apostles, is not the individuals involved, but the potential danger for the apostle posed by the scenario. The point of the story is not that a particular individual persecuted the apostle, but that many could. The conflict it illustrates was a general threat to the Christian community.

### The Resurrection of the Young Man

A second multiform in the *Actus Vercellenses* involves a series of three resurrections performed by Peter as he faces Simon in the forum (*AcVer* 25–28). Agrippa places a young man, a favorite of the emperor, before the two contestants. Simon slays him with a word. At this moment, a poor Christian widow cries out to Peter that her only son is dead; Peter instructs her to bring the body to the forum. Agrippa complains that his candidate for resurrection is still lying unattended; Peter commands him to raise up the boy by the hand, and the boy lives again, to the acclamation of the crowd. The widow's son now arrives, and Peter raises him, too. After this, a senator's mother requests that Peter raise her son, Nikostratos. Peter lets Simon have the first shot at this, but Simon succeeds only in making the man's head nod and open its eyes. Agrippa pushes Simon away, and the man lies dead as before. After securing from the mother a promise that all the slaves who had been freed upon the man's death would retain their freedom and that the money that would have been spent on his funeral would be given to the Christian widows, Peter raises Nikostratos.

In this case, again, the author of the *Actus Vercellenses* is completely conscious of the parallelism of these stories. Though the first two resurrections are juxtaposed in a rather baroque fashion, the intent is sophisticated: to heighten suspense of the account by delaying the conclusion of the first resurrection. The Greek vellum fragment (*P. Oxy* 849) spans the transition from one episode to the other, so we know that the intercalation was part of the Greek text. The third resurrection story (*AcVer* 28) stands on its own, and manifests the same redactional concerns apparent in the Marcellus sections of the narrative: the conversion of the senatorial elite and their duty to provide for the less fortunate in the Christian community.[104] This third story, however, has characteristic elements known from other allusions to the contest in the forum. In Pseudo-Hegesippos, Simon also tries to deceive the crowd by moving nothing more than the man's head (Ussani 184.26–185.2):[105]

> Simon approached the dead man's bed and began to chant and murmur horrifying spells. The man who had been dead was seen to move his head. A colossal outcry arose from the pagans that he was already alive and that he was talking to Simon. . . . Then the holy

apostle called for silence and said, "If the dead man is alive, let him speak; if he has been revived, let him rise up, walk, talk to us."

The corpse remains unable to do these things, and Peter proves the superiority of the power of his God by raising the man completely.

*Nereus and Achilleus* contain the same details in their account of the contest (*Nereus* 12):[106]

> Then, by invoking the *daimones* with his magical procedures, Simon began to make the body of the dead man jerk about. When the crowd saw this, they began to shout in praise of Simon, and to cry out in favor of Peter's execution. Then Peter, barely managing to silence them, said to the crowd, "If he is alive, let him speak, let him walk about, let him take food, and go back to his home."

Although this account is similar to the third resurrection in the *Actus Vercellenses*, it also describes the dead man as the only son of a widow, as does the second resurrection in the *Actus Vercellenses* (chaps. 26–27). The description of the resurrection of the only son of a widow is already modeled on Luke 7:11–17, which is in turn based on Elijah's resurrection of the son of the widow at Zarephath (1 Kings 17:17–24). To sort out the various processes that led to these multiple versions is difficult.[107] The third resurrection in the *Actus Vercellenses* does seem to be a literary elaboration within the development of that narrative: it expresses the redactional concerns of this text transparently and seems to provide a counterpart to the story of the poor widow and her only son by presenting a rich senatorial mother of an only son. Pseudo-Hegesippos and *Nereus and Achilleus* provide the details of Simon's failed attempt to heal the dead man, but they do not follow the *Actus Vercellenses* in describing three resurrections in the contest between Simon and Peter.

### The Paralytic Daughter

A third multiform within the *Acts of Peter* trajectory involves Peter's daughter and the gardener's daughter. Augustine is the only source that attests the two accounts together (*contra Adimantum* 17, see Chapter Two). The Coptic fragment of the *Act of Peter* contains an extended series of related stories. The first tells of the temporary healing of Peter's daughter: a crowd of people asks Peter why he has not healed his beautiful virgin daughter, who is paralyzed on one side. Peter responds that God alone knows; it is not God's powerlessness that causes her to remain infirm. He then proceeds to heal his daughter, who walks unaided to the acclamation of the crowd. Peter reiterates that God is not powerless and then tells his daughter to return to her paralysis, "for this is profitable for you and for me." The crowd laments. Peter then goes on to tell them that the girl was paralyzed on the night she was taken to the house of Ptolemaios; this happened in accordance with a vision given to Peter upon her birth that she would become a temptation to many if her body remained healthy. Two further stories about the conversion of Ptolemaios follow this account.

*Nereus and Achilleus* likewise know the story. The two accounts, however, develop the story of the suitor differently. In the Coptic account, Ptolemaios carries off the daughter. In the later account, Petronilla turns down the proposal of *comes* Flaccus. The story of the gardener's daughter is attested in the epistle of Pseudo-Titus:[108]

Consider and take note of the happening about which the following account informs us: A gardener had a girl who was a virgin. She was also his only daughter, and therefore he besought Peter to offer a prayer for her. After he had prayed, the apostle said to the father that the Lord would bestow upon her what was expedient for her soul. Immediately the girl fell down dead.

O reward worthy and ever pleasing to God, to escape the shamelessness of the flesh and to break the pride of the blood!

But this distrustful old man, failing to recognize the worth of the heavenly grace, i. e., the divine blessing, besought Peter again that his only daughter be raised from the dead. After she had been raised, some days later, nearly immediately, a man who passed himself off as a believer came into the house of the old man to stay with him, and seduced the girl, and the two of them never appeared again.

Both accounts have characters and motifs in common: the virgin daughter, the father, Peter, the suitor, a bodily affliction that keeps the girl chaste, and the reversal of a miracle. Yet the verbal overlap is minimal, limited to the phrase, "what is expedient for her," which also turns up in Augustine's quotation. The stories are clearly related in some way, although the relationship between them has become so complicated that they no longer even have the same structure: the seduction is unsuccessful in one case, successful in the other. In the story of Peter's daughter, Peter and the father have been collapsed into one character.

Redactional touches have further complicated the picture. The point of the story of the gardener's daughter, expressed in the words "This is expedient/profitable for her," is that sexual abstinence is to be preferred over bodily health. The story about Peter's daughter contains this phrase as well and still affirms sexual abstinence as a desirable state of life. The major concern, however, seems to be the issue of nonhealing: healing fails to take place, not because God is unable, but because it is his will to leave the person in their present condition. There is a reason, but "it is evident to God alone why her body is not well."

Although the account in the epistle of Pseudo-Titus does not claim to be a quotation from the *Acts of Peter*—only Augustine supplies this information—it is a story attributed to Peter. What is this author citing? We can't know. There is no inherent claim in this text to preserve any source faithfully. The account in Pseudo-Titus is, in the last analysis, yet another retelling of the story.

It is in the realm of possible literary practices that a story such as that of the gardener's daughter would be elaborated in the direction of the story of Peter's daughter. The development of names and identities for anonymous characters, and their association with known figures, is a common secondary feature in many types of narrative.[109] The drama of the episode of Peter's daughter is further heightened by more vivid characterization: the anonymous daughter and her shadowy suitor known from the story of the gardener's daughter become definite characters with significant past-life events. The figure of the suitor is drawn more sympathetically in the account of Peter's daughter; he is given a name, Ptolemaios, and becomes a Christian convert. If one account developed from another, the multiforms of the gardener's daughter and of Peter's daughter would have resulted from the preservation both of the earlier version and its later expansion in the same text.

## Simon Airborne

Simon's flight over the city of Rome provides a last multiform: Simon takes flight not once, but twice, announcing his amazing feat a day in advance in each case. The first episode takes place when Simon first enters the city of Rome from Aricia, where he has been working miracles. He promises to the crowds, "Tomorrow you will see me at about the seventh hour flying over the city gate in the form in which you now see me speaking with you" (*AcVer* chap. 4). His flight over the city is what causes the apostasy of the entire Christian community at Rome. The second episode takes place after Peter routs Simon in the contest in the forum and continues to follow Simon through Rome, disproving and disputing everything that he does. Simon finally promises, "For tomorrow I will leave behind you who are utterly profane and impious, and fly up to God, whose power I am, although enfeebled" (*AcPetMart* 2; *AcVer* 31).[110]

At Peter's prayer, Simon falls in mid-flight and dies after undergoing treatment for his broken leg at Tarracina. Again, the text is aware of the parallelism of the two tales. In the Greek martyrdom account, though not in the Latin Acts, the text refers to the first flight over Rome, in which he "astonished the crowds by flying" (ἐξέστησεν τοὺς ὄχλους πετώμενος, *AcPetMart* 3; Lipsius 82.7-8), just before narrating the second flight.

## The Written Context of Multiforms

Multiforms are considered to be a smoking gun pointing to oral transmission. The presence of so many in the *Actus Vercellenses* strongly suggests that oral elaboration of the narrative played a role in the development of the stories about Peter. More germane to the present study, however, is the clear and conscious preservation of the multiforms in the written transmission of the *Acts of Peter*. The text is aware of the parallelism between multiforms and often makes the similarity of the stories yet more apparent by placing them near one another or referring to one story while introducing another. There is no awareness, however, that the accounts are different versions of the same basic event: each multiform is treated as a separate historical event, and all of them are presented as actually having taken place at some point in time. The text simply places each individual unit at the appropriate point in the narrative: the resurrections all cluster in the contest section, for example. The author of the *Actus Vercellenses* has reconstrued the multiformity resulting from oral circulation (or its written analog): each recasting of the same event becomes a real event in itself, lovingly preserved by a text that wants to lose none of the deeds done by Peter.[111]

Accounts such as the Linus text, *Nereus and Achilleus*, and Pseudo-Hegesippos necessarily lose some of this multiformity by truncating the narrative. The Linus text, because of its close relation to the *Actus Vercellenses*, does preserve both Albinus and Agrippa, though it loses the parts of the narrative containing the other three multiforms. Neither Pseudo-Hegesippos nor *Nereus and Achilleus*, however, contains three resurrections, but only one each. The Greek vellum fragment (*P. Oxy.* 849) proves that a version of the *Actus Vercellenses* containing at least two resurrections was in circulation in the late third or early fourth century, before the date of composition of both these later texts.

The later texts did not preserve the complete account of the contest because the narrative context demanded epitome.[112] Both are epitomizing the content of the *Acts of Peter* in a text the aim of which is not primarily to report the deeds of Peter; Pseudo-Hegesippos is providing an excursus within a translation of Josephus, and *Nereus and Achilleus* provide an account of later martyrs. For both, it is sufficient to show that Peter vanquished his opponent at one point. In this shorter scope, the multiplicity of events in the earlier sources is compressed to the one event that is dramatically necessary.

Among the multiforms, treatment of major and minor figures differs dramatically. Minor figures are extraordinarily elastic: the gardener's daughter becomes Peter's daughter, who is identified as Petronilla in *Nereus and Achilleus*; the suitor becomes Ptolemaios, who develops a story of his own, or *comes* Flaccus; the son of the poor widow becomes the senatorial son of a rich matron. Only the basic structure of the narrative is preserved from one version to another; the requisite role can be played by an Agrippa or an Albinus, or both.[113] The major characters, however, never change. Peter always raises the dead man or men and always in the context of his contest with Simon. No one other than Simon ever deceives the masses by flying above the city of Rome. And it is Peter who paralyzes or kills the young virgin. Simon and Peter have the same persistence among the multiforms that secondary characters such as Agrippa and Albinus show throughout the written versions.

## Conclusion

The purpose of this chapter is not to catalog every point of similarity or difference among the various versions of the *Acts of Peter*, but rather to isolate traces of the narrative techniques and compositional processes at work in this trajectory in order to clarify the question of the purpose and reception of these works—and of other early Christian texts like it. Six characters in the *Acts of Peter* are all known from first-century sources independent of the *Acts of Peter* narrative trajectory: Peter, Simon, Marcellus, Nero, Agrippa, and Albinus. Although the considerable divergences show that there is no question of literary dependence, the various *Acts of Peter* texts transmit not only their names, but other information that is "accurate" vis-a-vis these first-century sources. With the exception of Agrippa, Marcellus, and Albinus, who land in a different city, the characters all appear in approximately the same geographic and temporal location attributed to them in the earlier texts. Their basic deeds also remain constant: Simon disputes with Peter, Nero executes Peter, Agrippa arrests Peter, Marcellus embezzles money and defaces imperial statues. Beyond this, however, the characters are elastic to the extent that narrative exigencies will allow. Their actions do not change, but their motivations often do; the narratives may add information about their social class or family connections or may attribute additional deeds to them. Despite this flexibility, the characters are retained with considerable tenacity from one version to another, even when this causes temporal or dramatic difficulties. Their very elasticity ensures their survival; if the storyline alters, they tend to change roles rather than be omitted.

On the other hand, the story itself can be remarkably fluid. Individual narrative units persist—Simon's flight over Rome, the resurrection of the youth in the forum—but the narrative framework itself also admits elasticity. It is not the basic topic that changes:

these texts always tell the story of Peter's martyrdom in Rome. The conflict at the root of the narrative, that between Christianity and the Roman ruling classes, also reappears from one version to another. The specific terms of the conflict alter, with the causation of events and the motivations of the characters showing the greatest flux from one version to another.

The presence of numerous multiforms, as well as the occasionally perceptible chronological telescoping, suggest that oral circulation or its textual analog was the method of transmission. The stories began forming in the first century, which is the temporal location of its characters, and the written record demonstrates that the process of recasting and rewriting the narrative continued for several centuries. Differentiating between oral and textual *composition* is all but impossible and is of little phenomenological importance for this study. The same *methods* known from oral traditions are evident even on a textual level; the written versions show the same fluidity, the same tendency to create multiforms, the same telescoping of chronology, that one would expect in oral transmission. The later work of classicist Albert Lord and the research of anthropologists Ruth Finegan and John Miles Foley demonstrate that, in cultures with high residual orality, written compositions are treated as single performances, just as an oral performance would be treated. As Foley remarks, "we are learning from the comparative study of oral traditions worldwide that orality, literacy, and texts form a complex and interactive continuum rather than discrete categories, so it is no longer a contradiction to speak of oral traditional features in a written document."[114]

These findings clearly have ramifications for the evaluation of the purpose and reception of the *Acts of Peter*. Though admitting much opportunity for the free play of imaginative expansion, these fluid narratives were inherently conservative. The presence of traditions gave limits to creativity. Among the versions of the *Acts of Peter*, the tendency is to conserve characters, episodes, and multiforms from one text to another. They are not primarily texts of individual authorial creativity. Although individual texts of the *Acts of Peter*—the Linus text, for example—exist as independent creations of high literary value, each of the texts also appears as part of a narrative tradition and so exists as a work created between the freedom of imagination and the constraints of previous tradition.

# 4

## Narrative Fluidity as
## a Generic Characteristic

### Methodological Considerations

Although blessed with a relatively extensive and variegated set of witnesses, the *Acts of Peter* lack any extended testimony to the original Greek text beyond that of the martyrdom account, extant in two manuscripts. The only other testimony emerges from the fourth-century vellum fragment (P. Oxy 849). None of these three Greek witnesses attests the *Acts of Peter* in their original form. Each of the manuscripts of the martyrdom account (Codex Patmos 48 and Codex Vatopedi 79) represents an independent excerpting from the longer version of the *Acts of Peter*, for they begin the martyrdom account at different points. Vatopedi begins with the episode of the rich and promiscuous benefactress Chryse (=AcVer 30), but Patmos begins only after the death of Simon, at the episode concerning Agrippa's four concubines (=AcVer 33). The vellum fragment (P. Oxy. 849) is also a truncation of the longer narrative.

Not only the Greek texts, but also the various translations all represent some type of editorial activity on the Greek text. The *Actus Vercellenses* shortened a Latin translation of the *Acts of Peter*. The Coptic account of Peter's daughter is also an excerpt. The other translations of the *Acts of Peter* contain only the martyrdom account: this exists in Syriac, Armenian, Ethiopic, Arabic, and Old Church Slavonic.

The *Acts of Peter*, understood as a complex of narrative units, were clearly read and relished by many in antiquity, even beyond the limits of individual languages. Two of these four texts, Marcellus and *Nereus and Achilleus*, were available in both Greek and Latin, and the Marcellus text also exists in Armenian, Old Church Slavonic, and Coptic, and in two distinct recensions.[1] But its translators and editors seem to have perceived no compulsion to remain faithful to any particular version of the text or storyline; they preserve only the individual episodes of the fabula intact, and even these have a new spin put on them.

Students of the *Acts of Peter* are thus faced with the remarkable lack of anything resembling an "original text." Precisely this absence is significant in assessing the reception of the *Acts of Peter*, that is, the type of written work it was considered to be by its ancient audience. The process of excerpting, abridging, redacting, and translating that led to its variegated manuscript tradition, usually held to be so problematic, is in fact not problematic at all, but meaningful in itself. For, though the audience of the *Acts of Peter* remains difficult to reconstruct, it is patently clear that the individuals who excerpted, translated, and reedited the text also read the *Acts of Peter* with singular care. Their actions on the text, which resulted in our manuscript tradition, reflected their assessment of it. And the attitudes of the ancients are valuable for any treatment of the genre and purpose of the *Acts of Peter*.

One of the defining characteristics of the *Acts of Peter* narrative trajectory is its fluidity. The feature of "narrative fluidity" can also be found in related texts. The Clementine literature, though ostensibly about the contest of Simon Magos and Peter, does not preserve any of the individual narrative events of the fabula of the *Acts of Peter* trajectory; it represents an independent tradition. Yet it bears a striking relationship to those texts in that it, too, is available in more than one version; and, like the *Acts of Peter*, these two versions cannot be explained as a phenomenon of simple literary dependence. Scholars argued for decades about whether the *Homilies* depended on the *Recognitions*, or vice versa, and finally settled on the hypothesis that a common source, a *Grundschrift*, explains the close relationship of these texts. Debate still rages, however, about the exact nature of this text.[2] From the standpoint of narratology, the *Recognitions* and the *Homilies* are texts based on the same fabula. Since the narrative units common to both do not occur in the same order in both texts, they even vary on the level of storyline. As in the case of the *Acts of Peter*, it is the individual units of the fabula that are preserved in both versions.


## Narrative Fluidity among Novelistic Works in Greek

The *Acts of Peter* and the Clementine literature are not unique. The phenomenon of narrative fluidity is widespread in various types of "novelistic" literature in antiquity. Though the Apocryphal Acts are so often compared with these novelistic works, no attention has been devoted to this characteristic abundantly shared among both novelistic works and the Apocryphal Acts. The phenomenon of fluidity is not confined to that genre, however, nor even to narrative works. Fluidity is also a characteristic of other genres, such as oral epic, performative texts such as magical spells, and ethical codes such as the Pentateuch. Nonnarrative texts can be helpful analogs for the *Acts of Peter* by elucidating the reasons that texts would exist in fluid forms at all: what is the function of fluidity? As nonnarrative texts, however, they do not provide generic models for the *Acts of Peter*. Epic or ethical texts of great antiquity clearly possess a fluid transmission because they were passed down as oral tradition in the absence of widespread literacy: their fluidity is not surprising. It is precisely the narrative nature of the *Acts of Peter*, and its existence as a text in a literate world, that makes its fluid nature so difficult to explain. Novelistic narrative works are thus the best focus for a discussion of this phenomenon. Even within the novelistic genre, the degree of fluidity varies greatly among the five late Greek erotic novels and texts such as the Alexander romance and the considerably earlier Jewish novellas.[3]

## The Novels and the Alexander Romance

Recently published papyri of Achilles Tatius, a novel in Atticizing Greek composed in the second century C.E., show a degree of narrative fluidity striking for an ancient literary text; the papyri[4] contain surprisingly numerous variants, mostly on the level of the phrasing and word order. The fragments of text are relatively brief: *P. Rob.* 35 and *P. Colon.* 901, two extensive fragments of the same roll, amount to about seven and one half pages of a standard-sized printed edition when placed together. In this short scope, the papyri that overlap in the part of the text that they preserve (P[4]= *P. Rob.* 35 and *P. Colon.* 901; and P[5]=*P. Oxy.* LVI 3836) frequently disagree with one another, but have the support of one of the later codices, except in four cases in which P[4] stands alone in a correct reading against the combined witness of P[5] and the codices. Only once do the two papyri agree against the vellum codices; so the flux entered the manuscript tradition early.[5]

Although this is a striking degree of narrative fluidity for an ancient literary text, it pales by comparison with texts such as the Alexander romance and the Jewish novellas. With the Alexander romance, one is no longer on the familiar terrain of fixed texts and of manuscript traditions that can be reduced to neat genealogical relationships. The textual variants in other ancient Greek literary texts, even including the five late novelists mentioned above, can usually be reduced to a neat, half-inch textual apparatus at the bottom of each printed page of their editions. But the Alexander romance of Pseudo-Kallisthenes shows such variation among the manuscripts that the work itself—quite aside from the later translations, versions, and rewritings of it that proliferated throughout the middle ages, about eighty of them so far[6]—exists in no less than five Greek recensions: A, β, λ, ∈, γ, all edited and printed as separate editions of the same text.[7] The first two recensions (A and β) are earlier, but the three later Byzantine recensions often offer valuable readings that witness an earlier form of the text.[8]

Variants in the Alexander romance are more substantial than those in other literary texts, more than a matter of a word or two, or even of alternate phrasing, as is the case in Achilles Tatius.[9] The various recensions of the romance include and omit entire episodes. Recension β presents an extensive letter from Alexander to his mother, Olympias, in which he narrates his journey to the edge of the world (2.23–41); this letter does not appear at all in recension A. Recension γ, a Byzantine recension, has the letter and includes in it further episodes not known from β, such as encounters with giant ants, rivers of sand (2.24–31), and centaurs (2.42). Recension β, however, is not even necessarily the "longer" of the two ancient recensions (A and β) of the Alexander romance. It omits substantial sections known from recension A, such as the account of Alexander at the Isthmian games after the sack of Thebes (1.47) and his conflict with the Athenians (2.1–6). Thus it is not the case that β is a simple expansion of A.

Evaluation of the smaller variants, those on the level of words and phrases, is impeded by a contamination among the manuscripts so severe that the most recent text critic judges it to be impossible to set up a stemma of manuscripts, even within each of the five recensions.[10] The transmission of the Alexander romance is unusually rich, and copyists were in the habit of collating one manuscript against the other, introducing readings from one family of manuscripts into another.[11]

The modern reader of the Alexander romance is apt to find the account episodic, easily unraveled into a number of independent constituent units. Many of the constituent episodes of the Alexander romance did, in fact, circulate independently and had their own textual tradition; this situation is analogous to that of the Greek martyrdom accounts of the *Acts of Peter*. These independently circulating episodes have generally been judged to represent the sources from which the Alexander romance was compiled, though they apparently circulated alongside the more extensive versions that used them as sources. The piece that closes the romance, "Alexander's Last Days" (3.30-33), survives in an independent Latin translation; a Greek fragment of this text has been found on papyrus (*P. Vindob.* 31954). In these witnesses, the story of Alexander's death is narrated in a more complete manner than it appears in the Alexander romance, and those details of historical sequence that the Alexander romance confuses appear in the correct order. They were thus probably source documents rather than later excerpts.[12] The letter of Alexander to Aristotle, in which he describes the wonders that he saw in India (3.17), is likewise more complete in the independently circulating Latin translation. Recension A and codex L epitomize different parts of this text; the Latin translation, the more complete version, again represents the source document.[13] Alexander's conversation with the Gymnosophists (3.6) is preserved separately in a Greek papyrus (*P. Berol.* 13044), as are some of the letters between Alexander and various kings (such as Darius and Poros) that appear in the romance (*P. Soc. It.* 1285 = Romance 2.10; and *P. Hamb.* 129 = Romance 2.17).

The fluidity of the transmission and combination of these various episodes is striking. In some cases, independent episodes were combined with other material to make a longer work, as when the text, "Alexander's Last Days," the letter to Aristotle, and other works were combined to create the Alexander romance. The various recensions of the Alexander romance even diverged in the way in which the episodes were combined. Conversely, a complete, previously published work, an epistolary novel, forms one of the base texts of the Alexander romance; this work was dissected into bits and pieces and swallowed up, completely anonymously, into the later Alexander romance.[14] A striking doublet suggests that even this earlier epistolary novel circulated in more than one recension.[15]

Unlike the five late Greek erotic novels, the Alexander romance was translated early into Latin and into several other languages before the end of antiquity. Julius Valerius created the earliest surviving Latin translation of the Alexander romance around 300 C.E.; this translation is actually a rather free version, so free that one often cannot tell which Greek recension Valerius was using.[16] The Armenian translation and the much later Latin translation by a certain archpresbyter Leo in the tenth century are more faithful witnesses of a distinct recension. Of the other twenty-two languages into which the Alexander romance has been translated or adapted, the other relatively early witnesses to the original Greek text are the Syriac and Ethiopic translations. The *Acts of Peter* are similar to the Alexander romance in this respect as well; they were translated into Latin early, in the mid-fourth century, a bit later than the period when Julius Valerius was making his translation of the romance.

Within the trajectory of the Alexander romance, one can also find examples of the process of the creative development of a story to accommodate a new historical context, similar to what can be seen in the later texts of the *Acts of Peter*. The example of the death of Darius well illustrates this sort of elaboration. After his defeat by Alexander at Arbela, Darius was taken prisoner by some of his own satraps. But Alexander was so fast on their heels that they eventually wounded Darius and left him behind so that they could beat a hastier retreat. Darius later died of his wounds, and the corpse was found by the Macedonians; so reads Arrian, probably the most reliable extant history (3.21). Biographers of Alexander such as Plutarch and Curtius Rufus tell us, however, that a Macedonian soldier named Polystratos, while looking for water, came upon Darius while he was breathing his last. Polystratos offered the monarch a sip of water, and the dying king commissioned the simple soldier to carry to Alexander an expression of gratitude for his kind treatment of his family and his request that he be avenged on his disloyal satraps.[17] Sources read by Diodorus Siculus report that it was Alexander himself who discovered Darius as he lay breathing his last, lamented over him, and responded personally to Darius's request by taking an oath to avenge the murder.[18] In the Alexander romance, the scene takes place, not in the disorder of the Persian retreat, but in the palace of Darius itself, where the king, now deserted by all, lies dying. Alexander is so chivalrous that he entreats Darius to rise again and rule the Persians under the Macedonian conqueror's support and protection; but when it is clear that the king will die, Alexander offers of his own initiative to wreak vengeance on the murderers, without even waiting to be requested by Darius to do so (2.20).[19] These examples show how minor details of a base story can be progressively embroidered to heighten the dramatic effect, without completely distorting the two major points: that Darius requested Alexander to avenge him, and that Alexander showed sympathy for a fallen fellow monarch.

Other Greek novelistic works show similarities to the Alexander romance. As Jan Bremmer has pointed out, the *Metamorphoses* of Apuleius offers a parallel to the Apocryphal Acts in that Apuleius "translates" a Greek original, the *Metamorphoses* of Lucius of Patrae. He also inserts independent stories and new episodes and changes numerous small details in the text.[20] The *Historia Apollonii Regis Tyri* would furnish a similar example, a novelistic text which exists in several Latin recensions, of which the recensions A and B form the basis of most modern editions. As one of its recent editors notes, the "numerous groupings . . . defy reconciliation and result in a different text for each grouping."[21] Although the Latin recensions date to the fifth to sixth century C.E., the other of its recent editors, Georgius Kortekaas, and its most recent translator, Gerald Sandy, believe that it is based on a Greek original that dates to the second century. Sandy cites in particular the similarities of its plot to the other ancient novels. Its present narrative form suggests a process of elaboration similar to that found in the Alexander romance. Sandy notes that the style has "wild fluctuation from simple, almost primitive narrative to stylized and elaborate forms of expression,"[22] which would indicate that several authors had a hand in its composition. Among the Greek novels, there exists a continuum of fluidity, with the ideal romances less fluid, the *Metamorphoses* more so, and the story of Apollonius, and the Alexander romance, forming the extreme.

### The Jewish Novellas

The Jewish novellas[23] show a degree of flux nearly as striking as the Alexander romance. The book of Daniel, for example, shows two early stages of composition. The first six chapters are early, a collection of five independent narratives concerning the experiences of Daniel at the court of the various eastern monarchs, formed perhaps in the third or early second century B.C.E. The individual units are linked into a narrative whole by means of simple literary techniques: the story of Nebuchadnezzar's loss of reason (and consequent bovine culinary habits), narrated obliquely in chapter four, is recounted in direct discourse in chapter five (vss. 18–21), and an introductory chapter begins the collection. Chapters 7–12, the well-known apocalyptic sections probably written during the Maccabean revolt (167–164 B.C.E.), were added later to the already extant chapters 1–6. The form of Daniel changed once again some time after the Maccabean revolt, by the beginning of the first century B.C.E., when the existing narrative was enriched by three new episodes. These three additions appear only in the Greek translation of Daniel in the Septuagint, although it is unclear whether this is their original language. The prayer of Azariah and the Song of the Three Young Men in the furnace, added to chapter three, may have been composed in Hebrew. The story of Susanna, an erotic plot telling of the eventual vindication, through the offices of Daniel, of a young Jewish matron who resists the attempts of two elders to seduce her, was added to the beginning of the book of Daniel. The narrative of Bel and the Dragon, in which Daniel destroys the dragon who resides in the temple of Bel, idolatrously worshipped by the Gentiles, was added to the end.[24] Thus, the original collection of stories in the first six chapters of Daniel changed shape at least three times, as various other stories concerning Daniel agglomerated.

The book of Esther exhibits even greater fluidity, to the extent that Wills calls it "not so much a single, unique text, as it is a snapshot of a literary tradition in progress."[25] One of the exemplars is the "canonical" Hebrew version, the text printed in the Jewish and Protestant Scriptures based on the Hebrew original; this version probably dates to the later Hasmonean period, after 165 B.C.E., although the source documents may be considerably older. Another, the "canonical" Greek translation, printed in the Greek Orthodox and Catholic Scriptures, is a relatively faithful translation of the Hebrew work but contains six significant additions, such as a dream of Mordecai and its interpretation, prayers by Mordecai and Esther, two royal decrees, and other expansions of the narrative. These additions subtly change the nature of the narrative. The royal decrees add a historiographic tone and are composed in a sophisticated, rhetorical Greek that raises the literary level of the work. The prayers add a theological dimension to the narrative, which otherwise does not mention God. A further ancient Greek version, the Greek A version, contains these same six additions but varies sharply from the texts of the other Greek version, especially toward the end. The divergence is so great that it has been suggested that the Greek A version and the canonical Greek and Hebrew represent two different endings added to a text which originally concluded at 8:2. In the rest of the narrative, the Greek A text also varies somewhat from the two canonical versions and is considered to represent an older form of the text, closer to the Hebrew original.[26] The various Greek versions of Esther seem to have arisen in the early first century B.C.E.

In addition to the Greek versions, there are two Aramaic translations that stand on their own. None of the three versions, then, including the canonical Hebrew, represents the original text of the book. All are expanded versions of a more concise telling of the story, which can be isolated in the canonical Hebrew version on the basis of its historically earlier form of Hebrew.[27] The concise form of the story, for example, seems to have lacked some of the narrative detail that lends the later version its color and historical flavor, such as the descriptions of the court in chapter one or of the harem in chapter two; neither did it contain the passage describing the institution of Purim at the end (9:20–32).[28]

The book of Esther provides a close analog to the *Acts of Peter*, for which, likewise, no original exists; even the closest approximation of an early Greek version of the text, the *Actus Vercellenses*, is an excerpt of a translation of an earlier Greek text, which in its turn was subject to a redaction and shows detectable traces of source documents. And, as with Esther, many of the changes and additions, though carrying theological import, operate on a literary level; they chiefly alter the nature of narrative.

It would be possible to multiply further examples of Jewish novellas, but one more, *Joseph and Aseneth*, a treatment of the marriage of the Jewish patriarch Joseph to an Egyptian woman dating to the first century C.E. or later,[29] merits mention because of the similarity of its manuscript tradition to the Alexander romance. Like it, and like the *Acts of Peter*, the situation of the text is both complicated and enriched by the existence of numerous early translations: *Joseph and Aseneth* exists in Syriac, Armenian, two Latin translations, Serbian Slavonic, Modern Greek, Rumanian, and Ethiopic. The sixteen Greek manuscripts (there are seventy total when one counts the translations) fall into four different recensions. In each of the first three groups, the text is fairly unified; one of these represents a revision, no later than the tenth century, that improves the style of the original Greek (a), and the third is an epitome, no later than the eleventh century (d). But the fourth group (b), which also contains seven of the eight translations, is a grab bag: it contains the oldest witnesses (the Armenian and Syriac translations) and represents the widest geographical distribution, and yet it offers little help for arriving at the *Greek* text, since the four Greek manuscripts in this group, all very recent, differ greatly in the wording of the story and even in its length.[30] The scholar presently at work on a new edition of the Greek text, Christoph Burchard, writes, "The book is an author's work, not a folk tale which has no progenitor. There was an original text." Yet, the most that he can presently offer toward realizing this text is the observation that, "often the witnesses agree literally or to a degree that the general run of the text is unmistakable even if the wording is not."[31] The overlap between the manuscripts, then, is at the level of storyline, rather than text. If there was an original text, it was not respected by the various individuals who transmitted the manuscript. On logical grounds, it is not possible to reconstruct the original text on the basis of the available evidence; on methodological grounds, such an exercise may not be the most productive response to this textual phenomenon.

## Observations on Authorship

Burchard's comments on *Joseph and Aseneth* raise the issue of authorship in relation to narrative fluidity. The papyri of Achilles Tatius suggest that the texts of novelistic literature, in general, may have been less stable than those of other literary texts in antiquity. Works such as Esther, Daniel, *Joseph and Aseneth*, the *Acts of Peter*, and the Alexander romance, however, show a degree of textual instability that, when compared with the five late Greek erotic novels, is a difference in degree constituting a difference in kind. Each of these texts exists in several recensions, each was translated more than once, and all except *Joseph and Aseneth* had significant portions added to them over the course of their history.[32]

All of these works, moreover, are arguably anonymous, and most do not even have fixed titles in the manuscript tradition. Only the visions of Daniel in chapter 7-12 are spoken in the first person by "I, Daniel," thus not anonymous, but pseudonymous. The Alexander romance is sometimes attributed pseudonymously to Kallisthenes in the manuscript tradition, but the absence of any preface indicating authorship shows that it, too, is anonymous. The two early Latin translations of it, however, carry the name of an author. The various versions of the *Acts of Peter* are anonymous in the earlier part of their history. The *Actus Vercellenses* have neither author nor title; they simply follow a text of the Clementine *Recognitions* in the Vercelli manuscript. But later versions of the *Acts of Peter* are pseudonymously attributed to named figures, for example, to Linus or Marcellus or Josephus. Tertullian identifies the author of the *Acts of Paul* without giving his name (*de baptismo* 17). The *Acts of Andrew* are preserved in an anonymous *Laudatio* and *Narratio*, though the later Latin epitome is rightly attributed to Gregory of Tours. The five late Greek erotic novels, on the other hand, all carry the names of their authors. Only "Xenophon" of Ephesos might be considered a nom de plume: there are three Xenophons mentioned in the *Suda*, the work of each of which is titled by an ethnographic adjective, which has led some scholars to conclude that these names were pseudonyms, indicating the intention to market as a type of local history the works that bore them.[33] Significantly, the *Ephesiaka* of Xenophon, which may thus be pseudonymous, is the only one of the five late Greek erotic novels that may be preserved solely in a form radically divergent from the original text. Inconsistencies in plot and diction have led to perennial, though not uncontested, theories that parts of the *Ephesiaka* are an epitome.[34] The most anonymous of the erotic novels would also then be the most subject to textual alteration. Moreover, the text of Xenophon itself shows knowledge of Chariton and, because of similarities of plot, might even be described as a reedition of Chariton.

A direct relationship thus holds between anonymity and narrative fluidity among ancient novelistic texts. Perhaps ancient scribes perceived less obligation to protect the *ipsissima verba* of texts unsanctioned by the name of an author. Yet, as noted, there seems to be also a slight degree of flux even for some of the five late Greek erotic novels, so other features play a role: the fact that these works do not belong to a recognized genre, as well as their imaginative nature, may have also offered the scribe greater license. In Greek style, literary conventions, and generic affinities, the *Acts of Peter*, the Alexander romance, and even the five Greek erotic novels are far less sophisticated than the "highbrow" literary products of a Polybios or even a Philostratos.[35]

Many of these works appear on codices rather than the scrolls generally used for works of literature during the earlier Roman Empire. The papyrus fragments of Achilles Tatius, as noted above, appear in three out of six instances in codices. The fourth-to fifth-century Coptic papyrus fragment of the *Acts of Peter* edited by Carl Schmidt is likewise a codex, with numbered pages, as is the fourth-century vellum fragment in Greek (*P. Oxy.* 849). The *Acts of Paul* appear in the Hamburg Greek papyrus (ca. 300 C.E.) and in the Heidelberg Coptic papyrus (6th c. C.E.), both of which are codices, as is *P. Oxy.* 1602, in vellum (4th-5th c. C.E.). The early Coptic fragment of the *Acts of Andrew* is likewise a papyrus codex (*P. Copt. Utrecht* 1).[36]

In the case of works such as the Alexander romance, the *Acts of Peter*, Esther, and *Joseph and Aseneth*, the multiplicity of translations is evidence that the Greek style of the originals was not considered to be the primary literary characteristic of these works; such style as they possessed would be lost in translation. It was the narrative content that attracted the Latin- or Syriac-speaking reader, and this could be read out of any more-or-less faithful translation, regardless of which Greek text the translation followed. The fixed original text of an author was accorded little value.

This is a matter of reception, however. The originals were clearly literary productions on one level, not *Kleinliteratur*, a mere transcription of anonymous oral tradition produced by a community. Burchard is right, for example, in recognizing that even an anonymous work such as *Joseph and Aseneth* is not a folktale, but the deliberate composition of an author. This is true of all the other anonymous works. Among the Apocryphal Acts, the *Acts of Andrew* not only possesses the most polished Greek style, but shows a complex and consciously worked web of allusions to Homeric literature. Ancient readers did not, however, always follow the lead of the author. Dennis MacDonald, a recent investigator of the *Acts of Andrew* concludes that, although the author intended the work to be read against the background of the Homeric works, it is not clear that any ancient readers ever did so.[37] None of the reports about this work in the patristic sources show any awareness of these allusions, nor do the readers who translated, copied, or excerpted the work. The *Acts of Andrew* were subject to the same fluid reception as all the other Apocryphal Acts.[38]

The readers of this literature seem to have lacked any sense of an inviolate original text. The *Acts of Peter* clearly had an early Greek version, that is, the continuous Greek text, which would count as an "original text" for modern scholars. Like the text of *Joseph and Aseneth*, however, this "original text" is presently unattainable. Even if a felicitous manuscript discovery should make it available, the value of such an item should not be overestimated. The "original text" meant little to those early compilers and editors who loved, read, and preserved the *Acts of Peter*, and works like them, in these multifarious forms.

The predominance of such fluidity in the transmission of works such as the Alexander romance and the *Acts of Peter* has important ramifications for the evaluation of a whole complex of issues generally considered to be implicit in particular generic definitions of these works, and one of these is authorship. Even if we grant the existence of an "original text" written by a single author, we must reckon with a series of readers who did not strive to preserve this original text, but took the liberty to go about rewriting it in their own fashion. Some of the people who had a hand in transmitting these works were compilers—or authors—rather than mere scribes.[39] The various exemplars sometimes differ to a degree that each seems to be a unique performance of the work. The copyist here approaches the freedom and autonomy that we generally associate with a performer—or an author. Their relationship to the original creator is not that of redactor to author, but of author to author. The original text is not a monolith, but functions as a basis for further retellings.

The generic definition that arises in the minds of modern scholars when they classify, for example, the Apocryphal Acts as "novels," even ancient ones, stands in sharp contrast to this. A novel is considered to be the product of a single author, an imaginative creation that results in a distinct text. In the case of the Apocryphal Acts, this preconception has had the unfortunate result that these works have often been neglected as meaningful constructions of history and theology that represented the opinions of large groups of people—this neglect despite their obvious popularity. A broader survey of the history of the *Acts of Peter* in manuscript tradition reveals that even the select group of people who had a hand in shaping the text, the translators and editors, was large. The reuse of the *Acts of Peter* in so many documents is evidence of the continued reading of them over a span of centuries.

On the score of narrative fluidity, the *Acts of Peter* are much closer to works such as the Alexander romance or the anonymous Jewish novellas than to the five late Greek erotic novels, to which they have often been compared. The processes of translation, excerpting, expansion, and reedition that the *Acts of Peter* underwent bear more similarity to these anonymous novelistic works, works that, like the *Acts of Peter*, recounted the life and deeds of a founding figure of a nation or community: Peter, Alexander, Joseph, Esther, Daniel.

Moreover, all the Apocryphal Acts share with the *Acts of Peter* the feature of narrative fluidity. With the exception of the *Acts of Thomas*, they have all come down to modern editors as mere collections of excerpts. In each case, the martyrdom section of the Acts enjoys the best attestation and translation into the most numerous languages, because this part of the text was significant for the developing liturgies of the saints' days. The *Acts of Paul and Thekla*, from the *Acts of Paul*, are the best-known example of an excerpt from the Acts that is not a martyrology. It, the correspondence between Paul and the Corinthians (the so-called *3 Corinthians*), and the martyrology all circulated independently. It was only the Heidelberg papyrus (*Coptic P. Heid.* 1) that first proved that these excerpts existed as components of a continuous narrative of the *Acts of Paul*.[40] The manuscript tradition for the travel accounts that comprise the body of the *Acts of John* is separate from the attestation of the central section, which contains the mystic dance and the address about the cross; they have been transmitted as though they were separate works.[41] The *Acts of Andrew* have been preserved as a continuous text only in the sixth-century Latin epitome of Gregory of Tours, the *Liber de miraculis*. The *Acts of Andrew and Matthias*, which is the first portion of the material that Gregory epitomizes, circulated separately in Greek, Latin, Syriac, Coptic, Ethiopic, Armenian, Old Church Slavonic, and Anglo-Saxon. The martyrdom of Andrew likewise has a rich attestation in many languages as an independent document. Last, although the *Acts of Thomas* have been preserved as a complete text, there is a problem in determining the "original" text, since it is not clear whether the Greek or the Syriac is prior.[42] The Syriac is more likely to be original, but has been subjected to much heavier orthodox alteration than the Greek.[43]

Many other early Christian works may show features analogous to the Apocryphal Acts of the Apostles. From this vantage point, the canonical gospels appear to be closely related. In addition to the similarities of language, scope, and topic, the gospels exist as related texts of the same fabula, although Matthew and Luke are each much more closely related to Mark than are any of the texts of the *Acts of Peter* among themselves. Within their individual histories, as well, the gospels display the same sort of narrative fluidity documented here. The *Gospel of Mark* may have undergone from two to four recensions.[44] The *Gospel of John* seems to have undergone several stages of transmission.[45] This phenomenon is not limited solely to gospel literature, of course; some of the Pauline epistles may be editions and compilations of several earlier letters, with 2 Corinthians being the most persuasive case. On a more fundamental level, many of the miracle stories of Jesus exist in multiforms: the canonical version of Mark contains two closely similar "catenae" of miracles, and some of these also find echoes in the *Gospel of John*.[46] Similarly to the *Acts of Peter*, the gospels preserve multiforms of the same narrative units and present them as separate events in the life of Christ, such as the feeding of the five thousand (Mark 6:33–44) and the feeding of the four thousand (Mark 8:1–9). Moreover, although the collection of books that form the New Testament writings became fixed, the text of the New Testament was not fixed by any means. Like the Apocryphal Acts, individual scribes willfully altered the text of the New Testament in transmission.[47] The alterations may have been smaller in scope, but likely had greater historical implications. As Bart Ehrmann rightly notes, these types of alterations are the beginnings of interpretive commentary on the meaning of the text.[48]

## The Historical Consciousness of Primary Orality

What features of the uses and functions of these texts led to this constant stream of alteration? For the Greek erotic novels, the fluctuation seems great only in comparison with the Greek "classics"[49] and suggests that the readers and copiers were aware that this type of literature differed from the canon of Greek literature, central in primary and secondary education. But even the most radical alteration of one of these texts, the epitomization of Xenophon, is not a change in substance—only in length—and mirrors the process undergone by many texts in antiquity, in the express interest of preserving the entire plot of the work, and all its constituent episodes.

The successive alterations that one finds in the other novelistic literature, from the Jewish novellas to the Alexander romance and the *Acts of Peter*, result in the text wearing a different face at various points in its history. For many of these texts, it is clear that the alterations express the shifting concerns of the editors and copyists of the text over a span of time. As Merkelbach and others have demonstrated, the various versions of the Alexander romance mirror the changing political concerns of its tradents. The text, "Alexander's Last Days" (3.30–33), which circulated independently and was later incorporated into the work of Pseudo-Kallisthenes, betrays the political concerns of the *diadochoi*.[50] By the time of Pseudo-Kallisthenes, however, the political concerns are largely those of Greeks living in Egypt: the founding of Alexandria (1.30–33), the cult of Alexander (3.34), and his descent from the last Egyptian pharaoh, Nektanebos (1.1–8). This same process of accommodation to changing times appears in the text of the *Acts of Peter* as well. The figure of Marcellus, for example, is a polytheist benefactor in the continuous Greek text. In the late second-century Greek redaction, however, Marcellus becomes a lapsed Christian, apparently for the purpose of facilitating a discussion on the possibility of being forgiven for grave sins such as backsliding into immoral behavior or heretical beliefs, an issue in late second-century Asia Minor.

This adaptation of narratives about the past in the interest of reflecting current social realities has been called the "homeostatic organization of cultural tradition" by students of primary oral communities. The past is not remembered as such, but is continually retold to reflect present history and social relations. In the absence of written records, only memory contains information about the past. Study of oral traditions shows that they are extremely unstable in the absence of formal or ritual techniques for their preservation.[51] Since memory, in this case, is more or less limited in its powers of information storage and retrieval, telescoping and selective forgetting of irrelevant data form the process by which the number of things that must be remembered can be reduced and organized meaningfully.[52]

Moreover, memory never works in a disinterested manner; items are not remembered accidentally. The traditions that are preserved relate to social groups or institutions that have developed sufficient identity, power, and duration in time to foster the transmission of traditions meaningful to them: aristocratic families, classes of priests, city-states, or cult organizations. The critical conflicts decisive in forming this identity are popular topics for oral traditions: in Greek history, the Trojan war and the Persian war are examples. In the case of the *Acts of Peter*, the one conflict that appears even in the shortest martyrologies is that between the apostle and the Roman authorities who execute him.

Homeostatic organization persists even when writing is known; the mere existence of fixed written records does not mean that they will be preferred to homeostatically organized information. Among the Tiv peoples of western Nigeria, for example, orally transmitted genealogies provided the basis of most legal decisions. Recognizing their importance, the British colonial government kept written records of the genealogies from the time that they began to administer the province. The Tiv genealogies changed over the four decades during which records were kept. When the British governors pointed out the discrepancies between the current oral tradition and past written record, however, the Tiv considered the written records to be the incorrect ones. The presence of the written documents led to greater conflict, rather than to greater consensus because of increased accuracy.[53]

This type of historical consciousness is not limited to primary oral societies, however. Studies of medieval European society also show the persistence of homeostatic attitudes toward the account of past events even when writing was known and practiced by the tradents.[54] Though literacy in the Hellenistic age and the early Roman Empire was probably much higher than for the earlier Middle Ages,[55] there remained a great deal of overlap between oral and written modes of communication throughout antiquity, in a manner that Walter Ong terms "cheirographic."[56] Manuscripts were less stable than modern printed texts because copying by hand allowed both for error and deliberate modification. Reading aloud was certainly the norm, although silent reading was not unknown.[57] Authors published their books, not by the issue of countless scrolls, but by public reading; even literature as sophisticated and demanding as ancient histories were published in this fashion.[58]

Moreover, the feature of homeostasis is not so much a characteristic inextricably intertwined with primary orality, but rather with a preference to view the past chiefly from the perspective of the present. Though primary oral societies, in the absence of sophisticated mnemonic technology, are consigned to perceive the past in this fashion, homeostasis may be the chosen mode of historical consciousness in societies that know writing. Change in the perception of the past is not a necessary concomitant of the introduction of writing. Relationships between writing, oral tradition, and historical consciousness show a great deal of variation in individual societies.[59]

One motive for the reedition of accounts of the past such as the Alexander romance and the *Acts of Peter* may have been the persistence of a homeostatic orientation toward the past. This would explain why these two works, or Jewish historical novellas such as

Esther, underwent much more serious alteration than the five late Greek erotic novels. For these late works have only the most tangential relationship to history writ large:[60] although most of them seem to be set in the past, they do not purport to be the stories of individuals with lasting historical significance. But with figures of world-political significance, the situation is different: Peter, Alexander, Joseph, and Daniel were important figures for the ethnic communities that claimed them. Martin Braun's comment on the numerous multiforms of the national hero romances hits the mark: "In this lasting topical interest and popularity of national heroic figures lies the ultimate reason why their tradition is so inconsistent and so full of interpolations."[61]

## The Effect of Performance

Narrative fluidity is not, however, confined solely to narratives about the past. It exhibits itself in many types of ancient text: oral epic, magical spells, liturgical texts. What these texts all have in common is a performative aspect. The closest examples to the early Christian texts are several varieties of ancient Jewish religious texts, all of them nonnarrative in nature. The most striking case is that of the Hekhalot literature, postrabbinic texts that chiefly school the individual devotee either on how to ascend to heaven or how to adjure an angel to come to earth and reveal wisdom.[62] Each "text" comprises many smaller units of the most variegated genres: midrashim, apocalypses, words of adjuration, hymns that are sung before the heavenly throne (the "heavenly liturgy"), descriptions of heavenly journeys, and ascetic preparations for the procedures described in the texts. Each manuscript of a text is markedly different from any other. The order of the component textual units varies, as does the actual wording of the texts, and the various smaller elements are alternately included or excluded from the macroforms. It is even unclear from the manuscripts where the individual texts begin and end; scholars disagree, for example, on which unit forms the last portion of *Hekhalot Zutarti*, and the same problem emerges at both the beginning and the end of the *Merkavah Rabbah*.[63] Peter Schäfer, who published the most recent critical treatment of the manuscripts, dispensed with the more traditional approach of editing the manuscripts into one text. Instead, he printed a synopsis of seven manuscripts of the same text.[64] He explains, "Every 'work' in this literary genre that I have investigated more closely proves to be astonishingly unstable, falls into smaller and smaller editorial units and cannot be precisely defined and delimited . . . [this] can be generalized as a striking characteristic feature of the whole literary genre."[65] In an important set of articles, Schäfer argues that many rabbinic texts display an equal degree of flux in the manuscript tradition. He claims that, in such cases, an "original text" may never have existed. The attempt to determine an "original text" is really the arbitrary choice of one form of the text as a "zero point" on the continuum: all versions of the text before it are then classed as source documents, and those after it are redactions.[66] Alternately, the final redaction may be chosen as the text, but as Schäfer writes, "is the final redaction merely the more or less incidental discontinuation of the manuscript tradition?"[67] Instead of this approach, Schäfer advocates the "documentation and description of a dynamic manuscript tradition."[68]

Daniel Harrington and Anthony Saldarini, the editors of Targum Jonathan for the major prophets, an Aramaic paraphrase of the Hebrew Bible used in synagogue services in antiquity, cite Schäfer's work on the Hekhalot in the introduction to their edition of the text. They conclude, "The individual manuscripts of what we call *Targum Jonathan* tend almost to constitute separate works. The process by which these works were shaped was so varied and fluid that the search for the 'one' text or the 'original' text may be illusory."[69] Rebecca Lesses emphasizes that narrative fluidity in the Hekhalot literature results from its nature as a performed text: the manuscripts record adjurations that were meant to be spoken to be effective, and the scribes who preserved the texts may also have been practitioners of the rituals contained in them. Such fluidity as one finds in the manuscript transmission of the Hekhalot literature is problematic for a magical text. One would expect that magical words would be recorded in the same way in each manuscript, since it is presumably their form which carries the power. Lesses explains the variance in terms of performance:

> It is more fruitful to view each manuscript as a script for performance of the various units of the Hekhalot tradition (the "formulas"), rather than asking the traditional question of textual criticism—"what is the *Urtext*"—which assumes the existence of one unique author who composed the written form of the ritual at one sitting. . . . Each written version gives instructions for a slightly different performance of the incantation.[70]

The different forms of the words of power, then, can be attributed to the character of the manuscript as a descriptive record of performance, rather than as a prescriptive manual of procedures.[71]

Most of the other Jewish texts also have a strong background of oral performance. The Targumim were meant to be spoken to an audience. Rabbinic texts themselves underwent an extended process of oral transmission before their reduction to writing and were always learned alongside additional interpretive traditions transmitted orally.[72]

In the case of texts such as the *Acts of Peter*, *Joseph and Aseneth*, or the Alexander romance, it may be advisable to view each manuscript of this text as a separate performance, similar to descriptions of oral tradition. The impulse to create a new version of the story with each retelling of it has more affinity with oral habits of performance than with the modern print-conditioned tendency toward exact reproduction. A "performance" attitude toward written texts was common and widespread in antiquity and was a component of the educational system. The oral expansion of a base narrative was a fundamental exercise in elementary education, which inculcated both oral and written composition. The *Progymnasmata*, elementary rhetorical exercises practiced in antiquity, suggest that anyone receiving even slight education would have been taught how to expand or condense a story at will. Here is the expansion of a *chreia* in a teachers' manual by the first-century C.E. rhetorician Theon:[73]

> For example, a concise *chreia*: Epameinondas, as he was dying childless, said to his friends: "I have left two daughters—the victory at Leuctra and the one at Mantineia." Let us expand like this: Epameinondas the Theban general was, of course, a good man in time of peace, and when war against the Lacedaemonians came to his country, he displayed many outstanding deeds of great courage. As a Boeotarch at Leuctra, he triumphed over the enemy, and while campaigning and fighting for his country, he died at Mantineia. While he was dying of his wounds and his friends were lamenting, among other things, that he was dying childless, he smiled and said: "Stop weeping, friends, for I have left you two immortal daughters: two victories of our country over the Lacedaemonians, the one at Leuctra, who is the older, and the younger, who is just now being born at Mantineia."

The writers and rewriters of the Alexander romance and the Acts of Peter would have been familiar with these techniques of expansion and epitome; if they were educated at all, exercises such as the one above would have been drilled into them at an early age. Perhaps even attitudes to finished texts were similarly fluid in antiquity. The written text of the Acts of Peter may have been meant to serve only as a resource for later retellings. The continuing use of the Acts of Peter as a base text for later versions would suggest that this was the case.

This state of affairs has important ramifications for broader theoretical consideration of orality and literacy in antiquity. The Acts of Peter would be evidence of continuity between oral and written modes of communication: the written text here displays an "oral," performance-based attitude on the part of its transmitters. Similarly, the aspects of the Acts of Peter considered to be worth conserving have little to do with our concept of authorship, as noted above: not the Greek style, nor the particular form of the work, nor even the author's specific manner of structuring the plot, none of these were preserved—only the base storyline, the individual characters, and the salient details remain fixed from one version of the text to another. These were the significant aspects of the work to those who preserved them, not the particular twist that any individual author might give to the storyline. Moreover, the interpretation of the causation of events was equally fluid: the motivations for the martyrdom of Peter change with every retelling of the text.

The importance of texts such as the Acts of Peter, the Alexander romance, and Esther to religious communities gives further impetus to their fluidity. The ritual reading of the martyrdom from the Acts of Peter on the day in the liturgical calendar commemorating his death was standard religious practice in late antiquity.[74] The festival of Purim likewise affords opportunity for the ritual use of Esther.[75] An example from Hindu tradition illustrates even more explicitly the effect of religious practice on the oscillation of a text between oral and written modes. The Râmacaritamânasa is a version of the Râmâyana epic by the poet Tulsîdâs (d. 1623 C.E.). It is a written version of an originally oral epic; the advent of the printing press to India seems to account in large part for its great diffusion. It has become steadily more popular over the last two centuries (the first edition was printed in 1810); in 1983 alone, 200,000 copies were made of a single edition of the text by one printing house, Gita Press. But the text functions in oral fashion: professional reciters tell the work at festivals, rural and urban singing groups perform it, and a few stanzas a day are recited by Brahman schoolboys.[76] Thus a single narrative has proceeded from oral epic, to written composition, and back to oral recitation, because of its ongoing life in a religious community as a meaningful narrative about the past.

# 5

## The Acts of Peter *among* the Novels and Histories

### The Novelistic Elaboration of Historical Characters

The complicated compositional processes among the various versions of the *Acts of Peter* would not incline the observer to class it among the works of ancient historiography. Histories are works of known authors, written with literary aspirations. Several features of the *Acts of Peter*, however, show that the purpose of the narrative was historiographic, although the nature of the historical consciousness differs radically from that found in the more literary historical texts of antiquity. The first of these features is characterization. Although the *development* of the characters in the *Acts of Peter* shows distinct similarities to novelistic processes, the *types* of characters chosen and their precise treatment have very few points of comparison with the five surviving erotic novels, but find their counterparts among the historical and biographical novels.

Even the erotic novels are historical novels in some sense, however, so the lines of definition must not be drawn too sharply. The treatment of characters in the *Acts of Peter* finds its closest analog among the erotic novels in Chariton. His protagonist, Kallirhoe, the daughter of the Sicilian general Hermokrates known from Thukydides,[1] also appears in Diodorus Siculus and Plutarch.[2] Although these texts present her as an anonymous figure, they contain striking overlaps with Chariton's novel. In the histories, the girl is said to have married Dionysios I of Syracuse, to have been assaulted by soldiers, and to have died of her injuries, or, alternately, to have committed suicide because of the outrage of the attack. In Chariton, she also marries a Dionysios, but it is the otherwise unknown Dionysios of Miletos, and it is her second marriage. Her first husband, the youthful Chareas, appears, to the readers, to have killed her early in the romance by kicking her. She does not die of her injuries, however; this being the world of the romance, her death is only apparent. Like Simon, Marcellus, and Agrippa in the *Acts of Peter* trajectory, Chariton still retains in his novel the two or three data generally known about the life of Kallirhoe, as transmitted by Plutarch and Diodorus. The novel and the historical accounts belong to the same fabula. The storyline, however, diverges radically in the novel: different causes are attributed to the events, and the motivation of the characters diverges from the historical accounts.

*Metiochos and Parthenope*, perhaps also written by Chariton,[3] presents a more attenuated example. The story takes place at the court of Polykrates, tyrant of Samos, and
includes an appearance by the pre-Socratic philosopher Anaximenes.[4] The two title figures are, respectively, the son of the Athenian Miltiades and the daughter of Polykrates.
Both children are mentioned in Herodotos, the daughter of Polykrates at 3.124 and
Metiochos at 6.39–41. Though peopled with characters from "real" history, this novel
does not grant them the centrality that such characters receive in the *Acts of Peter*. Although the fathers of Metiochos and Parthenope, like the father of Kallirhoe, were famous individuals, about whose lives much information is available, they appear only
on the borders of the novels; their children, the central figures, whiled away their lives
quietly, receiving only brief mentions in the historians. These daughters and sons of
leading political figures do, however, illustrate the genealogical relationship between
history and novel. Like the main characters themselves, these novels are descendants of
political historiography.

   *Kallirhoe* and *Metiochus and Parthenope* are, however, the earliest of the erotic novels
and are exceptional in their relationship to history. In the other erotic novels, none of
the characters possesses a historical pedigree to this extent. The characters in Longos,
Achilles Tatius, Heliodoros, and Xenophon are happily obscure. The evidence suggests
that, earlier in the development of the novel, the relationship to history was closer. Unlike
the later erotic novels, in the pre-Sophistic novels, historical figures are the primary
characters. The collection and publication of the fragments of the Greek novel have
only increased the number of works pertaining to this category, which Susan Stephens
calls "nationalistic novels." Ninos the founder of Nineveh, Sesonchosis the Egyptian
conqueror, Rhodanes the king of Babylon, and Calligone, a South Russian figure, are
all attested in novel fragments.[5] The *Ninos* novel is based on a legendary Assyrian king.[6]
He, like Joseph from *Joseph and Aseneth*, doubtless possessed great significance for his
ethnic community. The novel, however, is still far from a historical account. The part of
his life that becomes the subject of the novel is the period about which no other author
shows any knowledge. The *Ninos* novel treats the years of his youth. In the surviving
fragments, he is only sixteen years old and is wooing the thirteen-year-old Semiramis
between his campaigns against various armies in the Mediterranean basin.[7] Similarly,
*Joseph and Aseneth* fills out the span of the single verse in Genesis (41:45) that narrates
the courtship and marriage of one of the patriarchs of Israel. So even in the case of the
earlier "historical" novels, the story develops on the margins of history, twining its flow-
ers in the lacunae left by surviving historical traditions.

   The *Acts of Peter* embellish their characters using the same means as the novels, but
the relationship to historiography differs considerably. The novels, both erotic and historical, avoid direct reference to commonly known historical events. Although the *minor*
characters may be drawn directly from historical figures, neither the *main* characters nor
the story refers to the events or public figures who populate historical discourse. In texts
such as the *Acts of Peter*, however, the narrative focuses directly on figures of great public significance to the tradents. And it is precisely the most noteworthy events in the
lives of the characters that become the province of the Christian writers and storytellers.
This is certainly true of Simon and Peter, and even of secondary figures such as Marcellus.
However historically worthless or distorted the information in the *Actus Vercellenses*
may be, the objective is not to tell something that *may* have happened in the past, using

history for décor, but to retell the most significant and well-known events from the public life of an individual; a narrative about noteworthy events of the past is the main objective. The Alexander romance provides the best generic parallel among the novelistic products of the Roman Empire. Alongside all of the imaginative and improbable occurrences that form the fabric of the narrative, the romance also narrates all the best-known events of Alexander's life.

Though the texts of the *Acts of Peter* respect the basic deeds of their characters, the transmitters show a striking license that leads to the elaborations and recastings of the narrative enumerated above. The imaginative and creative embellishment of a "historical" narrative is one of the features that the *Acts of Peter* and related texts share with novelistic literature. Both types of text employ similar narrative techniques to achieve this end. The referential worlds created by the two classes of literature, however, differ sharply. The erotic novels provide space for imaginative embroidery by focusing on the margins of history or by presenting the narrative as an elaboration (*ekphrasis*) of a painting, as do Achilles Tatius and Longos. In other words, imagination finds free rein in an absence of reference to a "historical" world outside the narrative. Texts such as the Alexander romance and the *Acts of Peter*, however, discover the potential for embellishment in the elaboration of the basic data about the lives and deeds of their characters. These texts are deeply referential to history and find creative liberty in the *manner* in which the tradition is transmitted. The presence of traditions about the characters does not set the boundaries of imaginative retelling, as in the case of the erotic novels; the traditions become the framework of the narrative.

## History in Multiform

The fluidity of such traditions allows them to remain useful to changing audiences over time by easily accommodating new political and social realities into the tradition. The genealogies of oral tradition will similarly alter over the course of time to include or exclude individuals and families to reflect those currently in power.[8] This is called "homeostasis" because the effect is to depict the past as essentially the same as the present: if things are a certain way now, it is because they always were so. In oral transmission, events and people are always remembered for a reason, and the irrelevant tends to be forgotten over time. One scholar has called this process "structural amnesia."[9] If the fluid organization of historical information is happening on a written level, as with the *Acts of Peter*, however, it is not a case of amnesia. Each of the *Acts of Peter* texts knows earlier written versions. The constant reformulation of the narrative, then, is not an accident of memory, but a chosen compositional technique. It is a way of maintaining a meaningful relationship to the past.

The narrative fluidity of these stories, their existence in multiple translations, redactions, abridgments, and expansions, is evidence of successive performances of a narrative such as the *Acts of Peter* and should be viewed as a positive characteristic of this category of literature, rather than the terror of the editor. This activity of transmission was inherently fluid; it allowed texts like the *Acts of Peter*, or the Alexander romance, to serve as texts of orientation for their tradents, expressing a meaningful past, identifying and explaining the conflicts that formed their group identity. This constant process of reformulation allowed the audience to use its history to renegotiate and revisualize its relationship to present political and social realities.

The example of the *Acts of Peter* demonstrates that the act of writing a text does not necessarily signify a desire to fix it. In the case of a narrative tradition with written texts, the fluidity of the tradition per se is not the result of the failure of human memory, but of a preference for treating the past *in this way*. However novelistic the trappings of works such as the *Acts of Peter*, history is also deeply important in them: the past is used as a reference point for orientation in the present. The unexpected and seemingly idiosyncratic treatment of history in such literature may seem so only because it offers a rare insight into an alternative mode of ancient historical consciousness.

Texts such as the *Acts of Peter* maintain their focus on individuals with heavy symbolic value. Martin Braun catalogs other such narratives, which he calls "national hero romances." The stories of Ninos preserved the historical memory of the Babylonian east, the Egyptians told stories about Sesonchosis and Nektanebos, and the Jews wrote novelized histories of Moses.[10] Most prominently, Alexander expressed Greek identity in numerous ways in the various traditions about him; the A and B recensions of the Alexander romance of pseudo-Kallisthenes reflect Egyptian-Greek concerns such as the founding of Alexandria.

To center on the deeds of one leading individual is a manner of organizing information about the past that gained currency even in elite historiography over the Hellenistic period. It is the written analog to the concentration of epic lore around larger-than-life figures within oral tradition.[11] In their successive editions, the narratives "map" the characteristic concerns of their audiences onto the experiences of one individual who is paradigmatic for the identity of the audience, whether it be Alexander for the Greeks or Peter for the Christians.

The individual figure, rather than any specific version of the story of his life, thus functions as the fabric of the narrative. This turns modern expectations on their head. Modern historiography tends to focus more on the causation of events, and their proper sequence, than on the guiding figures of history. The first thing one would like to know about Peter's martyrdom is not the name of the man who arrested him, but the reason he attracted the hostile attention of Rome. It is characteristic that this issue and others like it are precisely those that are left to swim among the texts of this narrative tradition.

When the characterization of the figures in the narrative does change, it is often to make them more suitable as paradigmatic figures. In the language of "speech acts," these alterations make the text more "felicitous," that is, adequate to the circumstances in which it is communicated.[12] Marcellus, for example, functions as a cipher for the ideal audience of the *Acts of Peter*. The rising fortunes of Marcellus among the later texts of the *Acts of Peter* reflect the social reality of the increasing acceptance of Christianity by ever higher classes of the Roman aristocracy. Second-century Christianity may have known one or two aristocratic converts. In the *Actus Vercellenses*, this new historical situation was retrojected into the very beginnings of the Christian movement to provide these new converts with a role model. Christians of less illustrious classes also wanted to read about powerful men giving benefactions to their community and converting to belief in their God. The narrative of the *Acts of Peter* places the ruling classes in the "proper" relationship to the Christian community, and not only to them, but to the founders of their community. Peter and Marcellus are not only friends; Marcellus places himself under the instruction of Peter, and, by the time he becomes the author of the "Passion of the holy apostles Peter and Paul," the Marcellus text, he calls Peter "my lord." This increasing submission to a founding figure of the community occurs in tandem with the progressive social upgrading of the figure of Marcellus. In the Linus text and *Nereus and Achilleus*, Marcellus not only moves closer to the center of the Christian community, he is more aristocratic. His actions, his patronage, and his testimony to the Christian faith are ideal actions of upper-class Christian converts.

The outset of the Alexander romance narrates that Alexander is not really the son of Philip of Macedonia, but of Nektanebos, the last Egyptian pharaoh (1.4–8 in the β recension). He flees Egypt at the coming of the Persian army. While Philip is away, he appears at the Macedonian court and tells the queen Olympias that she is destined to bear the child of the Libyan god Ammon. He then causes her, by magic, to dream this herself. Ammon appears in Olympias' bedroom, not surprisingly, in the form of Nektanebos; the queen accepts him without complaint and bears the child of Nektanebos, Alexander.

The lineage of Alexander is thereby altered in the romance. The more usual alternative story about Alexander's lineage is that Ammon visited Olympias in the form of a snake: this is widely distributed and can be found, for example, in Plutarch's *Alexander* (chap. 2). Why Nektanebos? Other features of the Alexander romance show that Greeks of Egypt had a hand in composing the work: the story shows an intense interest in the founding of Alexandria (1.32–34 in the β recension). The people who told and heard this story wanted to identify Alexander as one of their own, as truly an Egyptian Greek, half Egyptian and half Macedonian. The text itself indicates an identity between Nektanebos and Alexander. When, after Nektanebos is accidentally killed, Alexander sees to it that he is properly buried, we read the comment: "It is one of Providence's notable marvels that Nektanebos, an Egyptian, received a funeral in the Greek style in Macedonia, but that Alexander, a Macedonian, received a funeral in the Egyptian style."[13] So the account claims as a hometown boy one of the major figures of world history. His epigones then became the longtime rulers of Egypt, the Ptolemies. In the birth story of Alexander, the relationship between Egyptian and Macedonian is inverted: Nektanebos, the last native Egyptian king, becomes the source of Macedonian rule. Thus Macedonian rule of the Egyptians is really the rule of Egyptians by Egyptians, for Alexander is the son of the Pharaoh.

The motif of the conqueror who is really a secret descendent of the people whom he conquers appears frequently in ancient literature. In Herodotos, the Persian king Cyrus, who conquered the Medes, was said by the Egyptians to be the son of a Median princess,[14] and Cambyses, the conqueror of Egypt, was said to be son of an Egyptian woman.[15] The situation in the *Acts of Peter* is analogous in that it claims the Roman rulers for the Christian community and creates a world in which the rulers do not persecute the Christians, but rather identify themselves as Christians. Since this is not an ethnic identity, but a religious one, changed loyalties and conversions—as with the case of Marcellus—take the place of genealogical descent. The aim, however, is the same as the stories which subvert the historical conquerors by altering their genealogy: powerless people—and this could even designate the Christian leadership—tell tales that reenvisage their relationship with the powerful. These tales create a vision of a different world, one in which the powerful become sponsors of the powerless in the Christian community. As propaganda directed at upper-class sympathizers, the texts are a first step to realizing a new relationship with the powers that govern their world. The text is not descriptive, but prescriptive, and acts as an instrument to achieve its vision. The text was not only propaganda aimed at the Roman elite, but also changed the way the Christians themselves viewed their world and, by motivating actions consonant with this new outlook, changed the world itself.


## The Trouble with Audiences

To assess genre from an Aristotelian standpoint means to classify a work by the overt signs embedded in its text: it is prose or poetry, tragedy or comedy. Structuralist critics were the first to break the link between the physical text and its genre. As Todorov writes, "We have postulated that literary structures, hence genres themselves, be located on an abstract level, separate from that of concrete works. We would have to say that a given work manifests a certain genre, not that this genre exists in the work."[16] The text can then be viewed not as an inert object, but as a communication between author and reader, and not simply that, but between an implied author and an implied reader. The physical author, in other words, presents him or herself as a persona within the text, one that differs from the "real" author. The implied reader is also one that has its true existence only within the text, as the persona to whom a work is addressed. The relationship between implied author and implied audience is the location within which genre is communicated.

Foucault has noted that "authors" of any type do not really exist. Not only are they constructs located within texts, the determination of authorial function itself is one that depends on historical factors, on the particular cultural context within which texts are read.[17] Analogously, one could conclude that the audience function is similarly historically conditioned. If both author and audience, as functions of texts, are historically conditioned, then so are notions of genre.[18] This historicization of the process of reading opens the possibility of multiple generic designations of a literary work dependent on the historical context.

Glen Bowersock has argued that the Christian gospels represent a new type of narrative fiction in the form of history, one which entered the ancient literary scene during the reign of Nero, a period he considers crucial in Roman cultural history. He argues that the Christian fictions stimulated the growth of secular novelistic narratives by offering a fiction that was "true" in some sense, a fiction as history.[19] Throughout his lectures, Bowersock reverses the accepted directionality of influence;[20] the Christian works as he presents them were not mere passive recipients of the literary techniques and conventions of ancient fiction, but also contributed to its development.

Bowersock has time on his side: four of the five ideal romances were written in the second century or later and thus were composed before the gospels. He is also to be commended for taking the early Christian narratives out of the quarantine in which they are placed both by scholars of classics and by scholars of early Christianity. Christian texts cannot be isolated behind a semipermeable barrier through which literary influence can be received, but never given. In the second century, Christian writings had sufficient circulation to be read by curious polytheists such as Celsus. Moreover, Bowersock shows good observation in concentrating on the "pseudo-historians" of the Neronian period, such as Diktys and Dares, or works such as the *Heroica* of one of the Philostrati. These texts were playing with the boundaries between history and fiction, but theirs was a serious game, for they focused on the primal text of Greek identity, the *Iliad*.

The exact relationship between the Christian works and novelistic literature, however, is obscured by Bowersock's treatment. Although there is a close generic relationship between texts such as the gospels and the "fictions as history" of Diktys and Dares, the novel itself had a parallel and partially independent development. The first- and second-century novels in which Bowersock finds the influence of the Christian gospels actually form the endpoint of a literary development that began, in the case of the Jewish examples, at least two centuries before the composition of the gospels; even the *Ninos* novel existed well before the gospels entered the literary scene.[21] The Christian narratives may indeed have entered and enriched a trend in literature already well underway and furnished the Sophistic novels with some of their favorite motifs, such as resurrection and cannibalism.[22] But the gestation of the novel is to be located elsewhere, since the novel is temporally prior to the gospels.

Bowersock's major claim is that these medial works, such as Diktys, Dares, and the gospels, are toying with the genre of history, presenting fictitious content within historiographic trappings. Common to the novels, and to the "fictions as history" such as the gospels and the Apocryphal Acts, is the relationship they hold to public history. All these, as prose works about past events, are histories of some ilk, at least in an Aristotelian sense. One cannot, however, treat all these works as an undiffierentiated block. History is more central to the gospels, the Apocryphal Acts, the Alexander romance, the Jewish novellas, and the pseudo-histories. These are all "referential" texts that narrate major historical events, however constitutive novelistic techniques of embellishment may also be for their genre. The erotic novels, on the other hand, avoid this sort of referentiality, focusing on the private events of obscure characters.

From another perspective, however, Bowersock's reading of not only the Apocryphal Acts but also the canonical gospels as essentially fictitious may not be so wide of the mark.[23] If the choice is between fiction and history, then the Christian texts are not historical in any formal generic sense of the word. In the case of the *Acts of Peter*, an example he does not mention,[24] the narrative begins almost without introduction to narrate a tale set in the past. Though treating events in the past, the domain of historiography, it lacks all the external generic conventions appropriate to this category of literature. No preface introduces the author, no metatextual statements of method or purpose in writing intrude on the narrative, the text provides no indication of its sources, the author never explicitly weighs evidence, nor writes excurses providing divergent analyses of the causation of individual events. Although the genre of history admitted considerable breadth of topic by the end of the Hellenistic period, the subject of the *Acts of Peter*, the progress of a religious movement, is not the typical fare of political or military history, which forms the center of the ancient genre of history. Moreover, the only large-scale historical figure, Nero, appears on the edge of the narrative. The rest is a tale of the travels and deeds of a certain Peter largely unknown to people outside the Christian community.

The learned historian likely replicates the response of an ancient polytheist to texts such as the *Acts of Peter*. The closest analog to the *Acts of Peter* for an *uninformed* ancient reader would be works such as Chariton's *Chareas and Kallirhoe* or his *Metiochos and Parthenope.* These narratives are also set in the past and present themselves as straightforward accounts unburdened with any particular concern for sources and evidence. Like the *Acts of Peter*, they take place in a distinct historical nexus: the Samos of Polykrates in *Metiochos and Parthenope* parallels the Rome of Nero in the *Acts of Peter* as a glamorous setting for a story. In these novels, as well, the uninitiated ancient reader would find all the historical figures on the sidelines, providing the setting for a protagonist far more obscure, such as Chareas or Peter.

Tomas Hägg defines this type of work as a "historical novel": the pleasure of reading them derives from the "juxtaposition of the real and the imaginary."[25] According to Hägg's definition, these tales narrate the affairs of fictitious characters, include some historical events in the public sphere affecting the personal fortunes of the characters, are set at least one or two generations back, and demonstrate historical verisimilitude. Works like the Alexander romance, the *Cyropaedia*, the *Life of Aesop*, and the *Life of Homer* would fail this definition because the central figure is historical; he considers these to be romanticized biography. As Hägg and others have noted, however, it is entirely possible that most readers would have accepted even the "fictitious" or "imaginary" aspects of these historical novels as true and accurate;[26] the point is not that Daphnis and Chloe are fictitious or imaginary, but that they are obscure and unknown outside the world of their own narrative.

Hägg's restrictive definition of the historical novel would contain only two ancient works, *Chareas and Kallirhoe* and *Metiochos and Parthenope.*[27] The other erotic romances are not historical enough. In terms of passive generic conventions, the various versions of the *Acts of Peter* could have been considered historical novels by a large segment of their possible ancient audience, that is, as a dramatized and naively straightforward prose narration set in the past in which the major historical figures appear as décor alone and the action is carried by lesser lights. To this extent, those who would describe the Apocryphal Acts as novels have evidence for their claims, and Bowersock is correct that Christian narratives would have primarily influenced fictitious works such as the Sophistic erotic novels. As others have pointed out at length, the similarity exists not only on the level of substantive indices, "motifs," but also in narrative technique. The manner in which the narrative of the *Acts of Peter*, or any of the Apocryphal Acts, is elaborated owes much to literary techniques familiar from the novels.[28]

The term "historical novel" is problematic for several reasons, however. As a hybrid genre that implicates both novel and history, it has been used inconsistently in the secondary literature on the ancient novel. Tomas Hägg provides an excellent example. His statement above is directly contradicted in one of his earlier works, in which the Alexander romance appears, not as a non-novelistic "romanticized biography," but as the quintessential historical novel:[29]

> On the other hand, private individuals unburdened by historicity stand at the centre [of the five erotic novels], and therefore it may be more correct to reserve the designation 'historical' for those novels that really do follow a historical course of events, in however imaginative a way. . . . Not until the *Alexander Romance* do we find a complete living specimen of the genre.[30]

Hägg's two definitions are thus self-contradictory, which indicates a serious theoretical difficulty. The problem, I would submit, is one of referentiality. The determination of whether a work is historical—and thus less fictional—depends on the nature of its reference to history, which is something beyond the pale of the text proper. The extent to which a text can be considered a "history" thus cannot be described in the text-immanent fashion in which most modern literary criticism is conducted. One must make a judgment about the knowledge of realities outside the text that was available to its readers. By invoking "history" as a generic component, the reception of the text is unwittingly drawn into the definition of genre.

If such a definition accords only partially with modern understandings of text and genre, this manner of distinguishing between history and fiction has the advantage of being much closer to literary distinctions practiced in the ancient world. Ancient rhetoricians distinguished three types of narrative: history, myth, and *argumentum* or πλάσμα, a word without direct English equivalent. History and myth differed in that history is true and myth is fantastic; it does not even *seem* true.[31] The defining characteristic that distinguished πλάσμα (fiction) from ἱστορία (history) was not its verisimilitude—both showed this as a defining feature—but whether or not the things narrated actually happened. As an example of a "true thing that happened," Sextus Empiricus gives the fact that Alexander died in Babylon because he was poisoned by plotters against his life. Πλάσμα, on the other hand, are things that did not happen, but that are related in a similar fashion to things that did happen: "*plasma* [is] the exposition of events that did not happen, but are told in a manner similar to [events] that have happened, such as the plots of comedies, and mimes" (*adversus mathematicos* 1.263-66).[32] The issue is evidentiary. Thus, according to the ancient distinction between history and fiction, proper genre can only be determined if one has knowledge beyond the text. The text is only historical if it is referential to events outside the text itself. Significantly, the historical event that Sextus mentions is narrated at the end of the Alexander romance, a novelistic work. Sextus uses it as an example precisely because every literate person would know that it actually happened. By Sextus's definition, then, novels such as Chariton's would not qualify as historical in any sense, even as "historical novels."

Hägg's first definition of the historical novel, as a tale of fictitious characters against a historical backdrop, is thus at odds with ancient literary sensibilities expressed theoretically. Symptomatically, such a restrictive definition would leave large numbers of ancient works unclassifiable. If Chariton is the center of the genre of "historical novel," what is to be done with those that fall in between because they are more historical than Chariton and yet not history proper? Chariton and the Alexander romance are clearly two different sorts of things, but the example of *Ninos* does not fall neatly into Hägg's distinction between "historical novel" and "romanticized biography." *Ninos* is an erotic novel, but its centerpiece is a legendary figure, not a fictitious character. The range of these novelistic works clearly falls on a continuum, ranging from the least historical of the erotic novels, such as Longos and Achilles Tatius, through exemplars with a progressively more central historical focus: Chariton, *Ninos*, the Alexander romance. If Longos can be called a "historical novel," and by Hägg's definition, it can, the continuum runs from "historical novel" to "novelized history."

Employing the term "historical novel" has utility, if this designation is defined broadly enough to include works such as the Alexander romance, the Gospels, and the *Life of Aesop*. Although the surface analysis of the *Acts of Peter* might indicate that it is a novel in the same sense as Chariton, this judgment is belied by the history of the transmission of the *Acts of Peter*. Whereas the individual texts, as single points in the narrative trajectory, may seem to be novels like Chariton's to the uninitiated reader, the entire complex of related texts as a phenomenon is unparalleled among the erotic novels. In evaluating the various translations, excerpts, interpolations, and redactions present even in the earliest written exemplar of the *Acts of Peter*, and the continuing stream of closely related but not literarily dependent recastings of the narrative, a second segment of the ancient audience comes into view. Each of the recastings of the narrative is a discrete act of reading by an ancient reader. The transmission of the *Acts of Peter* shows the most similarity, not to the erotic novels, but to novelistic texts such as the Alexander romance or *Joseph and Aseneth* or Esther, stories of the lives of individuals who were not only historically significant to their communities but often stood at the center of their cultic life.

The identity of the protagonist is the single most significant factor in determining the shape of the transmission of these texts. The impulse to recreate and update the narratives concerning historically significant individuals, the heroes of Martin Braun's "national hero romances," is an index of their popularity among the tradents of these stories. No variant versions exist for the stories of Daphnis and Chloe, or Habrokomes and Anthia, because the narratives about them were finished on the day the author composed them. No later editor took a hand to them because little was at stake; as David Konstan has observed, "It does not make sense to say that Longus . . . added or subtracted episodes. There is nothing in the cultural tradition for Longus to have been mistaken about. The only presumed witness to the actions of Daphnis and Chloe is the novel itself."[33] No revision of the story was ever necessary, since it did not refer to the changing external world in the same way that the histories of Herodotos or even the Alexander romance did.

To compare the last two might seem a precipitous action. The Alexander romance is hardly responsible history; it swims with errors. The distinction between novel and history, however, is not based on their relative accuracy. The difference between Herodotos and the erotic novels is that, in the case of Herodotos, there is something about which to be wrong. Although the chronology of the Alexander romance goes askew, it still offers enough connection with "historical" events, that is, public and well-known events, to construct a relationship between the "historical" chronology and the "novelistic" one. The relationship between the narrative and the external world is crucial, and this was perceived by the authors of the *Acts of Peter* in that they constantly reformulated the narrative to attain a more "felicitous" relationship with the external world.

For a Christian reader, Peter was no anonymous figure, but one of the guiding personalities of the early Christian community. Although the secondary personages appearing in the *Acts of Peter*, Agrippa, Albinus, and Marcellus, may no longer have retained significance for the second-century community apart from their appearance in the narrative of Peter, their existence as first-century figures suggests that the narratives about Peter began in the first century. The narrative sprung up not far removed from its dramatic date, then; as it began to be told, it was not set in the distant past, as were, for example, Chariton's work(s), or the *Ninos* romance. Again, the Alexander romance provides the closest parallels. Some of its sources, such as the last will and testament of Alexander and the memoirs of Alexander's generals, developed in the decades immediately following his death.[34]

The persistence of the secondary figures throughout the various exemplars of the *Acts of Peter* also shows the basic tendency of the narrative to conserve traditional materials. The impulse is toward retention of the significant details of Peter's life and works, primarily organized around named characters. The appearance of multiforms in the *Actus Vercellenses* shows the same desire to lose as little as possible of the narrative trajectory about Peter; variant versions of the same eposide are simply inserted at the appropriate point in the fabula of the *Acts of Peter*.

The generic evaluation of a work like the *Acts of Peter*, then, depends on the particular reading audience. The passive features in the text, by which the genre would be defined in a Aristotelian sense, would lead the uninitiated reader astray. Readers outside the communities in which Peter was a significant figure would have been apt to read the works about him as they would have read any prose text about an obscure character from the past; for these individuals, Peter's tale would be closer to that of Habrokomes and Anthia than to the Alexander romance. This reader would be encountering the text of the *Acts of Peter* at one point in time and would be unlikely to know of the other recensions and exemplars. In other words, this hypothetical reader would have been far from the ideal reader of the text; he or she would have lacked critical information. Indeed, because the texts in the *Acts of Peter* trajectory allude to other early Christian works, and even to other Petrine narratives, not only the ideal reader but even the implied reader would have had familiarity with the world of early Christian texts.

A reader in the Christian community would be able to take on the persona of the implied reader. He or should would not only have known Peter as a historical figure of great significance, but may also have been aware of other versions of the *Acts of Peter* and other Petrine narratives. The *Acts of Peter*, then, have a surface level generic classification based on the physical features of the text, and a deeper generic classification that presupposes the inside knowledge provided by a reading community, not encoded in any of the passive generic conventions in the text.

The *Acts of Peter* would be considered history according to Sextus's classification, for, to its implied reading community, the events narrated in it truly took place. In a more absolute sense, the narrative of a text of the *Acts of Peter* refers to events outside itself. Although external attestation of the events of Peter's life cannot be found in unrelated works of history, any version of the *Acts of Peter* does refer to something beyond its own text: it refers to the other texts of the *Acts of Peter* trajectory.

## The *Acts of Peter* and the Historical Monograph

The problem with works such as the Alexander romance, and the Apocryphal Acts, is whether they should be called novels at all, since, once admitted to this class, they must be called historical novels. The centrality of the protagonist in the narrative raises the question of whether these works should be classed as biographies. And to call them "romanticized biographies" has the advantage of assigning them to another genre. There is no question that these works bear great generic similarity to the Christian gospels, which have repeatedly been compared to ancient biographies,[35] especially the lives of the philosophers.[36] These latter have the advantage of providing a model in which emphasis is devoted not only to the figure of the philosopher, but also to his disciples and teachings. Moreover, many of these works are similar to the gospels and the Apocryphal Acts in not containing birth stories. Last, the genre admits considerable range: not only Diogenes Laertius, but even the biography of Apollonios of Tyana may be included.[37] Genre can be defined dynamically, so that one can even speak of a genre trajectory between biography and novel, with some overlap possible.[38] Lawrence Wills is right in emphasizing that the "popular, novelistic biography of the extraordinary person," such as the *Life of Aesop* or the *Life of Secundus the Silent Philosopher* provide models of the biographical genre closer to the gospels than are Plutarch or Diogenes Laertius.[39]

Even within this range, however, one must question whether the Apocryphal Acts present their figures as a biographer would. Biography is not primarily a historical genre. Although biography refers to history in that it narrates the lives of public figures, it often narrates events about these figures that are private rather than public. As he writes in the first chapter of his *Life of Alexander*, Plutarch often preserves the smaller and less historically significant actions because they provide a better key for illuminating the psychological aspects of a character. Ancient biography differs from an account of the deeds of leading individuals, which had become a standard subgenre within history by the Hellenistic period.[40] Since the interest of a biography is not in events, but in the character who is the subject of the biography, it is not a requirement that the events narrated refer to public historical events. The referent of the text is the person described, although this person refers to a historical context to the extent that he or she is a figure of public significance.

In the Apocryphal Acts, on the other hand, the events narrated are all public events, not anecdotes about private life that would illuminate the character of the main figure. The Gospels and the *Acts of Peter* focus rather on the most public and best-known deeds of their characters. They also focus on only one event from the course of the apostle's life that pertains directly to the apostle as a private individual: his death. The other events narrated are events within the community of Christians: miracles, the refutation of false teachers, conversions. We learn nothing, for example, of the lineage or families of the apostles, of their education or secular occupations.[41] Even the interest in the apostle's death is not purely private, for the apostle serves as an example of martyrdom for the rest of the community, and the day of his death becomes a public holiday. Texts such as the Alexander romance, Apocryphal Acts, *Life of Aesop*, and the gospels all exhibit this focus on the public life of their protagonists. Moreover, they all share a similar literary form, described in the previous chapter. As David Konstan has written, "All such wise-man tales have in common an episodic structure, in which the several scenes are concatenated like beads on a string until they culminate in the extraordinary death of the hero. As a result, they are easily subject to expansion, reduction, and variation of incident, and they tend accordingly, like the Alexander Romance and the Gospels, to survive in multiple redactions."[42]

Even in the case of the Gospels, the biographical model has not taken the field as their unqualified generic description. Mary Ann Tolbert argues that the novels present a useful model for the genre—and audience—of Mark, in that they are all entertaining prose narratives in a less elevated style.[43] She would place Mark among the historical/biographical novels such as the *Cyropaedia*, the Alexander romance, and the *Ninos*, though she notes that this grouping of novels is too fragmentary a basis on which to postulate a subgenre.[44] Wills also agrees that the gospels do bear a close relationship to the novel, though he observes that this similarity lies more in technique than in form, for the novel supplies the means by which the individual, character, and psychology are developed. As he writes, "The novel, or more precisely, the indigenous novelistic literature of the ancient world, is what prepared the way for the gospel."[45] Among the ancient novels, Wills finds that the Gospels bear the most similarity to the historical novels, because of their lack of a truly fictional aspect. On balance, the work of those who use literary models to describe the genre of the Gospels[46] suggests that they are a hybrid genre: novelized biographies, novelized histories, or historical novels. The *Acts of Peter* are thus not ancient biographies in any typical sense.

Charting the distance between novel and history is extraordinarily difficult. A strict dichotomy between novel and history in antiquity is untenable because of the close literary relationship of these two genres and because, as Bowersock argues, the very notions of fiction and truth were under discussion at precisely the point in time that the Christian writings were developing. The *Acts of Peter*, however close to novelistic texts, would have been unusual but certainly not impossible as a work of history on the basis of its topic: a short and entertaining account of the public exploits of a leading figure of a community. In a well-known letter[47] (5.12, ca. 56 B.C.E.) to a literary friend, a certain Lucceius, Cicero pleads with him to interrupt his work on the universal history he was writing in order to narrate a single episode in Roman history, the conspiracy of Catiline. Cicero considers himself to have played an important role in this event[48] and expresses his desire to have the pleasure of reading an account of his deeds while he is still alive. He suggests to Lucceius not to wait until he comes to the proper place in his general history (*perpetuam rerum gestarum historiam*, 5.12.6), but to disregard the canons of history (*ut . . . in eo leges historiae neglegas*, 5.12.3) and treat the conspiracy as a separate account, since it differs from the wars against enemies and allies that Lucceius was otherwise narrating.

This practice of writing a short historical account, a monograph, was common. In the same letter, Cicero mentions several Greek writers (Kallisthenes, Timaios, and Polybios) who narrated the events of a single war as a self-contained volume (5.12.2).[49] Sallust's *Jugerthine War*, an account of a series of Roman campaigns in Numidia (112–105 B.C.E.), is comparable in extent to these. Cicero's suggestions to his friend about the extent of the proposed work are close to the chronological limits of Sallust's other work, the *Conspiracy of Catiline*: Cicero thinks that a good-sized volume (*modicum quoddam corpus*) can be made from the events starting from the beginning of the conspiracy to Cicero's return from exile (5.12.4).[50]

The existence of historical monographs as a live option for writers in the late Republican period would have little to do with the Apocryphal Acts were it not for Cicero's description of the merits of such a piece. These correspond more closely to our conception of a dramatized documentary (5.12.4–5):

what has happened to me will supply you with an infinite variety of material, abounding in a sort of pleasurable interest (*plenam . . . cuiusdam voluptatis*) which could powerfully grip the attention of the reader. . . . For there is nothing more apt to delight the reader (*nihil est enim aptius ad delectationem lectoris*) than the manifold changes of circumstance, and vicissitudes of fortune, which . . . will certainly afford entertainment (*erunt iucundae*) in the reading . . . the regular chronological record of events interests us . . . little (*ordo ipse annalium mediocriter nos retinet*) . . . but the uncertain and varied fortunes of a states-man . . . give scope for surprise, suspense, delight, annoyance, hope, fear.[51]

In this description, Cicero is less interested in an accurate record of the past than in a product to please the reader; he calls the envisaged work *hanc quasi fabulam rerum eventorumque nostrorum* ("this sort of drama about my deeds and experiences," 5.12.6). Although the accuracy of Lucceius's general outline of the events is probably assumed, since Cicero offers to draw up some notes on the events (*commentarios*, 5.12.10) for Lucceius, and hints that his friend will take his point of view and thus vindicate him against his enemies (5.12.4), such a monograph could have functioned primarily as entertainment. Polybios's repeated censure of the Hellenistic historians who wrote be-fore he did (200–118 B.C.E.; fl. 144–133 B.C.E.), along with the surviving fragments of the Hellenistic historians, demonstrate that this dramatization of history, the emphasis on the (literally) "pathetic," had been in practice in historiography for some time. Thus, it is difficult to distinguish between particularly "novelistic" literary techniques and the general stock-in-trade of ancient historiography from the Hellenistic period onward. The focus on a single character, as Cicero writes, "the uncertain and varied fortunes of a statesman" is also a standard subgenre within Greek historiography from the Hellenis-tic period onward, as noted above.

Indeed, in terms of topic alone, the work that Cicero proposes, the Alexander ro-mance, and the *Acts of Peter* are comparable. As Hägg notes, the Alexander romance differs from some of the other novels in that it is not about the private experiences of a fictitious character, but about "the public life and exploits of a world-historical figure himself."[52] Martin Hengel also recognizes the historical monograph as a subgenre within ancient history and argues that the Acts of the Apostles would fit well within this ge-neric description.[53] Adela Yarbro Collins has applied this designation also to the gos-pel of Mark,[54] a work with many similarities to the Apocryphal Acts.

If the *Acts of Peter* are a type of history, however, they are a product radically differ-ent from standard ancient histories. The motivations and causation of events are con-stantly in flux, even on a written level. They alter to reflect the current social and politi-cal realities of their tradents and audiences. Though this attitude toward the transmission of history is commonplace among primary oral cultures, its existence in the *Acts of Peter* trajectory, a conglomeration of written texts, shows that this historical consciousness is not determined by the failure of human memory. Rather, to view the causations and motivations of such events as Peter's arrest in a fundamentally fluid fashion is a chosen means of appropriating the past. The transmission of the past becomes an arena for representing and renegotiating relationships of power in the present.

To some extent, this is true of all historiography. In selecting events worthy of re-counting, the criteria for evaluation always emerge from the present of the historiogra-pher. Hayden White has pointed out that the meaningful aspect of all historiography is its fictitious component: not the drab chronicle of events, but the mythological pattern according to which the data are arranged and interpreted.[55] The degree to which past record is shaped by the vantage point of the present is simply greater in works such as the *Acts of Peter*.

As in many other exemplars of ancient history and epic history, the narrative trajectory of the *Acts of Peter* is organized around primary conflicts. In the *Actus Vercellenses*, the conflict with Simon Magos shapes both the miracle stories taking place in Marcellus's house and the contest in the forum. The conflict with the Roman governing classes is the leitmotif of the arrest and execution of Peter. The conflicts narrated also shift in their prominence as the social and political context of the audience changes. In the later versions of the *Acts of Peter*, the conflict with Simon Magos shrinks, while the arrest and execution become the focus of these texts. Interreligious competition between Christianity and polytheism, in which each demonstrated its validity through supernatural signs, became less relevant as Christianity attracted adherents from the ruling classes and eventually became the religion privileged by the Roman government. As long as there was a polytheist minority among the ruling classes, however, the stories of Peter's arrest and execution still retained relevance.

## The *Acts of Peter* as Historical Novel

The *Acts of Peter*, the Apocryphal Acts, and the Christian Gospels all do make implicit claims to be histories. They are prose narratives about important figures from the past. And yet, they exhibit a distance so great from ancient historiography that few have successfully argued that their genre is history without making significant qualifications. Often the objections are that they are too entertaining, too propagandistic, have too much pathos, and rely too much on miracles and the supernatural. Yet even the best ancient histories are filled with entertaining episodes, including miraculous interventions by gods. It was also a stock criticism of the Hellenistic historians that they relied too much on the pathetic and dramatic. One might also exclude the Acts and the Gospels from the genre of history because they are about a topic not generally appropriate to history proper, the deeds of the leading figures of a religious movement. The historical genre, however, also had many subgenres, one of which was the *praxeis* of famous men, a genre that approximated the Apocryphal Acts. And all histories are propaganda of some sort; they are usually political propaganda, however, rather than religious propaganda, and thus closer to the tastes of some modern interpreters.

There are, however, more important objections to the designation of the Apocryphal Acts as histories. The first is that the Apocryphal Acts nowhere have the standard indicators of the historical genre, as noted. More disturbing are the two features that have been the center of this investigation, the narrative fluidity and homeostatic orientation of the *Acts of Peter*, and with them the Apocryphal Acts. Standard ancient histories simply do not display the same fluidity in the manuscript tradition, the bewildering array of excerpts and translations. And no ancient historian would postulate that the motivation or causation of an event in the first century should vary depending on whether the story is told in the second or fourth century.

Once the generic classification of "history" is abdicated, however, the Apocryphal Acts and works like them drift into the camp of the novel. There is much in favor of this identification. The motifs and narrative techniques of the Christian works stand closest to the novel. It is important to note, however, that the concept of novel in antiquity does not necessarily imply fictiousness. Fiction is not simply falsehood or bad history. The Alexander romance is bad history, but it does not thereby become fictitious. As David Konstan has written, fiction in the ancient world differs from history in that its plot has no referent outside the world of the text. Fiction does not refer to "a specific repertoire of shared narrative materials."[56] History does. In the sense that Konstan uses the word, Homer is not fictitious, since, however mythological and lacking historical veracity, it nevertheless refers to "a culturally acknowledged phenomenon."[57]

Bowersock and others have argued, I think correctly, that there is no clear dividing line between history and fiction. This insight is usually employed to play up the fictionality of ancient histories. Thus if even history is fictitious, there is no question about the fictionality of the novels, hence J. P. Morgan's dictum that, "whereas all novels are fictions, not all fictions are novels."[58] But if "fiction" in this sense – a decidedly modern one – characterizes such a broad number of ancient prose works, it then loses descriptive value in generic characterizations. Alternately stated, the dichotomy should not be between our modern constructs of ancient history and ancient fiction, but between our constructs of ancient history and ancient novel. Since these two generic descriptors exists not as ideal forms, but as points on a continuum, the theoretical problem is then describing the more tenuous cases between the two points, such as the *Acts of Peter*.

Modern discussions of the fictionality of ancient works, while fascinating in their own right, often imply the issues of verisimilitude and "fictional complicity," that is, the suspension of disbelief by the readers. These were not deciding factors in ancient literary classification.[59] By ancient standards, literary works that told of real events, no matter how novelistically, were histories; the works of Dictys and Dares were considered reliable historical sources by later readers. And works that told of events that did not take place, no matter how verisimilar, were *plasma*. If one leaves aside the obfuscating issue of fictionality, one must only account for two features in the generic classification of the *Acts of Peter*, and works like it: first, the recognition, based in ancient literary theory, that they would have been understood as histories, not *plasma*, by their implied and ideal reading audiences, because they are accounts of events that are part of the shared past of a society or subculture; and second, our recognition as modern literary theorists that these works bear little formal relationship to the works that we usually classify as ancient histories. Those literary works that exemplify both these features are best described as "historical novels." Conversely, this term should not be used to describe works such as Chariton's, which, though referring to past events, do not refer to the common past of the society from which their audience is drawn.

There is nevertheless a close relationship between the historical and erotic novels. The historical novel is a precondition of the erotic novel. The historical novels begin to narrate those parts of the lives of great figures not covered in the culturally shared matrix of narratives, such as the *Ninos* novel, with its account of Ninos's youthful romances alongside the better-known battles. In the erotic novel, the relationship of the main characters to history is first attenuated by making them relatives of great figures, as in Chariton. Then it is severed completely.

The *Acts of Peter* fall between novel and history. The lack of the generic indicators of historiography does not completely disqualify them from being histories or push them into the preliterary or nonliterary realm of *Kleinliteratur*, which is considered to be the transcription of oral tradition rather than the creative work of an author. There is some-

thing between this and high literature:[60] a straightforward Koine without generic adorn-
ments was commonly used for informational works in antiquity.[61] The very fluidity of
the *Acts of Peter*, however, sets them apart from both history proper and the erotic novel
that is the endpoint of the development of the novel. Neither of these genres admits
such narrative instability from one version to another, not even in the case of fiction,
though tales do get retold and rewritten within fictional works. But as Konstan writes,
"fictional narratives . . . are not versions of anything else, which is another way of saying that there is no body of traditional lore to which they refer."[62]

The feature of fluidity is common enough among these medial works between history and novel that it may be indicative of the transition. Each of these traditions, of
Peter, Ninos, Alexander, Joseph, or Esther, were works that referred, not to a matrix of
narrative materials shared by the culture as a whole but to a narrative complex known
to a subset of the society. The generic trappings are lacking because the literary aspirations were lower, but also because they were unnecessary. The intended audience was
already familiar with the constellation of characters and events. The very multiformity
of the narrative trajectory created a point of reference for each text within it. Ancient
erotic novels refer primarily to the narrative world of the individual text. These historical novels refer not just to their own individual texts but to all the texts in the narrative
trajectory, that is, to the fabula.

The homeostasis of the narrative is also intrinsically interwoven with the medial nature of historical novels such as the *Acts of Peter*. David Konstan posits the lack of a universal myth as one of the motive factors in the development of the referential autonomy of
fiction.[63] Its self-valorization in the absence of appeals to complexes of culturally shared
narratives allowed it to fill a vacuum, to narrate stories with the small, individual values of
family, marriage, and hometowns. The erotic novels achieved relevance by eschewing reference. The historical novels, all of which pertained to nonelite subgroups in the Roman
Empire, achieved relevance by reading current concerns into the malleable constellation
of traditional characters and narratives. Both the historical novel, and later the erotic novel,
became a meaningful conveyor of values by the diminution of reference to a larger cultural
script. When Christianity became the "new universal myth"[64] in the consolidation of the
Christian empire in the fifth and sixth centuries, the development of the Apocryphal Acts
ceased, and they became fixed "service texts" within Christian liturgy.

There are thus strong phenomenological ties between the novels, both erotic and
historical, and the Apocryphal Acts. It has been the argument of this study, however,
that the *Acts of Peter* are not fiction in the same sense as the five erotic novels. They
must be read against the background of their fluid manuscript transmission. To ignore
this tradition is to erase the referent of the *Acts of Peter* and to eclipse the deeply historical side of its hybrid nature.

## Conclusion

If narrative fluidity is the normative condition for historical novels, because of the historical consciousness that guides them, the question is not so much "Why fluidity?" but
rather "Why fixity?" Perhaps the degree and type of fluidity described in this study is
actually the norm for this category of texts.

The gospels show great similarity to the *Acts of Peter* in their treatment of the past. The narrative trajectory of the gospels organizes the material about the life of Christ around primary conflicts: the miracles of Christ arouse the suspicion of the religious authorities of his day, and his execution pits him against both the Jewish and Roman governing classes. Similarly, the narratives in the *Acts of Peter* trajectory are organized around the conflict between Peter and the Roman ruling classes. Both the gospels of Jesus and the narratives of the *Acts of Peter* exist in multiforms that vary to reflect the changing evaluation of this conflict by authors and their audiences over time.

Both the Gospels and the Apocryphal Acts were products of a particular period of transition in the cultural development of the Roman empire, as the empire absorbed its subject peoples in the east, along with their highly developed cultural heritages. The Gospels and Apocryphal Acts, for the audiences and authors that read and treasured them, were histories of their particular subculture within the larger empire, histories focusing their pride in their past and hopes for the future. The two troubling features that mar the historiographic aspirations of these texts, their multiformity and their homeostatic organization of historical data, are both explained by their location within these subcultures of the Roman empire. The multiformity of the texts was the very factor that created a world of self-referential texts, a library of previous oral and written versions in which any new performance of the narrative could develop and could find the field of references that made it meaningful. Multiformity created referentiality. The homeostatic nature of the texts allowed them to retain relevance within these same subcultures, who did not have the trappings of a continuous universal history on which to fall back. Instead of continuing a universal historical narrative, the authors within these subcultures simply rewrote the same narrative again and again.

In creating their own referential world within a group of related texts, however, and in using the guise of a straightforward and unadorned narrative prose, along with the many other "novelistic" techniques not foreign to historiography, the Gospels and Apocryphal Acts belong to the world of the historical novels, if this definition also includes "nationalistic novels" such as those of Alexander, Sesonchosis, Moses, Ninos, Esther, and Joseph and Aseneth. All these works display the features of narrative fluidity and homeostatic historiography to some degree, and all of them carry the cultural memory of subcultures within the larger Roman empire. These shared characteristics make them very similar in both form and function to the Gospels and Apocryphal Acts of the Christians, who had themselves developed a quasi-ethnic self-description in the very word Χριστιανοί.

To the extent that these texts all celebrate revered figures directly related to cultural foundation myths, and identified with particular cultic complexes, they are also religious texts. Thus, even if not read in a formal cultic ceremony, the texts of the *Acts of Peter* are religious texts. All religious texts admit elasticity over time. Though ostensibly transmitting timeless truths, religious texts are bound up in time, in the time of their composition, and the time of their interpretation. To communicate meaning in the historical context of interpretation, which necessarily differs radically from the context of the formation of the text, a certain elasticity is necessary, or else the text will cease to be meaningful in changing historical circumstances. Fixed canonical texts achieve this elasticity, this space for new interpretation, in the penumbra of hermeneutical and exegetical traditions surrounding the text. One learns the accepted procedures by which to manipulate the text so that it retains its meaning over time. Texts such as the *Acts of Peter* possessed this elasticity in their very narrative fluidity and in the homeostatic manner in which the narrative itself was constantly updated to accord with changed historical contexts. The timeless truth of the narrative was not in a fixed text but in the figure of Peter itself, in a life of overriding significance meant to serve as a paradigm for human action generally.

# Appendix One

## Overview of the Ancient Editions of the Acts of Peter

### Actus Vercellenses

*Text and story:* An account of Paul's departure from Rome for Spain, Peter's arrival in Rome, his various contests with Simon Magos, and his martyrdom.

*Languages, attestation, and source relations:* Latin translation of a Greek text. The account of the martyrdom is also preserved in Greek in two separate manuscripts. A Greek vellum fragment provides the text of a passage from the contest between Simon and Peter.

*Date:* The vellum fragment dates, on paleographic grounds, to the third or fourth century C.E. (Grenfell and Hunt) and represents a second-century original. The Latin translation dates from 359 (mention of *curiosi*) to 385 C.E. (use by Priscillian).

### The Linus Text

*Text and story:* An account of Peter's martyrdom and the events leading up to it.

*Languages, attestation, and source relations:* Latin. At times, the text follows the Greek martyrdom known from the *Actus Vercellenses* very closely, though as a paraphrase, not a translation. It contains additional episodes not known from these texts. The correct and specific topographic references suggest it was written in Rome.

*Date:* Mid to late fourth century C.E.: the biblical quotations are closer to the *Vetus Latina* than the Vulgate; the meter suggests a mid-fourth-century date. The *Acts of Nereus and Achilles*, a Greek text, mention a Greek martyrdom written by Linus; this does not seem to refer to our Linus text, since the text known there contains the martyrdoms of both Peter and Paul.

### Pseudo-Hegesippos

*Text and story:* This account appears as an episode in a Latin translation of Josephus's *Jewish War*. It narrates the contest between Simon and Peter before Nero, and the martyrdoms of both Peter and Paul.

*Languages, attestation, and source relations*: Latin. The passage has the conciseness of an epitome. Though it knows some of the stories of the *Actus Vercellenses*, it also transmits other stories known only from the Linus text, or which appear later in the Marcellus text.

*Date*: The account was used by Ambrose of Milan; it probably dates to around 370 C.E.

## Acts of Nereus and Achilleus

*Text and story*: A narrative about two later saints that touches on the contest between Peter and Simon. Peter's disciple Marcellus recounts these episodes in a letter to the protagonists.

*Languages, attestation, and source relations*: Greek. No close textual relationship exists with any other versions, though *Nereus and Achilleus* retells some episodes known from them: the dog episode, the resurrection performed by Peter, and the episode of Peter's paralyzed daughter (the latter is only known from a Coptic fragment). A Latin translation exists that depends on one of the recensions of the Greek text.

*Date*: Fifth century C.E. The text mentions a church of Petronilla that has been found and dates to the 390s C.E.; the thirteen Flavian-period martyrs named in the text begin appearing in the calendars in the fifth to sixth centuries C.E. The *Acts*, however, do not give the dates of their festivals, but do give their places of burial, so I consider them prior to the calendars.

## The Marcellus Text

*Text and story*: An account of Paul's arrival in Rome while Peter is working there, their disputations with Simon before the emperor Nero about the reality of Christ's miracles, Simon's untimely death as a result of Peter's prayer, and the subsequent martyrdoms of Peter and Paul.

*Languages, attestation, and source relations*: Greek, with a Latin translation of one of the Greek recensions. There is no close textual relationship with any of the other versions. Although many characters appear who are known from the other versions, the narrative content is substantially different, except for the account of Simon's death and Peter's death on the cross. There are, however, some allusions to episodes known from the other versions.

*Date*: Fifth to sixth centuries C.E., on the basis of internal linguistic and theological information.

# Appendix Two

### Intertextual Relationships between the *Actus Vercellenses* and Other Early Christian Literature

N=narrative overlap; Q=quotation in text

## Coptic fragment

brought sick to Peter to heal them: Acts 5:16-17, Mark 6:55, Matt 4:24
made blind to see, deaf to hear, and lame to walk: Matt 11:5 par.
selling land and not keeping back price: Acts 5:1-11 (Ananias and Sapphira)

## *Actus Vercellenses*

### Chapter 1

Quartus the prison guard: Rom 16:23
N-Quartus gives Paul permission to go through city: Acts 28:30
not seeing Paul again (farewell scene): Acts 20:38
destroying human teachings and traditions: Col 2:8-23
like children without a mother: John 14:18
Paul as God's chosen servant: Acts 9:15-16
N-Paul's trip to Spain: Rom 15:28

### Chapter 2

adulteress taking Eucharist: 1 Cor 11:27-28, Acts 5:1-10
the living God, who scrutinizes the heart: Rom 8:27, Acts 1:24, 15:8
the one who is able to blot out your sin, he is faithful: 1 John 1:9
unquenched fire and outer darkness: Matt 8:12 par., Matt 25:30
forgiving what was done in ignorance: Acts 17:30, 3:17
arm your inner person: Eph 6:11
firstborn of all creatures: Col 1:15

confirmed all things by your word: Ps 33:6

N-I was once a persecutor, now I suffer persecution: Acts 8:3; 9:1, 15-16, Phil 3:6, Gal 1:13

I have received forgiveness: 1 Tim 1:12-14

*Chapter 3*

Lysimachus who belonged to the household of Caesar: Phil 4:22

Narcissus: Rom 16:11

*Chapter 4*

N-Simon the Great Power of God: Acts 8:10

N-Timothy and Barnabbas to Macedonia: Phil 2:19-21, Acts 19:22

*Chapter 5*

mighty works of God: Acts 2:11, Sirach 36:7

grace which has no bounds: Wis 7:13

baptize in name of Father, Son, and Holy Spirit: Matt 28:19 (liturgical)

*Chapter 6*

stand fast in the faith: 1 Cor 16:13, Eph 6:11

infirmity in the flesh: Gal 4:12

tempts the whole world by his angels: Rev 12:9

placing things beneath the feet of the faithful: Rom 16:20

Q-if anyone causes stumbling: Mark 9:42 par., note use of lemma and free completion of logion

Narcissus: Rom 16:11

*Chapter 7*

God sent his son into the world: John 3:16

principles and powers: Col 1:16

N-Peter walked on water: Matt 14:29

N-Peter witnessed signs and wonders: gospels

N-Peter denied Christ three times: Mark 14:30, 66-72 par.

Q-wicked dogs surround: Ps 22:16 "as said the prophet of the Lord"

N-the Lord turned toward me: Luke 22:61, a detail peculiar to Luke

weakness of my flesh: Mark 14:36-37

Satan aims arrows: Eph 6:16

be strong: Eph 6:10

son of perdition: John 17:12, 2 Thess 2:3

the Lord, father of our Lord Jesus Christ: Col 1:3

[God] whom no one has seen: John 1:18
understand whence the temptation comes: 1 Cor 10:13
mighty works of God: Acts 2:11, Sirach 36:7
no one should look for another one [but Jesus]: Acts 4:12
Jesus, this Nazarene, crucified: Acts 4:10

### Chapter 8

N-Simon the power of God: Acts 8:10
building a fire for the day of wrath: Rom 2:5
rapacious wolf: Matt 7:15, Acts 20:29
N-Judas, fellow apostle who betrayed Christ: gospels
N-Herod and Pharaoh: Matt 2:16-18, Luke 23:11, Exod 7:3
N-Caiaphas handed over Jesus to the crowd: Matt 27:2 has him handed over to Pilate
poisoned arrows: Eph 6:16
doors, stealing sheep: John 10:12

### Chapter 9

many more were added: Acts 2:47
N-Simon stunned: Acts 8:13

### Chapter 10

Q-Jesus commands to hate no one: Matt 5:43-44 par. Luke 6:27, said to have been learned from Paul
Simon, the young god: Justin Martyr *Apol.* 1.26
giving property to save soul: Mark 8:36 par.
considering sons nothing compared to faith: Matt 10:37 par.
Q-faith of grain of mustard: Matt 17:20, Marcellus says that Christ said in Peter's presence
N-Peter doubting on the water: Matt 14:28-31
Jesus as shepherd of sheep once lost: Mark 14:27 par.
sheep gathered as one in thee: John 10:11

### Chapter 11

N-demoniac story: Philostratos, *Apollonios of Tyana* 4.20
God, through whom all things are possible: Mark 10:27 par., Luke 1:37

### Chapter 12

dumb animal with a human voice: 2 Pet 2:16, but this is a reference to Balaam's donkey in Numbers 22. It is possible that 2 Peter is here referring to the narratives in the *Acts of Peter* texts
outer darkness: Matt 8:12 par., Matt 25:30

*Chapter 13*

Peter explained the writings and prophets and the things which our Lord Jesus Christ has done both in words and deeds: cf. Acts 1:1, cf. Eusebios, *Ecclesiastical History* 3.39.15

*Chapter 14*

Jesus a carpenter's son: Matt 13:55

*Chapter 16*

N-Jesus abused, mocked, and spat upon: Passion narratives
Jesus present when believers ask for signs and prodigies: Mark 16:15
works of his father (the devil): John 8:44

*Chapter 17*

N-Simon put to flight in Jerusalem: Acts 8:11
mighty works of God: Acts 2:11, Sir 36:7
God the judge of the living and the dead: Acts 10:42
no other hope except Jesus: Acts 4:12
angel of Satan: 2 Cor 12:7

*Chapter 20*

light inapproachable: 1 Tim 6:16
N-transfiguration: Mark 9:2–8 par., some details from Matt (deprived of sight, gave me hand) and 2 Pet 1:16–18 (holy mountain, majesty; although the direction of dependence is again a question in this case)
borne our weaknesses and carried our offenses: Isa 53:4
Q-he bears our sins and suffers for us, but we thought him to be in anguish and enduring blows: Isa 53:4, direct quotation of "the prophet"
he is in the father, and the father is in him: John 10:38, 17:21
he is himself the fullness of all majesty: Col 2:9
N-he defended me [Peter] when I sinned and strengthened me: probably a reference to the aftermath of Matt 26:69–75
he whom flesh has not seen and now is seen: John 1:18
Jesus the door, light, way, bread, water, life, resurrection, refreshment, pearl, treasure, seed, abundance, mustard seed, vine, plough, grace, faith, word: parable traditions
to him be praise, world without end: Rom 16:27, Gal 5:4, Eph 3:21, Phil 4:20, 1 Tim 1:17, etc. (liturgical)

*Chapter 22*

those whom I have approved for your service: 2 Tim 2:3

*Chapter 23*

N-did you not fall at my feet and Paul's in Jerusalem . . . you said, "take payment from me, as much as you will": Acts 8:18–19, Peter says to Simon
Jesus the son of a carpenter: Matt 13:55


*Chapter 24*

Q-his generation, who will declare it: Isa 53:8, "the prophet says of him"
Q-he possessed neither beauty nor grace: Isa 53:2, "another prophet says"
Q-a boy born of the Holy Spirit, whose mother knows not a man: Isa 9:6, Matt 1:18–19, Luke 1:34–35
Q-she has given birth and not given birth: attributed to Ezekiel by Tertullian, *de carne* 22
Q-is it a small thing for you to contend? Isa 7:13
Q-behold, a virgin conceives in her womb: Isa 7:13–14
Q-we have neither heard her voice nor has a midwife entered: cf. *Ascension of Isa* 11.14 "another prophet says"
Q-he was not born from the womb of a woman, but he descended from a heavenly place: "yet another prophet says"
Q-a stone was cut without hands and has struck down all kingdoms: Dan 2:34
Q-a stone which the builders rejected, this was placed at the head of the corner: Ps 118:22, cf. Mark 12:10 par., Acts 4:11, 1 Pet 2:7
Q-a chosen and precious stone: Isa 28:16
Q-behold, I saw one coming on a cloud like the Son of Man: Dan 7:13, cf. Mark 13:26 par., "again, the prophet says of him"
it was necessary for the kingdom of God to come to completion through a mystery: Rom 16:25


*Chapter 25*

N- my son has died, the only one I had: Luke 7:12–15
we ask through you and obtain: Matt 7:7 par., Mark 11:24, John 14:13–14, 16:23
rise and walk to your mother, as long as you are useful to her: Luke 7:14


*Chapter 28*

I am one of you, a flesh-bearing human being and a sinner: Acts 14:15
I do not do this by my own power: Acts 3:12
unquenchable fire: Matt 8:12 par., Matt 25:30
Q-we have not learned to return evil for evil: Matt 5:38–42, Rom 12:7, 1 Thess 5:15, 1 Pet 3:9
Q-we have been taught to love our enemies and pray for our persecutors: Matt 5:44
N-If even this man is able to repent, it would be better: Acts 8:22
let him enter the light of Christ: 1 Pet 2:9
his father the devil: John 8:44

*Chapter 29*

N-placing at his feet whoever was sick: gospel tradition
N-they worshipped him as a god: Acts 14:8–18
a speaking sacrifice to god: Rom 12:1

*Chapter 31*

those who trusted Christ were healed of every bodily disease, and many were added to
the Lord's grace each day: Acts 2:47
God, whose power I am: Acts 8:10
I am going up to my father: John 20:17
they stoned you who were chosen by him: Matt 23:37, John 8:59, Acts 14:19

*Chapter 33*

Peter remained in Rome rejoicing in the Lord and giving thanks day and night for the
crowd who were being led to the holy name of the Lord's grace daily: Acts 2:47, 4:12

*Chapter 34*

Gk, there was a great disturbance in Rome, vs. Latin: when no little stir had been aroused,
Acts 19:19

*Chapter 36*

he will establish you in himself and cause you, whom he planted, to grow in him: 1
Cor 3:6, 10–11
as long as the Lord wishes me to be in the flesh, I will not object, but when he wishes
to take me, I will rejoice and be glad: Phil 1:22–24
soldiers of Christ: 2 Tim 2:3
he will come and reward everyone according to his deeds: Matt 16:27
signs and wonders: Acts 2:11, Sir 36:7
his father's activity: John 8:44

*Chapter 38*

Q-the things on the right as the things on the left: 2 *Clem* 12:2, *Gospel of Thomas* 22,
*Acts of Philip Martyrdom* chap. 34, *Acts of Thomas*, "the Lord said in a mystery"
Q-what is the Christ, but the word, the sound of God: Ignatius, *Magn.* 8.2, "the Spirit
said"

*Chapter 39*

Q-eye has not seen, nor has ear heard, nor has it entered the human heart: 1 Cor 2:9,
*Gospel of Thomas*, "he (Jesus) says to you"

*Chapter 40*

Q-leave the dead to be buried by their own dead: Matt 8:22, Luke 9:60, "have you not heard the saying of the Lord"

*Chapter 41*

Nero upset because Peter had made disciples of some of his close friends: Phil 4:22, *Martyrdom of Paul* 1

# Appendix Three

## Comparison of the *Actus Vercellenses*, the Greek Martyrdom Account, and the Linus Text

Greek Martyrdom, chap. 7; Linus, chap. 10; *Actus Vercellenses*, chap. 36

Text: Greek Martyrdom: Lipsius, 90.15–17; *Linus*: 12.3–5; *Actus Vercellenses*: 91.2–3.

| AcPetMart 7 (parallel to *Actus Vercellenses*) | Linus 10 | AcVer 36 |
|---|---|---|
| καὶ νῦν πρὸς τὸν Ἀγρίππαν μὴ πικραίνεσθε· διάκονος γάρ ἐστιν τῆς πατρικῆς αὐτοῦ ἐνεργείας. | nolite aduersus Agrippam saeuire et amaro animo in eum esse. ille enim minister est alienae operationis. | et nunc nolite furere in Agrippa praefecto. minister est paternae aenergiae et traditionis illius. |

Greek Martyrdom, chap. 4; Linus, chap. 2; *Actus Vercellenses*, chap. 33

Text: Greek Martyrdom: Lipsius, 84.14–23; *Linus*: 2.14–3.7; *Actus Vercellenses*: 85.12–20.

| AcPetMart 4 | Linus 2 | AcVer 33 |
|---|---|---|
| συνήγοντο δὲ καὶ αἱ παλλακίδες τοῦ πραιφέκτου Ἀγρίππα πρὸς τὸν Πέτρον, τέσσαρες οὖσαι, Ἀγριππῖνα καὶ Νικαρία καὶ Εὐφημία καὶ Δῶρις. | ubi coeperunt frequentare ad[1] illum quatuor concubinae praefecti Agrippae,<br><br>quarum erant uocabula Agrippina Eucharia Eufemia et Dionis. | conueniebant autem ad eum et concubinae praefecti |

ἀκούουσαι τὸν τῆς
ἀγνείας λόγον καὶ
πάντα τὰ τοῦ κυρίου
λόγια,
ἐπλήγησαν τὰς ψυχάς,

καὶ συνθέμεναι
ἀλλήλαις ἁγναὶ τῆς
Ἀγρίππα κοίτης
διαμεῖναι ἠνοχλοῦντο
ὑπ' αὐτοῦ.

ἀπορούντος οὖν τοῦ
Ἀγρίππα καὶ
λυπουμένου περὶ
αὐτῶν–καὶ μάλιστα
τούτων ἦρα–
ἐπετηρεῖτο οὖν καὶ
ὑποπέμψας ὅπου
ἀπήρχοντο, μανθάνει
ὅτι πρὸς τὸν Πέτρον.
ἔλεγεν οὖν αὐταῖς
ἐλθούσαις·

Μὴ κοινωνεῖν ἐμοὶ ὁ
Χριστιανὸς ἐκεῖνος
ἐδίδαξεν ὑμᾶς.

quae audientes ab eo
castitatis sermonem et
omnia domini nostri Iesu
Christi mandata,
tabescebant et molestabantur
{esse}[2] sub thoro Agrippae.
unde castitati se deuouentes
pactum consilii alterutrum
inierunt et confortatae a
domino Iesu Christo nullo
modo ei obsequio
concubitus adquiescere
ulterius decreuerunt.
subtrahentibus autem se
isdem[3] non solum a
complexu uerum et ab
omnimoda coniunctione
Agrippae,
coepit idem super hoc ualde
taedere et maestus esse;

mittensque sollicitos ac
sollertes exploratores
didicit eas studiosissime
ad beatum Petrum
prorumpere.[5] quibus ad se
reductis dixit
vehementissima amoris
captus insania: Scio unde
uenitis.
ille Christianus uos docuit
mecum non coire et a
debito thoro subtrahere.

audientes castitatem debere
obseruari

et conlocutae inter se
abstinebant se a concubitu
Agripae praefecti,

et cum illis molestus esset,
excusationibus adueniendo[4]
aporiabant eum. cumque
ille bilem pateretur
praeterea diligens eas,
exposuit eis curios‹os› ut
sciret ubi prodirent. et
scierunt quoniam ad
Petrum conueniunt. dixit
eis Agrippa:

Petrus uos prohibuit n‹on›
communicare mecum; ille
vos ha‹ec› do‹cuit›.

# Notes

## Chapter One

1. A collection of translations is available in B. P. Reardon, *Collected Ancient Greek Novels* (Berkeley: University of California Press, 1989). Tomas Hägg provides an introduction (*The Novel in Antiquity* [Berkeley: University of California Press, 1983]). Texts for the five *scriptores erotici* (see below) are readily available. A fine edition of the fragments is now available (Susan A. Stephens and John J. Winkler, *Ancient Greek Novels: The Fragments: Introduction, Text, Translation, and Commentary* [Princeton: Princeton University Press, 1996]).

2. I consciously adopt the term "novel" over "romance." Both are inadequate in that they erroneously suggest relationships to later bodies of literature: on the one hand, to the chivalric romances of the medieval period and, on the other, to the modern novel as it began its rise in the nineteenth century. I find the latter association to be the less problematic because I observe structural analogies to the rise of the Hellenistic novel. In both cases, a body of imaginative literature, the earliest representatives of which were historical or epistolary in form, developed during a period of increasing literacy and book-production, reflected individualistic longings and concerns rather than civic, and devoted greater space to the private sphere, and, consequently, to the lives of women. I do employ the term "Alexander romance" consciously because the tales of Alexander did indeed become romances in the generic sense in the middle ages.

3. On the relationship of the novel to other genres, see M. M. Bakhtin, "Epic and Novel," in Michael Holquist, ed., *The Dialogic Imagination*, trans. Holquist and Caryl Emerson (Austin: University of Texas Press, 1981) 3–40.

4. A good example of this is the description of Miletos which follows the preface in Longos' *Daphnis and Chloe*. On the influence of rhetorical education on the ancient novel, see B. P. Reardon, "The Second Sophistic and the Novel," in G. W. Bowersock, ed., *Approaches to the Second Sophistic* (University Park, Pa.: APA, 1974) 23–29, esp. 25–26. Shadi Bartsch argues that the authors of the erotic novels played on audience expectations engendered by rhetorical training (*Decoding the Ancient Novel: The Reader and the Role of Description in Heliodorus and Achilles Tatius* [Princeton: Princeton University Press, 1989]).

5. F. Jacoby discusses Hekataios and his context (s.v. in *Pauly's Real-Encyclopädie der classischen Altertumswissenschaft* 7 [1912], 2666–769).

6. B. P. Reardon's work limits the scope of discussion to the five erotic novels (Chariton, Achilles Tatius, Xenophon of Ephesos, Longos, and Chariton) and related fragments; his stated reasons are that the corpus of these works is well defined and that the plot and the effect on the

reader are predictable and recognizable (*The Form of Greek Romance* [Princeton: Princeton University Press, 1991] 6-7). One wonders whether these features are a mere accident of the survival of more works from this corpus than any other. Reardon does catalog other works that cannot be easily separated from the five erotic novels: fanciful historiography, romantic biography, utopian travel accounts, the Apocryphal Acts, and comic novels. E. L. Bowie's discussion is more inclusive; though admitting bewilderment at which features should be used to define the genre, he sees that related works bear on this question and notes the importance of *Joseph and Aseneth, The Wonders Beyond Thule*, and the three *Metamorphoses* works (the epitome attributed to Lucius of Patrae, *The Ass*, and Apuleius; E. L. Bowie, "The Greek Novel," in P. E. Easterling and B. M. W. Knox, eds., *The Hellenistic Period and the Empire*, Cambridge History of Classical Literature 1.4 [Cambridge: Cambridge University Press, 1985] 123-39, esp. 124-27).

7. The marginal cases are problematic: is Xenophon's *Cyropaedia* a novel? Or is the Alexander romance, which, in one of Hägg's analyses, is not a historical novel, but rather, "romanticized biography" ("The Beginnings of the Historical Novel," in Roderick Beaton, ed., *The Greek Novel A. D. 1-1985* [London: Croom Helm, 1988] 169-81, esp. 173-74). Moses Hadas prints the long excursus in Dio Chrysostom's seventh oration as a "novel," "The Hunters of Euboea" (*Three Greek Romances* [Indianapolis: Bobbs-Merrill, 1953] 129-42); Bowie concurs that it is at least related ("Greek Novel," 127). Richard I. Pervo defines the novel and provides a list of works that could be considered such (*Profit with Delight: The Literary Genre of the Acts of the Apostles* [Philadelphia: Fortress, 1987] 102-14).

8. See the important discussion of the contrast between our modern concept, "novel," and ancient literary classifications in Karl Kerényi, *Die griechisch-orientalische Romanliteratur in religionsgeschichtlicher Beleuchtung: Ein Versuch* (Tübingen: J. C. B. Mohr [Paul Siebeck], 1927) 1-23.

9. Among the three chief classifications of τὰ ἱστορούμενα, ancient novels would be πλάσμα rather than ἱστορία or μῦθος. Sextus Empiricus gives the Greek terminology (*adversus mathematicos* 1.263-69); the Latin is *argumentum, historia, fabula* (cf. *auctor ad Herennium* 1.12-13, Cicero, *de inventione* 1.27). See Reitzenstein's analysis of ancient theory in *Hellenistische Wundererzählungen* (Leipzig: Teubner, 1906) 84-99, 152-69. Glen Bowersock is concise and analytical on this point (*Fiction as History: Nero to Julian*, Sather Classical Lectures 58 [Berkeley: University of California Press, 1994] 10-19).

10. The emperor Julian advises against reading novels: ὅσα δέ ἐστιν ἐν ἱστορίας εἴδει παρὰ τοῖς ἔμπροσθεν ἀπηγγελμένα πλάσματα παραιτητέον, ἐρωτικὰς ὑποθέσεις καὶ πάντα ἁπλῶς τὰ τοιαῦτα (Epistle 89B 301b, see Bowie, "The Greek Novel," 123 n. 1). Philostratos the sophist, the same man who wrote the rather novelistic *Apollonios of Tyana*, also addressed a letter to one Chariton, asking why anyone would remember his λόγοι and calling him a nobody (Epistle 66, see Ben Edwin Perry, *The Ancient Romances: A Literary-Historical Account of Their Origins*, Sather Classical Lectures 37 [Berkeley: University of California Press, 1967] 98-99); this comment may refer to the novelist. In addition to *Kallirhoe*, Chariton perhaps also wrote *Metiochos* and *Chione*, two fragmentary novels that show affinities to *Kallirhoe* in language and style. See Albrecht Dihle, "Zur Datierung des Metiochos-Romans," *Würzburger Jahrbücher für die Altertumswissenschaft* n.s. 4 (1978) 47-55, H. Maehler, "Der Metiochos-Parthenope-Roman," *Zeitschrift für Papyrologie und Epigraphik* 23 (1976) 1-20. M. Gronewald edits the most recent fragment of Chione and discusses stylistic affinities to Chariton ("Ein neues Fragment zu einem Roman," *Zeitschrift für Papyrologie und Epigraphik* 35 [1979] 15-20).

11. The date of Dares is uncertain. The work exists in a fifth-century Latin translation, although the early-third-century writer Aelian knows of it. Most scholars believe there was a Greek original. For an insightful overview of both texts, see Stefan Merkle, "The Truth and Nothing but the Truth: Dictys and Dares," in Gareth Schmeling, ed., *The Novel in the Ancient World* (Leiden: E.J. Brill, 1996) 563-80.

12. It is an open question whether fiction existed in the ancient world in the sense that we understand it. There seems to have been some awareness that epic texts and mythological traditions narrated a world that was qualitatively different from the everyday world of the readers. Novelistic works with a dramatic setting in the historical world, however, may still have been believed to be substantially true by some parts of their audience. Hägg writes of Chariton's novel that "no doubt some believed the whole story to be authentic" ("Beginnings," 176). Granted, it is not of much consequence whether one believes that Chareas and Kallirhoe really existed or not; their actions do not have specific external referents, or, put differently, it is impossible to get their story wrong, since there is nothing about which it can be wrong; see David Konstan, "The Invention of Fiction," in Ronald F. Hock, J. Bradley Chance, et al., eds., *Ancient Fiction and Early Christian Literature* (Atlanta: Scholars Press, 1998) 3–17. Whether ancient readers "believed" a text or not is thus not a reliable criterion for distinguishing novels from other works. On the development of fiction, see Reardon, *Form*, 46–76. See also an entire volume devoted to fiction and mendacity in ancient histories and novels: Christopher Gill and T. P. Wiseman, eds., *Lies and Fiction in the Ancient World* (Austin, Tex.: University of Texas Press, 1993).

13. Rosa Söder, *Die apokryphen Apostelgeschichten und die romanhafte Literatur der Antike* (Stuttgart: Kohlhammer, 1932). Secondary motifs include sale into slavery, persecution, crowds, divine protection, oracles, and dreams.

14. *Apostelgeschichten*, 216. The novels and the Acts are aimed at different audiences: the Acts are "nicht so sehr für Gebildete, wie der Roman, bestimmt."

15. Erwin Rohde, *Der griechische Roman und seine Vorläufer* (1st ed. published 1876; 2d ed.; Leipzig: Breitkopf und Hartel, 1900).

16. Ernst von Dobschütz, "Der Roman in der altchristlichen Literatur," *Deutsche Rundschau* 111 (1902) 87–106.

17. Reitzenstein, *Wundererzählungen*.

18. J. Flamion, "Les actes apocryphes de Pierre," *Revue d'histoire ecclésiastique* 9 (1908) 465–90; 10 (1909) 5–29.

19. Eckhard Plümacher, "Apokryphe Apostelakten," *Supplement* to *Pauly's Real-Encyclopädie der classischen Altertumswissenschaft* 15 (1978) 11–70, esp. 63; the Apocryphal Acts are "kaum anders denn als christliche Varianten eben dieser Gattung [hellenistischen Liebesroman] zu begreifen. . . . sie setzen vielmehr . . . den voll ausgebildeten Roman als literarisches Vorbild für die Agg. voraus."

20. See, above all, Karl Kerényi, *Gnomon* 10 (1934) 301–9; Kerényi vociferously objects to the characterization of the Apocryphal Acts as novels. See also the extended evaluations of Söder's work in Virginia Burrus, *Chastity as Autonomy: Women in the Stories of the Apocryphal Acts* (Lewiston, N.Y.: E. Mellen, 1987) 15–22; Jean-Daniel Kaestli, "Les principales orientations de la recherche sur les Actes apocryphes des apôtres," in François Bovon et al., ed., *Les Actes apocryphes des apôtres: Christianisme et monde païen* (Publications de la Faculté de Théologie de l'Université de Genève 4; Geneva: Labor et Fides, 1981) 49–67, esp. 61–67; Plümacher, Eckhard. "Apokryphe Apostelakten," 56–65; and Philip Vielhauer, *Geschichte der urchristlichen Literatur* (Berlin: de Gruyter, 1975) 715, 717.

21. This aspect of Söder's work has been neglected or even misrepresented. Kaestli calls for renewed attention to the novel because, in his estimation, new papyrus finds, such as the *Ninos* romance, have altered the chronology of the novel since Söder wrote ("Orientations," 66). Although the full ramification of these finds had not yet been worked out, Söder is more up-to-date than Kaestli grants. She dates the *Ninos* fragments correctly (*Apostelgeschichten*, 41) and recognizes their importance for the development of novelistic literature (187). Söder's work is a distinct improvement over Flamion's treatment of this issue, in which he confines his analysis to the erotic novel ("Actes de Pierre" [1908, 1909]).

22. Vielhauer follows Söder on this point, assigning the Acts to the broader class of novelistic literature (*Geschichte*, 715-16).

23. Söder, *Apostelgeschichten*, 186-87.

24. "Second and Third Century Acts of Apostles: Introduction," in Schneemelcher, ed., *Apocrypha* (1965) 2.167-88, esp. 176. In the 1989 edition, Schneemelcher restates his position, but accepts more recent scholarship pointing to the influence of the novel. He believes that the Apocryphal Acts are not so much novels as the beginning of the *Rezeptionsgeschichte* of the novel and that elements of the *Praxeis* and *Periodoi* literature are also important, as is the question of the use of earlier traditions ("Second and Third Century Acts of the Apostles: Introduction," in idem, ed., *New Testament Apocrypha* [5th German ed., 1989, ed. R. McL. Wilson; Louisville, Ky.: John Knox, 1992] 2.75-86, esp. 78-83).

25. "La vie des apôtres: Traditions bibliques et narrations apocryphe," in idem, ed., *Actes apocryphes* (1981) 141-58, esp. 150-51.

26. "Early Christian Fiction," in J. R. Morgan and Richard Stoneman, eds., *Greek Fiction: The Greek Novel in Context* (London: Routledge, 1994) 239-54, esp. 239-41.

27. "The Ancient Novel Becomes Christian," in Gareth Schmeling, ed., *The Novel in the Ancient World* (Leiden: E. J. Brill, 1996) 685-711, esp. 689.

28. Léon Vouaux, *Les Actes de Pierre* (Paris: Letouzey et Ané, 1922) 62-63; Carl Schmidt, *Die alten Petrusakten im Zusammenhang der apokryphen Apostelliteratur nebst einem neuentdeckten Fragment* (TU n. s. 9.1; Leipzig: J. Hinrichs, 1903) 153-56.

29. Plümacher, "Apokryphe Apostelakten," 63; Vielhauer, *Geschichte*, 715-16; Reardon, *Form*, 165: "what Christian ideology could make of the romance form." Reardon oddly views Christian literature as impermeably isolated from the influence of Greek literature at large: "No 'model' was needed, certainly, for adherents of the Christian religion to use this method of capturing their tradition. The biographical gospels, one supposes, would have been composed whatever course Greek literature might have taken" (165). The hypothesis that any work of literature can be formed in total disregard of the generic and linguistic conventions of its society is difficult to sustain on a theoretical level.

30. Judith Perkins, "The Apocryphal *Acts of Peter*: A *Roman à Thèse*," *Arethusa* 25 (1992) 445-57; Tibor Szepessy, "Les actes d'apôtres apocryphes et le roman antique," *Acta Antiqua (Budapest)* 36 (1995) 133-61.

31. *Profit*, 121-35. Pervo also considers the Apocryphal Acts to be part of the history of reception of the novel ("Ancient Novel," 694). Robert Stoops, though not concerned primarily with this question, would also class the *Acts of Peter* as related to the ancient novel ("Miracle Stories and Vision Reports in the *Acts of Peter*," Ph.D. diss., Harvard, 1983; 286-87).

32. Hägg, *Novel*, 160-61; F. Morard, "Souffrance et Martyre dans les Actes apocryphes des apôtres," in Bovon, ed., *Actes apocryphes* (1981) 95-108, see esp. 107-8; Kaestli, "Orientations," 65-67; Helmut Koester, *Introduction to the New Testament*, 2 vols. (Philadelphia: Fortress, 1982) 2.324.

33. *The Ancient Novel: An Introduction* (London: Routledge: 1995) 22-26.

34. Alone among these scholars, Klaus Berger uses narrative structure to differentiate between Luke's Acts and the Apocryphal Acts. It is chiefly the fact that the Apocryphal Acts treat the deeds of one man, unlike Luke's Acts, that motivates him to classify them as πράξεις rather than history ("Hellenistische Gattungen im Neuen Testament," *Aufstieg und Niedergang der römischen Welt* 2.25/2 [1984] 1031-432, 1831-885 [index], esp. 1279). One wonders whether such a division is tenable; from the Hellenistic period onward, the deeds of leading individuals became an established subgenre within Greek historiography. See Charles William Fornara, *The Nature of History in Ancient Greece and Rome* (Berkeley: University of California Press, 1983) 34-36.

35. The stichometry of Nikephoros numbers the Acts of Peter at 2750 stichoi, the Gospel of Luke at 2600, and Luke's Acts of the Apostles at 2800. The Acts of Paul are considerably longer, at 3560 stichoi. On this, see Vouaux, Actes de Pierre, 35–36.

36. The major study is H. Ljungvik, Studien zur Sprache der apokryphen Apostelgeschichten (Uppsala Universitet Aarsskrift 8; Uppsala: 1926). See also now David H. Warren, "The Greek Language of the Apocryphal Acts of the Apostles," in François Bovon, Ann Graham Brock, et al., eds., The Apocryphal Acts of the Apostles: Harvard Divinity School Studies (Cambridge, Mass.: Harvard University, 1999) 101–24; and Evie Zachariades-Holmberg, "Philological Aspects of the Apocryphal Acts of the Apostles," in Bovon, Apocryphal Acts, 125–42.

37. The only other generic option entertained recently has been biography; see Charles H. Talbert, "Luke-Acts," in Eldon Jay Epp and Goerge W. MacRae, ed., The New Testament and Its Modern Interpreters (Philadelphia: Fortress, 1989) 297–320, esp. 310. Pervo offers an overview (Profit, 1–11).

38. Pervo, Profit, 12–85.

39. Schneemelcher, in the third edition of his handbook, even argues that the Apocryphal Acts were not theological in intention, though having a definite theological position ("Introduction [1965]," 169–74). In the fifth edition, he abandons this claim.

40. David Aune, The New Testament in Its Literary Environment (Philadelphia: Westminster, 1987) 149, 152. To his credit, Aune notes that both Luke's Acts and the Apocryphal Acts contain entertaining features; in his treatment, it is not the presence of these features, or the relative accuracy or inaccuracy of the account, but the conscious intention to entertain that sets off the Apocryphal Acts from Luke's Acts. He bases much of his argument on the presence of a prologue in Luke (79–80).

41. Books and Readers in the Early Church: A History of Early Christian Texts (New Haven: Yale University Press, 1995) 37–38.

42. "Créations romanesques et traditions ecclésiastiques dans les Actes apocryphes des Apôtres: l'alternative fiction romanesque–vérité historique: une impasse," Augustinianum (Rome) 23 (1983) 271–85, see esp. 277: "Ainsi, sauf exceptions, nous considérons que les épisodes des Actes apocryphes, c'est-à-dire les scénarios aussi bien que les données biographiques, sont des libres créations et non des reprises littéraires de traditions isolées."

43. Ancient Romances, 31.

44. For this reason, Vouaux objects to the designation "novel." He writes aptly, "et quand on désigne par le nom de 'romans' les apocryphes, c'est beaucoup plus pour en opposer le fond même, dépourvu à peu près de toute valeur historique, à celui du livre canonique, que pour marquer le contraste entre les formes que revêtent les deux œuvres" (Actes de Pierre, 62).

45. The Phoinikika by Lollianos is clearly picaresque (edited by Albert Henrichs, Die Phoinikika des Lollianos: Fragmente eines neuen griechischen Romans [Papyrologische Texte und Abhandlungen 14; Bonn: R. Habelt, 1972]), as may be Daulis, Iolaus, and Tinouphis. See the cogent remarks in Stephens and Winkler, Fragments, 4–8, and also Niklas Holzberg, "The Genre: Novels Proper and the Fringe," in Gareth Schmeling, ed., The Novel in the Ancient World (Leiden: E. J. Brill, 1996) 11–28.

46. The most convincing account is Perry, The Ancient Romances: a nearly inexhaustible source of insight.

47. Although Ninos has many correct Attic forms, the style has Hellenistic features. See θάρσος rather than the Attic θάρρος (col. A1, l. 11); διαίτησις for διαίτημα (col. B1, l. 30); ἤμην for ἦ(ν) in the first person singular imperfect (frag. A3, l. 38, but see the Attic form in col. A2, l. 26); the sigmatic future γαμήσεται instead of the liquid γαμεῖται (frag. A3, l. 10); and ἁρμόζομαι used with an accusative object rather than a dative (frag. A3, l. 14). The Greek text of Ninos is found in Stephens and Winkler, Fragments, 23–71.

48. Strictly speaking, only Achilles Tatius, Longos, and Xenophon of Ephesos are Sophistic. Heliodorus is generally dated much later, to the fourth century C.E., because of the similarities between the description of the siege of Syene described in book nine and the actual siege of Nisibis in 350 C.E. See J. R. Morgan, "History, Romance, and Realism in the Aithiopika of Heliodoros," *Classical Antiquity* 1 (1982) 221–65, esp. 253.

49. Ben Edwin Perry contrasts the pre-Sophistic (or non-Sophistic) with Sophistic novels (*Ancient Romances*, 108–15). On the historical background of the Second Sophistic, see Glen Bowersock, *Greek Sophists in the Roman Empire* (Oxford: Clarendon, 1969). More recently, see Graham Anderson, *The Second Sophistic: A Cultural Phenomenon in the Roman Empire* (London: Routledge, 1993) esp. 156–70 on the novels and related literature.

50. Xenophon, though not providing a dramatic setting as precise as that of Chariton, has almost no references to Roman officials or institutions, with lapses: the *eirenarch* of Kilikia (2.13.3 and elsewhere), an office only attested after 116–17 C.E. (David Magie, *Roman Rule in Asia Minor to the End of the Third Century*, 2 vols. [Princeton: Princeton University Press, 1950] 1.647, 2.1514–15); and the *praefectus Aegypti* (3.12.6 and elsewhere), which is post-Augustan. See E. L. Bowie, "The Novels and the Real World," in B. P. Reardon, ed., *Erotica Antiqua* (Bangor, Wales: [s.n.], 1977) 91–96.

51. Chariton's use of the first person, in contrast, is an authorial voice and recounts a story set clearly in the past.

52. *Contra* Perry, who believes it to be the sole erotic novel set in the present (*Ancient Romances*, 111–13).

53. Hermokrates enters the account at numerous points, first at 4.58, and at length in 6.72–80, in which he delivers two speeches.

54. Some 1400 years separate Ninos, a figure of the third millennium, from Semiramis, a ninth-century queen.

55. See the *Hellenika* and *Sikelika* as subgenres of history in Fornara, *History* 32–38.

56. This feature noted by Perry, *Ancient Romances*, 78, and Bowie, "Greek Novel," 125.

57. In addition to Xenophon of Ephesos, the Suda mentions that Xenophon of Antioch wrote the *Babyloniaka*, and Xenophon of Cyprus, the *Cypriaka* (noted in Reardon, *Form*, 166–73, and Perry, *Ancient Romances*, 35 n. 18).

58. See Lawrence M. Wills, "The Jewish Novellas," in Morgan and Stoneman, *Greek Fiction*, 223–38, and *The Jewish Novel in the Ancient World* (Ithaca: Cornell, 1995).

59. Bowie, as well, is inclined to see in *Joseph and Aseneth* an example of a popular version of the erotic novel that preceded the surviving, more literary versions ("Greek Novel," 125).

60. So Perry, *Ancient Romances*, 99–101.

61. *Ancient Romances*, 66–72.

62. On the significance of this papyrus find for the history of ancient literature, see the introduction to Albert Henrichs' edition (*Phoinikika*, 6–7, 11–12, 24–27).

63. Perry makes a distinction between the form and the purpose of the ancient novel; the form is history, but the characters treated are chiefly obscure, thus the purpose is not historical (*Ancient Romances*, 32–43); see Chapter Five below.

64. Bernard P. Grenfell and Arthur S. Hunt, eds., *The Oxyrhynchus Papyri* (London: Egypt Exploration Fund, 1908) 6.6–12.

65. Schmidt, *Petrusakten*; James Brashler and Douglas M. Parrott, "The Act of Peter," in Douglas M. Parrott, ed., *Nag Hammadi Codices V, 2–5 and VI with Papyrus Berolinensis 8502, 1 and 4* (Nag Hammadi Studies 11; Coptic Gnostic Library; Leiden: Brill, 1979) 473–93. For a detailed study of this manuscript, see Andrea Molinari, "Augustine, *Contra Adimantum, Pseudo-Titus*, BG 8502.4 and the *Acts of Peter*: Attacking Carl Schmidt's Theory of an Original Unity Between the *Act of Peter* and the *Acts of Peter*," in *Society of Biblical Literature Seminar Papers* (Atlanta: Scholars Press, 1999) 426–27; and idem, *"I Never Knew the Man": The Coptic Act of*

Peter (*Papyrus Berolinensis 8502.4*): *Its Independence from the Apocryphal* Acts of Peter, *Genre and Legendary Origins* (Quebec: University of Laval, 2000).

66. Printed as "Actus Petri cum Simone" in Richard Adalbert Lipsius, ed., *Acta Apostolorum Apocrypha* (Leipzig: Hermann Mendelssohn, 1891) 1.45–103.

67. Internal references show that the *Acts of Peter* began with a confrontation between Peter and Simon Magos in Jerusalem, but the *Actus Vercellenses* begin only with their continued confrontation in Rome. See Chapter Two.

68. See Chapter Two.

69. One can verify the Latin translation by checking it against the Greek of the martyrdom account (extant in two MSS) and *P. Oxy.* 849. The *Vita Abercii* also copies some of the speeches of the *Acts of Peter* verbatim in Greek.

70. D. De Bruyne, "Nouveaux fragments des Actes de Pierre, de Paul, de Jean, d'André et de l'Apocalypse d'Élie," *Revue Bénédictine* 25 (1908) 149–60, see esp. 151–53. Both the episode of Peter's daughter and that of the gardener's daughter are mentioned together in Augustine, *contra Adimantum* 17 (see Chapter Two for quotation and translation).

71. Also in Lipsius, *Acta*, under "Actus Petri cum Simone." A third Greek manuscript has been found in Ochrid (in the former Yugoslavia), *Bibl. mun.* 4, but remains unedited. See Maurice Geerard, *Clavis apocryphorum Novi Testamenti* (Corpus Christianorum; Turnhout: Brepols, 1992) no. 190.4.

72. Printed by Lipsius under the title, "Martyrium beati Petri apostoli a Lino episcopo conscriptum" (*Acta*, 1.1–22). See also the text of A. H. Salonius, "Martyrium beati Petri Apostoli a Lino episcopo conscriptum," in *Commentationes Humanarum Litterarum* (Helsinki: Societas Scientiarum Fennica; Leipzig: Harrasowitz, 1922–27) 1.22–58. For a collection of the ancient testimonies concerning Linus, see J. Hofmann, "Linus—erster Bischof von Rom und Heiliger der orthodoxen Kirche," *Ostkirchliche Studien* 46 (1997) 105–41.

73. Vouaux gives an overview of the question (*Actes de Pierre*, 134–37), and opts for the end of the fourth century to the beginning of the fifth, because, like Flamion, he views Pseudo-Linus as dependent on Pseudo-Hegesippos. Gérard Poupon argues successfully in an unpublished thesis that Pseudo-Linus neither depends on Pseudo-Hegesippos, nor does it use the Vulgate, as claimed first by Lipsius. Poupon holds that Pseudo-Linus was written before the decree of Gelasius around 382–84 C.E., which labeled as heretical the separation of the martyrdoms of Peter and Paul; this too confidently assumes that the decree would immediately have stifled all such writing. His other arguments could place the text anywhere in the late fourth century: the praise of asceticism, the treatment of Rome, which assumes that the events of 410 have not yet taken place, a change in meter from one based on quantity to one based on rhythm (Gérard Poupon, "La Passion de S. Pierre Apôtre," Magister diss., Université de Genève, 1975). I thank François Bovon for bringing this work to my attention.

74. Vincent Ussani, *Hegesippi qui dicitur historiae libri V* (CSEL 66; Vienna/ Leipzig: Hoelder-Pichler-Tempsky/ Akademische Verlagsgesellschaft, 1932) 1.183–87.

75. Hans Achelis, *Acta SS. Nerei et Achillei: Text und Untersuchung* (TU 11.2; Leipzig: J. C. Hinrichs, 1893).

76. Printed as μαρτύριον τῶν ἁγίων ἀποστόλων Πέτρου καὶ Παύλου in Lipsius, *Acta*, 1.118–77. He also prints an alternate Greek text as πράξεις τῶν ἁγίων ἀποστόλων Πέτρου καὶ Παύλου, 1.178–222.

77. Jean-Daniel Kaestli and Éric Junod have used these later redactions, or "avatars," to a limited extent in their treatment of the *Acts of John* (*L'histoire des Actes apocryphes des apôtres du IIIe au IXe siècle: le cas des Actes de Jean* [Cahiers de la Revue de théologie et de philosophie 7; Geneva/ Lausanne/ Neuchâtel: La Concorde, 1982] see esp. 6–7, 104–7). They view the process of redaction as an attempt to salvage the basic story and the entertaining and edifying quality of the narrative, while omitting all that would be doctrinally suspect, especially in the prayers,

speeches, and hymns, which tend to be cut or changed. Although I agree that this is a motivation, the explanation is too narrow to account for the basically fluid nature of the narrative, a quality that the Apocryphal Acts share with many other works (see Chapter Four below).

78. See Plümacher, "Apokryphe Apostelakten," and Kaestli, "Orientations."

79. Peter Nagel has argued that the Manichaean Herakleides knew a five-book corpus when he composed his *Laudationes* of holy women (preserved in the Manichaean Coptic Psalter, 192.25–193.3). The Coptic Psalter dates to the midfourth century, but Herakleides was a student of Mani himself, who died in 277 C.E. If the attribution is correct, the corpus of five acts is even earlier than its attestation elsewhere in the Coptic Psalter would suggest (142.17–143.15). See Peter Nagel, "Die apokryphen Apostelakten des 2. und 3. Jahrhunderts in der manichäischen Literatur: Ein Beitrag zur Frage nach den christlichen Elementen im Manichäismus," in Karl-Wolfgang Tröger, ed., *Gnosis und Neues Testament: Studien aus Religionswissenschaft und Theologie* (Gütersloh: Mohn; Berlin: Evangelischer Verlagsanstalt, 1973) 149–82, see esp. 152–53, 175–76. See also Knut Schäferdiek, "Die Leukios Charinos zugeschriebene manichäische Sammlung apokrypher Apostelgeschichten," in Wilhelm Schneemelcher, ed., *Neutestamentliche Apokryphen in deutscher Übersetzung* (5th ed.; Tübingen: J. C. B. Mohr, 1989) 2.81–93, see esp. 83–86.

80. *Christianizing Homer: The Odyssey, Plato, and the Acts of Andrew* (Oxford: Oxford University Press, 1994). MacDonald is acutely aware of the differences in the literary levels of the Apocryphal Acts. He began his work with the *Acts of Andrew* expecting to find evidence of oral folklore, as he had for the *Acts of Paul*, but discovered that he needed a more literary model for understanding the work (vii).

81. Warren, "Greek Language," 108–11, 117–18, 119, 121. Warren finds a striking contrast between the polished style of the *Acts of Andrew* and the monotonous prose of the *Acts of Andrew and Matthias*. This seriously undercuts MacDonald's arguments, against Jean-Marc Prieur and others, that the *Acts of Andrew and Matthias* and the *Acts of Andrew* were written by the same author (*The Acts of Andrew and the Acts of Andrew and Matthias in the City of the Cannibals* [Atlanta: Scholars Press, 1991] 6–47; Jean-Marc Prieur, *Acta Andreae* [Corpus Christianorum, Series Apocryphorum 5–6; 2 vols.; Turnhout: Brepols, 1989] 1.32–35). See also Zachariades-Holmberg, "Philological Aspects," 130–34.

82. Noted by Warren ("Greek Language," 111–15) as an important index of literary style.

83. MacDonald, *Christianizing Homer, passim*, esp. 307.

84. See Warren, "Greek Language," 111, 113–14, 122, 123–24, who notes that the *Acts of Peter* often sound "pretentious and even artificial" because the author shows "an ignorance of the classical standards in details of syntax." Similarly, see Zachariades-Holmberg, "Philological Aspects," 135–36.

85. With the concept of the implied author, structuralist theory also evades the intentionalist fallacy, that is, the position that author intent determines the meaning of a text. Since human intention can only be understood through communication to others, the only signs of author intent are in the text itself.

86. In my basically structuralist understanding of genre, I am close to the approach of Richard A. Burridge, *What are the Gospels? A Comparison with Graeco-Roman Biography* (Society for New Testament Study Manuscript Series 70; Cambridge: Cambridge University Press, 1992) 26–54. I have been most influenced by Tsvetan Todorov, Wolfgang Iser, Stanley Fish, and Michel Foucault.

87. MacDonald, *Christianizing Homer*, 290–91.

88. Dennis MacDonald, "Is There A Privileged Reader? A Case from the Apocryphal Acts," 71 (1995) 29–43, esp. 41–42.

89. Reinhold Merkelbach has put forth a related claim for the novel: while the novels clearly have a surface sense, they also contain a deeper meaning, a *Mysteriensinn*, which can only be construed by those readers who are familiar with the initiation rites of the various ancient mys-

tery religions (*Roman und Mysterium in der Antike* [Munich: Beck, 1962]). According to this analysis, the novels would have two audiences, an exoteric and an esoteric. Although it is helpful to differentiate among the various readings that an ancient work may have had, Merkelbach's thesis has not been successful, largely because it is impossible to prove that the rather contradictory system of allegorical readings on which his hypothesis depends would ever have occurred to an ancient reader. See most briefly Morton Smith, *Classical World* 27 (1964) 378.

90. François Bovon, "The Synoptic Gospels and the Noncanonical Acts of the Apostles," *Harvard Theological Review* 81 (1988) 19–36.

91. Christine M. Thomas, "The 'Prehistory' of the *Acts of Peter*," in Bovon, ed., *Apocryphal Acts*, 39–62.

*Chapter Two*

1. Christine M. Thomas, "Word and Deed: The *Acts of Peter* and Orality," *Apocrypha* 3 (1992) 125–64.

2. See the remarks in David R. Cartlidge, "Combien d'unités avez-vous de trois à quatre? What Do We Mean by Intertextuality in Early Church Studies?" in David J. Lull, ed., *Society of Biblical Literature 1990 Seminar Papers* (Atlanta: Scholars Press, 1990) 400–11.

3. Albert B. Lord, "The Merging of Two Worlds: Oral and Written Poetry as Carriers of Ancient Values," in John Miles Foley, ed., *Oral Tradition in Literature: Interpretation in Context* (Columbia: University of Missouri Press, 1986) 19–64, esp. 41.

4. See Rosalind Thomas, *Literacy and Orality in Ancient Greece* (Cambridge: Cambridge University Press, 1992) 44–51.

5. The term was developed by K. Schmidt and employed by Rudolf Bultmann and Martin Dibelius to indicate texts that ultimately derived from oral tradition, that were subliterary and thus lacking generic indictors, and that were anonymous products of a community rather than individual authors. For a brief discussion, see Harry Y. Gamble, *Books and Readers in the Early Church: A History of Early Christian Texts* (New Haven: Yale University Press, 1995) 11–17.

6. The fifth German edition of *Neutestamentliche Apokryphen in deutscher Übersetzung* repeats the position Schneemelcher has stated in the past ("Second and Third Century Acts of the Apostles: Introduction," in idem, ed., *New Testament Apocrypha* [1989, ed. R. McL. Wilson; Louisville, Ky.: John Knox, 1992] 2.75–86; earlier, see "Second and Third Century Acts of Apostles: Introduction," in Wilhelm Schneemelcher, ed., *New Testament Apocrypha* [3d ed.; ed. R. McL. Wilson; Philadelphia: Westminster, 1965] 2.167–88).

7. Schneemelcher treats this at greatest length in idem and Schäferdiek, "Introduction (1965)," 176–78. The fifth edition repeats the position, though retreating somewhat from it in favor of other literary models (Schneemelcher, "Introduction [1992]," esp. 78–79, 82–83).

8. Hans Conzelmann, "Zu Mythos, Mythologie und Formgeschichte, geprüft an der dritten Praxis der Thomas-Akten," *Zeitschrift für die neutestamentliche Wissenschaft* 67 (1976) 111–22.

9. Robert Franklin Stoops, "Miracle Stories and Vision Reports in the *Acts of Peter*," Ph.D. diss., Harvard, 1983. See also Martin Blumenthal, *Formen und Motive in den apokryphen Apostelgeschichten* (TU 48/1; Leipzig: J. C. Hinrichs, 1933), another form-critical study.

10. Virginia Burrus, *Chastity as Autonomy: Women in the Stories of the Apocryphal Acts* (Lewiston, N.Y.: E. Mellen, 1987); Dennis Ronald MacDonald, *The Legend and the Apostle: The Battle for Paul in Story and Canon* (Philadelphia: Westminster, 1983).

11. As is Stevan Davies, who also attributes the Apocryphal Acts to groups of Christian women, in his case continent widows, wives, and virgins (*The Revolt of the Widows: The Social World of the Apocryphal Acts* [Carbondale, Ill.: Southern Illinois University Press, 1980] ). Davies diverges from Burrus and MacDonald in viewing the Apocryphal Acts as primarily literary works

with no background of oral storytelling. He uses their similarity to the ancient novel as support for his argument on authorship, basing his assumption on the assertion of Rohde (!) that the novels are primarily women's literature (*Revolt*, 86, 101). The case for women's authorship is founded on the demonstration that women had the opportunity, means, and motive to write such works. Tertullian's explicit attribution of the *Acts of Paul* to a male presbyter is brushed aside as tendentious misinformation (*Revolt*, 95–109, esp. 108).

12. See MacDonald, *Legend*, 34–53; and the heading, "The Pastoral Epistles against 'Old Wives' Tales,'" 54; Burrus, *Chastity*, 81–112.

13. Brian McNeil, "A Liturgical Source in *Acts of Peter* 38," *Vigilae Christianae* 33 (1979) 342–46; R. H. Miller, "Liturgical Materials in the *Acts of John*," *Studia Patristica* 13 (1975) 375–81.

14. "Les traits charactéristiques de la théologie des 'Actes de Jean'," *Revue de théologie et de philosophie* 26 (1976) 125–45, esp. 125–27, 142–43.

15. "Créations romanesques et traditions ecclésiastiques dans les Actes apocryphes des Apôtres: l'alternative fiction romanesque–vérité historique: une impasse," *Augustinianum (Rome)* 23 (1983) 271–85, esp. 274–75. Eckhard Plümacher similarly claims that any possible sources of the Apocryphal Acts have left no trace in the language ("Apokryphe Apostelakten." *Supplement to Pauly's Real-Encyclopädie der classischen Altertumswissenschaft* 15 (1978) 11-70, esp. 66).

16. Richard Adalbert Lipsius, ed., *Acta Apostolorum Apocrypha* (Leipzig: Hermann Mendelssohn, 1891) 1.45–103, with introduction. See also idem, *Die apokryphen Apostelgeschichten und Apostellegenden: Ein Beitrag zur altchristlichen Literaturgeschichte* (3 parts in 2 vols.; Braunschweig: C. A. Schwetschke und Sohn, 1883–87) 2.1.109–42, 174–94.

17. Carl Schmidt, "Studien zu den alten Petrusakten: II. Die Komposition," *Zeitschrift für Kirchengeschichte* 45 (1926) 481–513; J. Flamion, "Les actes apocryphes de Pierre," *Revue d'histoire ecclésiastique* 9 (1908) 233–54.

18. Gérard Poupon, "Les 'Actes de Pierre' et leur remaniement," *Aufstieg und Niedergang der römischen Welt* 2.25/6 (1988) 4363–83. Poupon's arguments are based in part on observations already made by Adolf von Harnack and Léon Vouaux.

19. Poupon, "Remaniement," 4369–70.

20. Though the Coptic fragment could also date from the fifth century; see Carl Schmidt, *Die alten Petrusakten im Zusammenhang der apokryphen Apostelliteratur nebst einem neuentdeckten Fragment* (TU n. s. 9.1; Leipzig: J. Hinrichs, 1903) 2.

21. Grenfell and Hunt, *Oxyrhynchus* (1908) 6.8–9.

22. How much earlier is open to question. The initial three chapters of the present *Actus Vercellenses* are a later interpolation; since the interpolation dates from the late second century, and was probably done in Greek, it is possible that the fourth-century MS, of which the Oxyrhynchus papyrus is a fragment, would have contained these three chapters. If it did not, it would have contained more parts of the narrative unknown from the *Actus Vercellenses*. Whatever the case, the vellum fragment would still have been much shorter than the version of Nikephoros.

23. Incorrectly identified by Schneemelcher and Geerard as papyrus (Schneemelcher, *Apocrypha [1992]*, 2.278; likewise in Schneemelcher, *Apocrypha [1965]*, 2.269; and also Maurice Geerard, *Clavis apocryphorum Novi Testamenti* [Corpus Christianorum; Turnhout: Brepols, 1992] 101 §190). It is because the fragment is vellum and not papyrus that Grenfell and Hunt date it to the early fourth century rather than the later third. The script is of a type commonly used from the reigns of Diocletian to Constantine, but vellum is uncommon in Egypt before the fourth century. The stratigraphy is no help here, since the immediate context contained finds from the third to the fifth century (Bernard P. Grenfell and Arthur S. Hunt, eds., *The Oxyrhynchus Papyri* [London: Egypt Exploration Fund, 1908] 6. 6–12; see esp. 7).

24. The text parallels about twelve lines of the Latin *Actus Vercellenses* in the Lipsius edition (1.73).

25. *Contra* the hypothesis of Richard Lipsius that the text of Peter's martyrdom ascribed to Linus represents a direct and faithful translation from the original Greek text of the *Acts of Peter* (*Apostelgeschichten*, 2.1.109–35). Lipsius believes that the Greek original of the *Acts of Peter* has been lost and that the *Actus Vercellenses* is an abridgment of the Greek text. The two Greek codices that represent the shorter version of the martyrdom (in comparison with the translation of Linus) would thus be retrotranslations from the *Actus Vercellenses*. The Linus text does not preserve the passage contained in the vellum fragment (*P. Oxy.* 849), so no direct comparison can be made. But the terse style of the *Actus Vercellenses* at the point represented by the Greek fragment is consistent with the Latin style of the martyrdom section. The Greek codices thus have a text very close to the Greek from which the *Actus Vercellenses* was translated, and the Linus text is then a later reworking of the Greek text.

26. This sometimes leads to outright mistakes: the *Actus Vercellenses* misunderstands σὲ μᾶλλον καὶ τὸν διά σου θεὸν πειράσαι θέλων (*P. Oxy.* 849, ll. 20–21) as *confidens in te et in dominum tuum* (*AcVer* 26; Lipsius 73.23–24). For the *Actus Vercellenses*, the numbers refer to the page and line numbers of the Lipsius edition, which I have used for convenience, since the edition of Vouaux does not print the Latin of the martyrdom account (Léon Vouaux, *Les Actes de Pierre* [Paris: Letouzey et Ané, 1922]).

27. Comparison of the Greek and Latin versions of the martyrdom leads to the same conclusion. There is also no question that Greek was the original language of the *Acts of Peter*. Vouaux notes several passages in the Latin translation that are obvious misunderstandings of the Greek text (*Actes de Pierre*, 24): for example, the Greek must have read μαῖα instead of μία in chapter 30; the Latin translates this as *obstetrix* (Lipsius 79.20). See also Flamion, "Actes de Pierre (1908) 239–41, for an extensive list of such cases.

28. Text published in Schmidt, *Petrusakten*, 3–7 and again in James Brashler and Douglas M. Parrott, "The Act of Peter," in Douglas M. Parrott, ed., *Nag Hammadi Codices V, 2–5 and VI with Papyrus Berolinensis 8502, 1 and 4* (Nag Hammadi Studies 11; Coptic Gnostic Library; Leiden: Brill, 1979) 473–93.

29. Andrea Molinari, *"I Never Knew the Man": The Coptic Act of Peter (Papyrus Berolinensis 8502.4): Its Independence from the Apocryphal Acts of Peter, Genre and Legendary Origins* (Quebec: University of Laval, 2000) 13–25, esp. 22–25. Molinari's strongest argument is that, when a passage is excerpted from a larger work, the full title is generally employed (e.g. *Acts of Peter*), rather than some shortened version of the title (e.g., *Act of Peter*, as in the Coptic manuscript).

30. Latin text in Joseph Zycha, *Sancti Aureli Augustini* . . . (Corpus scriptorum ecclesiasticorum latinorum 25.1; Vienna: F. Tempsky and G. Freytag, 1891) 170: . . . *cum in apocryphis pro magno opere legant et illud, quod de apostolo Thoma commemoraui, et ipsius Petri filiam paralyticam factam precibus patris et hortulani filiam ad precem ipsius Petri esse mortuam, et respondent, quod hoc eis expediebat, ut et illa* [the edition reads *illi*] *solueretur paralysi et illa moreretur, tamen ad preces apostoli factum esse non negant.*

31. Faustus of Milevis and Philaster both refer around 400 C.E. to a collection of the five major Apocryphal Acts, which they attribute to a Manichaean, Leukios Charinos. See Knut Schäferdiek, "Die Leukios Charinos zugeschriebene manichäische Sammlung apokrypher Apostelgeschichten," in Schneemelcher, ed., *Apokryphen* (1989) 2.81–93. See more recently Jan Bremmer, "The Novel and the Apocryphal Acts: Place, Time, and Readership," in H. Hofmann and M. Zimmerman, eds., *Groningen Colloquia on the Novel: Volume IX* (Groningen: Egbert Forsten, 1998) 157–80, esp. 164. Bremmer argues that the five major Apocryphal Acts were translated in North Africa before the death of Priscillian (385 C.E.), who knew them in Latin.

32. Contra Molinari, *Independence*, 80–95 and idem, "Augustine, *Contra Adimantum* . . . Attacking Carl Schmidt's theory of an Original Unity Between the *Act of Peter* and the *Acts of*

Peter," *SBL 1999 Seminar Papers* (Atlanta, Ga.: Scholars Press, 1999) 426–47, esp. 431–35. In addition to the argument that the term *apocrypha* refers to other texts beside the Apocryphal Acts, Molinari states that the two stories, that of Peter's daughter and that of the gardener's daughter, are nowhere else associated in early Christian literature. While strictly true, one must note that other works familiar with the *Acts of Peter* also relate episodes concerning Peter's daughter. Both the *Acts of Nereus and Achilleus* (chap. 15) and the *Acts of Philip* (chap. 142) contain versions of it. Though neither of them cites a source, both are dependent at other points on materials from the *Acts of Peter* known from the *Actus Vercellenses*. Although it is possible to explain this association away, as Molinari does (*Independence*, 61–80, 95–116; Augustine," 436) by assuming that the two texts take their apocryphal Petrine stories from works other than the *Acts of Peter*, it is striking to find this association in two texts that know materials from the *Acts of Peter* well (see Schmidt, *Petrusakten*, 15–20, in addition to the treatment below of the *Acts of Nereus and Achilleus*). The story of the gardener's daughter is a multiform of the story of Peter's daughter (see Chapter Three). The theological disparities cited by Molinari ("Augustine," 442-47) between this account and both the Coptic *Act of Peter* and the longer *Acts of Peter* may be the result of the circulation of this tale separately from the version translated in the *Actus Vercellenses*. Once one recognizes the multiformity of the *Act of Peter* texts – and also their distinctness from other Petrine traditions such as the Clementines – one cannot assume that Augustine's copy, or that of his Manichaean interlocutors, was exactly the same as the second or early third-century version that is the basis of the *Actus Vercellenses*.

33. Carl Schmidt presents nine points of correspondence between the *Act of Peter* and the *Actus Vercellenses* (Schmidt, *Petrusakten*, 23–25, and idem, "Studien zu den alten Petrusakten," *Zeitschrift für Kirchengeschichte* 43 [1924] 321–48). All are refuted, some successfully, by Molinari (*Independence*, 26–59). Molinari argues that each of the lexical and theological correspondences is a motif that can be found elsewhere in early Christian literature, and thus none of them is specific enough to warrant a connection between the *Act of Peter* and the *Acts of Peter*. The thrust of Molinari's argument, however, misses the point: Schmidt's argument does not hang on any single correspondence, but on the combined weight of all of them.

34. Numerical references are to the page and line number of the codex itself, conveniently available in the editions of Brashler-Parrott and Schmidt. I have chiefly followed the text of Brashler and Parrott, with a glance at Schmidt's, occasionally adding punctuation not provided by either editor.

35. C. H. Turner suggests *eo quidem* which would, in any case, mean about the same thing ("The Latin *Acts of Peter*," *Journal of Theological Studies* 32 [1931] 119-33, see esp. 127).

36. Text reads *id*; Vouaux prints this emendation (394, ad loc.), attributing it to Lipsius, though it does not appear in that edition. Turner repeats the suggestion, apparently unaware that Vouaux had made it ("Latin Acts," 130).

37. So Molinari, *Independence*, 26–27.

38. ⲡⲉⲭⲁϥ ⲛⲁϥ ϫⲉ ... ⲉⲓⲙⲉ {ϭⲉ} ϫⲉ ⲛ̄ⲛⲉⲣⲉ ⲡⲛⲟⲩⲧⲉ ⲟ ⲁⲛ ⲛ̄ϭⲱⲃ ⲏ̄ ⲛⲁⲧϭⲟⲙ ⲉⲧⲣⲉϥⲭⲁⲣⲓⲍⲉ ⲛⲧⲉϥⲇⲱⲣⲉⲁ ⲛ̄ⲧⲁϣⲉⲉⲣⲉ. Except where noted, English translations are mine.

39. ⲉⲓⲙⲉ ϭⲉ ⲱ ⲡ̄ϩⲙ̄ϩⲁⲗ ⲛ̄ⲧⲉ ⲡⲉⲭ̄ⲥ̄ ⲓ̄ⲥ̄ ϫⲉ ⲡⲛⲟⲩⲧⲉ ⲣ̄ⲟⲓⲕⲟⲛⲟⲙⲓ ⲛⲛⲉⲧⲉⲛⲟⲩϥ ⲛⲉ ⲁⲩⲱ ϥⲥⲟⲃⲧⲉ ⲙ̄ⲡⲡⲉⲧⲛⲁⲛⲟⲩϥ ⲛ̄ ⲡⲟⲩⲁ ⲡⲟⲩⲁ. ⲁⲛⲟⲛ ϩⲱⲱⲛ ⲉⲙⲙⲉⲉⲩⲉ ϫⲉ ⲁ ⲡⲛⲟⲩⲧⲉ ⲟⲃ(ⲱ)ϥ ⲉⲣⲟⲛ.

40. As Stevan Davies notes, the Apocryphal Acts generally show great interest in widows, who are an order supported and respected by the church (*Revolt*, 70–94). In the contest with Simon, Peter raises the only sons of two widows, one rich and one poor. Before restoring the wealthy son, he exacts a promise that the money that would have been spent on the boy's funeral be devoted to the widows (chap. 28).

41. *Si est in uobis fides, quae est in Christo, si confirmata est in uobis, uidete sensu{m}* [Lipsius] *quod oculis non uidetis . . . hi{i} oculi iterum cludentur, nihil aliud uidentes nisi homines et boues et muta animalia et lapides et ligna; sed Iesum Christum non omnes oculi uident.*

42. Stoops also notes that the spiritualization of the miracle, that is, the emphasis on spiritual benefits over physical well-being, is present in this story ("Miracle Stories," 163, 182, 221).

43. It is true, as Molinari argues, that this phrase appears elsewhere in Greek literature as a commonplace. He was, however, only able to find four other attestations of equal or earlier date than the *Acts of Peter*; thus of the six attestations dating into the early third century, one is found in the *Actus Vercellenses*, the other in the Coptic fragment (*Independence*, 43–46).

44. Molinari, *Independence*, 31–34. It is only fair to note that Molinari discounts this *hapax legomenon* as unconvincing evidence because it was just one way of expressing a very common thought, that is, the totality of the body from head to foot. But to my mind it is precisely the lexically unique way of expressing the common thought that is especially telling, all the more so since the thought was so common.

45. A eucharist scene with bread alone, and neither water nor wine, occurs also in the *Actus Vercellenses* (chap. 5).

46. BHO 935, edited by Paulus Bedjan (*Acta martyrum et sanctorum Syriace* [1890–97; Hildesheim: G. Olms, 1968]); the work is a compilation of the canonical Acts, the Clementine literature, the "Syriac Preaching," and the *Acts of Peter*. The *Acts of Peter* owned by Nikephoros were about half again as long as the present *Actus Vercellenses*, according to his stichometry; he reckoned his version at 2750 lines. Theodor Zahn calculates that one-third has been lost; see Schmidt, "Studien II," 481–83. There are several back-references to the Judean portion of the narrative. Chapter 17 is a long narration by Peter of the final episode in the conflict in Judea, in which Peter proves to the wealthy Eubula that Simon is an impostor. Chapters 5, 9, and 23 also allude to Peter's conflict with Simon in Judea; see Schmidt, "Studien II."

47. See Schmidt, *Petrusakten*, 2, 13.

48. Brashler and Parrott, "Act of Peter," 475–76.

49. Noted by Vouaux, *Actes de Pierre*, 17. The interpolation comprises both sides of one leaf of the codex, pp. 363–64, which appears just before chapter 29 in the text, and follows four pages written in a different seventh-century hand, 359–62. The copyist's mistake here was recognized and corrected already in the eighth century.

50. Schmidt, "Studien II," 510–13.

51. These features noted also by Vouaux (*Actes de Pierre*, 27–33) and Poupon ("Remaniement," 4371–74), both of whom believe them to be interpolated. Gerhard Ficker (*Die Petrusakten: Beiträge zu ihrem Verständnis* [Leipzig: Barth, 1903] 30–32) and Schmidt ("Studien II," 494–97) hold the initial three chapters to be original.

52. *Orando autem plurima turba mulierum geniculantes rogabant beatum Paulum, et osculantes pedes eius deduxerunt in portum. sed Dionisius et Balbus ab Asia, {a}equites Romani, splendidi uiri, et senator nomine Demetrius adherens Paulo ad dexteram eius dicebat: Paule* [Lipsius; Vouaux prints dicebat: *Paulo; vellem fugere* (sic)], *uellem* fugere *ab urbe, si non essem magistratus, ut a te non discederem*. Item *de domo Caesaris Cleobius et Ifitus et Lysimachus et Aristeus, et duae matronae Berenice et Filostrate cum praesbytero Narcisso* (Lipsius 47.35–48.7).

53. Also considered an interpolation by Poupon ("Remaniement," 4370–74).

54. *iam instruebat deus in futurum Petrum in Hierosolymis, adimpletis duodecim annis quod illi praeceperat dominus, Christus ostendit illi uisionem talem* (Lipsius 49.21–24).

55. Vouaux notes this chronological inconsistency (*Actes de Pierre*, 93–100). Schmidt attributes this lapse to the artistic license of the novelist who wrote it ("Studien II," 499). Flamion, like Schmidt, blames the chronological and geographical inaccuracies on the genre of the work as a novel ("Actes de Pierre [1908]," 473–76). See Chapter Three below for fuller discussion.

56. *1 Clement* may allude to the deaths of both Peter and Paul, though the location is not clear from the text (*1 Clem.* 5–6); the letter shows greater knowledge about Paul than Peter. Dionysios of Corinth, writing to Rome around 170 C.E., is the first to say that the two apostles were martyred in the same era (κατὰ τὸν αὐτὸν καιρόν, in Eusebios, *Ecclesiastical History*

2.25.8) and that they taught together in Italy, though, again, he does not specify that Rome was the place of martyrdom. Tertullian is the first to claim that both were victims of the persecution under Nero (*Scorpiace* 15). In *adversus Marcionem* 4.5, he merely says that they were martyred together in Rome. Gaius, writing against the Montanists in the early third century, mentions τὰ τρόπαια of Peter and Paul and their locations on the Vatican and on the Ostian Way (in Eusebios, *Ecclesiastical History* 2.25.7). Jerome states that Paul was executed during the fourteenth year of Nero (ca. 67 C.E.), on the same day that Peter had been martyred (*de viris illustribus* 5).

57. This furnishes a framework for the elapsing of dramatic time within the *Actus Vercellenses*. All of the events are thought to take place within less than a year, including Peter's departure for Rome twelve years after Christ's death.

58. *sonus de caelis factus est, et vox maxima dicens: Paulus dei minister electus est in ministerium tempus vitae suae; inter manus Neronis hominis impii et iniqui sub oculis uestris consummabitur* (Lipsius 46.6–9).

59. This mode of analysis was suggested to me by the study of David H. Warren, "The Greek Language of the Apocryphal Acts of the Apostles: A Study in Style," in François Bovon, Ann Graham Brock, et al., eds., *The Apocryphal Acts of the Apostles: Harvard Divinity School Studies* (Cambridge, Mass.: Harvard University, 1999) 101–24.

60. The reference to Paul in chapter 23 may not be original. Poupon argues that the "Syriac History of Peter" (BHO 935) preserves the original reading ("Remaniement," 4366–72). In chapter 23 of the *Actus Vercellenses*, during the contest in the forum, Peter asks Simon, "Did you not fall at my feet and Paul's in Jerusalem?" Here the text of the "Syriac History" reads, "Did you not fall at my feet and at those of the other apostles in Jerusalem?" The reference to Paul is not here, presumably because it was not in the source of the *Actus Vercellenses*.

61. The transition from indirect to direct speech is so clumsy that one can only guess at which point to place quotation marks.

62. *dicebat enim Aristhon, ex ‹quo›* [Lipsius; MS *ex eo*] *Paulus profectus est in Spaniam, non fuisse neminem de fratribus ad quem refrigerare‹t›. praeterea Iudaeum quendam inrupisse in urbem, nomine Simonem. magico carmine a‹t›que* [Lipsius; MS *adque*] *sua nequitia hinc inde omnem fraternitatem dissoluit, ut etiam ego a Roma fugerem, sperans uenire Petrum* (Lipsius 51.25–30). Turner points out that the mistaken *ex eo* may derive from *co* in the *Vorlage*, a common early orthographic variant ("Latin Acts," 121).

63. Noted also by Poupon, "Remaniement," 4373–74.

64. *peruenit ad hospitium in quo solitus erat reuerti . . . erat autem ad quem reuertebatur nomine Ariston; hic timebat semper dominum, et se Theon cum illo committebat propter nomen* (Lipsius 51.15–18).

65. Vouaux argues that the first chapters were cobbled together from references to the New Testament and to the *Acts of Peter* itself (*Actes de Pierre*, 55–57).

66. Gérard Poupon, "La Passion de S. Pierre Apôtre," Magister diss., Université de Genève, 1975, 43–51.

67. Cf. the *Acts of Nereus and Achilleus*, in which Marcellus is simply a disciple of Simon until he realizes that his teacher is a thief and liar, after which he follows Peter (chap. 12; Hans Achelis, *Acta SS. Nerei et Achillei: Text und Untersuchung* [TU 11.2; Leipzig: J. C. Hinrichs, 1893] 11, lines 12–16): Ἐγὼ τοίνυν τούτου μαθητὴς ὑπῆρχον, θεωρῶν δὲ αὐτὸν λίαν πονηρόν, παιδοκτόνον τε καὶ φαρμακόν, κλέπτην καὶ γόητα, κατέλιπον αὐτὸν καὶ προσεκολλήθην τῷ κυρίῳ μου Πέτρῳ τῷ μακαριωτάτῳ ἀποστόλῳ.

68. *. . . ut non exequaris peccata mea, si qua est in te Christi vera fides quem tu praedicas, si praeceptorum eius memor es, neminem odire, nemini esse malu‹m›,* [Lipsius; MS *malus*] *sicut didici a Paulo coapostolo tuo. ne in animo inducas delictorum meorum. . . .* (Lipsius 57.16–19).

69. As noted also by Vouaux (*Actes de Pierre*, 292 ad loc.).

70. ὃν λέγεις θεόν / *deus tuus* (Lipsius 79.24).

71. Αὕτη τις μὲν ἔστιν τὸν ἄλλον βίον, οὐκ οἶδα / *Haec quae sit ignoro* (Lipsius 80.10–11, 81.10–11).

72. *mulier Eubola, honesta nimis in saeculo hoc* (Lipsius 63.2–3).

73. A small statuette weighing only two pounds, such as those described by Louis Robert, *Opera Minora Selecta* , vol. 5 (Amsterdam: A. M. Hakkert, 1989) 747–69. I thank Jan Bremmer for this reference ("Aspects of the *Acts of Peter*: Women, Magic, Place, and Date," in idem, ed., *The Apocryphal Acts of Peter: Magic, Miracles, and Gnosticism* [Leuven: Peeters, 1998] 1–20, esp. 7).

74. . . . *et uidⁱᵗ* [Lipsius; MS *uidet*] *turbam magnam uenientem et illos ligatos catenis. statim intellexit et fuga⟨m⟩* [Lipsius; MS *fuga*] *petiit, et non conparuit in Iudea usque in hoc tempus* (Lipsius 65.16–19).

75. *Eubola autem postquam recepit omnia sua dedit in ministerium pauperorum, credens autem in dominum Iesum Christum et confortata et contemnens et abrenuntians huic saeculo, tribuebat uiduis et orfanis et uestiens pauperos per multum tempus accepit dormitionem* (Lipsius 65.19–22).

76. Vouaux notes that this conclusion is more appropriate for the end of an ordinary narrative, rather than for a story told by Peter to encourage the Christian congregation (*Actes de Pierre*, 333 ad loc.). This may be a sign that chapter 17 was transposed here from an earlier point in the versions of the *Acts of Peter* used there.

77. The canonical Acts of the Apostles relates a similar tale regarding a prominent polytheist won over to Christianity by a miraculous feat. Paul and Barnabas present the Christian message to Sergius Paulus, proconsul on Cyprus, but are hindered by a Jewish magician named Bar-Jesus or Elymas. When Paul strikes Elymas blind, the proconsul converts to Christianity (13:6–12).

78. Poupon also suspects redaction in these chapters, and in chapter 30 ("Remaniement," 4372–74); Vouaux, as mentioned, believes that chapter 17 is an interpolation, in addition to the first three chapters (*Actes de Pierre*, 26–35).

79. Σίμων δὲ ὁ μάγος τῷ ὄχλῳ ἡμερῶν ὀλίγων διελθουσῶν ὑπισχνεῖτο τὸν Πέτρον ἀπελέγξαι. . . . ταῦτα δὲ πάντα ὁ Πέτρος ἀκολουθῶν διήλεγχεν αὐτὸν πρὸς τοὺς ὁρῶντας. καὶ δὴ ἀεὶ ἀσχημονοῦντος καὶ ἐγγελωμένου ὑπὸ τοῦ Ῥωμαίων ὄχλου καὶ ἀπιστουμένου ἐφ᾽ οἷς ὑπισχνεῖτο ποιεῖν μὴ ἐπιτυγχάνοντος, ἐν τούτῳ τούτων πάντα εἰπεῖν αὐτοῖς· Ἄνδρες Ῥωμαῖοι (Lipsius 80.20–21, 29–33).

80. *Sed post dies paucos Simon se dicebat Petrum vincere . . . nam Petrus sequendo Simonem magum dissoluebat eum, nam ab omnibus aporiabatur et nemo illi iam nihil credebat. nouissime autem dicit Simon: Viri Romani* (Lipsius 81.17–18, 26–29).

81. Ἐὰν ἀφῆς τοῦτον ποιῆσαι ὃ ἐπεχείρησεν, νῦν πάντες οἱ εἰς σὲ πιστεύσαντες σκανδαλισθήσονται καὶ ἔσται ἃ δι᾽ ἐμοῦ ἔδωκας αὐτοῖς σημεῖα καὶ τέρατα ἄπιστα (Lipsius 82.21–23).

*Si passus fueris hunc quod conatus est facere, omnes qui crediderunt in te scandalizantur et quaecumque dedisti per me signa erunt fincta* (Lipsius 83.14–16).

82. ἀφεώρων οἱ πιστοὶ εἰς τὸν Πέτρον. This passage is not translated in the Latin text (Lipsius 82.19).

83. ὅτε γὰρ εἰσίει εἰς τὴν Ῥώμην, ἐξέστησεν τοὺς ὄχλους πετώμενος. ἀλλ᾽ οὔπω Πέτρος ὁ ἐλέγχων αὐτὸν ἦν ἐνδημῶν τῇ Ῥώμῃ, ἥνπερ οὕτως πλανῶν ἐφάντασεν, ὡς ἐκστῆναι τινας ἐπ᾽ αὐτῷ (Lipsius 82.7–10).

84. Vouaux, on the contrary, believes that this passage is an interpolation by the Athos copyist, since that MS carries only the martyrdom account and a few chapters prior to it; the copyist is providing information from a part of the narrative that is not transmitted in his or her version (*Actes de Pierre*, 408 ad loc.). I would note here that the Vercelli MS often shortens the text and that the supposed interpolation really does not explain anything here or resolve any difficulty. Moreover, the text commonly makes back references to previous episodes; even if chapter 17 is suspect, there are three further references to Peter's expulsion of Simon from Judea in the Latin of the Vercelli ms (chaps. 5, 9, and 23).

85. Gerard Luttikhuizen objects to Poupon's hypothesis because he does not see a clear division between the encratite parts of the text, which would be assigned to the more stringent source text, and the parts advocating second repentence, which belong to the redaction. As he rightly points out, a concern with encratism is absent from the passage narrating the contest between Peter and Simon, which is doubtless one of the oldest parts of the narrative, and precedes the redaction. Luttikhuizen also doubts that the Coptic fragment about Peter's daughter and the fragment about the gardener's daughter belonged originally to the narrative about Simon and Peter, since these two episodes are markedly encratite, as is the martyrdom account ("Simon Magus as a Narrative Figure in the *Acts of Peter*," in Bremmer, *Acts of Peter*, 39-51, esp. 40-41). Luttikhuizen's critique is not entirely successful, since Poupon has more evidence at hand than the theological discontinuities in the document, such as the many literary details he marshals. Moreover, Luttikhuizen's conception of the history of composition of the *Acts of Peter* is too simple. The theological discontinuities he notes should not be assigned to the difference between text and redaction, but to the difference between the various sources of the text. The martyrdom and the contest clearly belonged together from an early date, but are nevertheless theologically heterogeneous, since they derive from different sources.

86. *Contra* Poupon, chapter 30, the story of Chryse, in which he also sees traces of redaction, does not illustrate the case of a lapsed Christian, or of forgiveness for adultery, but of a wealthy polytheist benefactress of the Christian church; it does not cohere with the level of redaction surrounding Marcellus, but rather with the concern of the previous version with non-Christian benefactors.

87. Poupon, "Remaniement," 4378-82.

88. Both Greek MSS read it. Flamion assumes that the Greek adds this passage because it does not preserve the allusion to Paul's return to Rome, which appears in the first chapter of the Latin ("Actes de Pierre [1908]," 243).

89. The beginning of chapter one, for example, evinces a Latin style influenced by a Greek original: *Pauli tempus demorantis Romae et multos confirmantis in fide contingit etiam quendam nomine Candidam . . . audire Paulum . . . et credere* (Lipsius 45.1-5) The genitive is unexpected here, and the entire construction looks more like a Greek sentence beginning with a genitive absolute than a Latin sentence.

90. For the sake of clarity, the term "continuous Greek text" will refer only to the unredacted Greek text that did not have chapters 1-3 and 41. The "Greek redaction," which contained these chapters, was the basis of the Latin translation in the *Actus Vercellenses*.

91. A point also noted by Vouaux, *Actes de Pierre*, 28, who nevertheless holds these chapters to be an interpolation.

92. Significantly, however, the eucharist in chapter 2 (called *sacrificium*) is with water and bread (Lipsius 46.12-13); in chapter 5 (*eucharistium*, Lipsius 51.3-10), and in the Coptic fragment, neither wine nor water are mentioned, only bread.

93. On the Roman topography known in this document, see Ficker, *Petrusakten*, 34-38.

94. For these arguments, see Ficker, *Petrusakten*, 38-46.

95. Bremmer, "Aspects," 14-16.

96. *Prosopographia Imperii Romani*$^2$ B 199.

97. A. H. M. Jones, *The Later Roman Empire* (Oxford: Oxford University Press, 1964) 2.578-80.

98. Bremmer, "Novel," 163-64; see also Bremmer, "Aspects," 19.

99. "The Language and Style of the *Acts of Peter*," in Benjamín García-Hernandez, ed., *Estudios de Lingüística Latina: Actas del IX Coloquio Internacional de Lingüística Latina* (Madrid: Ediciones Clásicas, 1998) 1063-72.

100. "Latin Acts."

101. Gérard Poupon, "L'Origine africaine des *Actus Vercellenses*," in Bremmer, *Acts of Peter*, 192–99.

102. See below.

103. Bremmer, "Aspects," 16–18.

104. Liuwe Westra, "*Regula fidei* and Other Credal Formulations in the *Acts of Peter*," in Bremmer, *Acts of Peter*, 142.

105. *1 Clement* 5–6, around 95 C.E.; Dionysios of Corinth, writing to Rome around 170, in Eusebios, *Ecclesiastical History* 2.25.8.

106. In Eusebios, *Ecclesiastical History* 4.23.6, cited by Ficker, *Petrusakten*, 41: οἵας δὲ οὖν ἀποπτώσεως εἴτε πλημμελείας εἴτε μὴν αἱρετικῆς πλάνης.

107. *sed et Marcellus* [Lipsius; MS *Marcello*] *in spiritu exaltabatur, quod tale signum primum inter manus eius factum fuisset. credens ergo ex totis praecordiis {u}suis in nomine Iesu Christi filii dei, per quem omnia inpossibilia possibilia sunt. sed Simon intus ad canem ita dixit: Dic Petro, intus me non esse. Ad quem canis coram Marcello ait* (Lipsius 59.28–34).

108. Vouaux also notes this difficulty, but attributes it to a translation mistake for a phrase such as ἐναντίον τῶν παρὰ τῷ Μαρκέλλῳ (*Actes de Pierre*, 305 n. 6 ad loc.).

109. *et canis renuntians quid gessisset cum Simone. haec autem locutus est canis: angel* [Turner ("Latin Acts," 126); MS *angelo et apostolo*] *dei uer* [Turner; MS *uere*] *Petre, agonem magnum habebis contra Simonem inimicum Christi ... multos autem conuertes in fidem seductos ab eo. Propter quod accipies mercedem a deo operis tui. haec cum dixisset canis, caecidit ante pedes apostoli Petri et deposuit spiritum* (Lipsius 60.14–20). If one does not follow Turner's emendation, the manuscript reading still results in a meaningful sentence ("the dog said to the messenger and apostle of God, 'Truly, Peter ...'"). Without Turner's emendation, Lipsius's emendation to *ueri* here makes grammatical sense, but does not seem particularly apt.

110. The Greek martyrdom displays a consistent mix of hypotaxis and parataxis throughout with the exception of chapters 37–38 and 40–41 (see above). The percentage of circumstantial participles from the total number of circumstantial participles and finite verbs runs at 35 to 40 percent for each of the individual chapters of the martyrdom account (chaps. 30–41), but dips to 20 to 21 percent in chapters 37 and 38. Chapters 37–38 reproduce a speech in which Peter cites a number of apothegms, and this may also affect the ratio.

111. See Thomas, "Word and Deed."

112. *cane{m} te arguente non es confusus; ego infans cogor a deo loqui et nec sic erubescis. sed te nolente, ueniente sabbato die alter te adducet in Iulio foro, ut adprobetur in te qualis sis* (Lipsius 62.6–62.9).

113. Parts of this section were presented as an address to the Seminar on Intertextuality in Christian Apocrypha at the Annual Meeting of the Society of Biblical Literature (20 November 1994): "One Never Steps into the Same River Twice: Response to Robert Stoops." Stoops's original paper is published as "Departing to Another Place: The *Acts of Peter* and the Canonical Acts of the Apostles," in *Society of Biblical Literature Seminar Papers* (Atlanta: Scholars Press, 1994) 390–404. For a more extensive treatment of intertextuality between the *Acts of Peter* and the New Testament, see Christine M. Thomas, "Canon and Antitype: The Relationship Between the *Acts of Peter* and the New Testament," *Semeia* 80 (1997 [1999]) 185–205. See also in the same volume Robert F. Stoops, "The *Acts of Peter* in Intertextual Context," *Semeia* 80 (1997 [1999]) 57–86, esp. 65–71, which are subtitled "Uses of Biblical Texts in the *Acts of Peter*." Stoops seems to be unaware of my treatment of the same topic in the same volume, although he himself edited the volume. Note especially the similar treatment of *AcVer* 23 (Stoops, "Intertextual Context," 65–66; Thomas, "Canon," 191–93); the similar treatment of *AcVer* 20 (Stoops, "Intertextual Context," 68; Thomas, "Canon," 188–89). Stoops moreover ignores my previous treatment of these topics in my 1995 thesis (Christine M. Thomas, "The *Acts of Peter*, the Ancient

Novel, and Early Christian History" [Ph.D. diss., Harvard University, 1995] 66-67 on chaps. 20 and 23).

114. Vouaux notes citations from every New Testament book save the Revelation, the Johannine letters, and the letter of Jude (*Actes de Pierre*, 45). See Philip Sellew, "*Laodiceans* and the Philippians Fragments Hypothesis," *Harvard Theological Review* 87 (1994) 17–28, for a similar example of a second-century document shedding light on the form and use of the text of the emerging New Testament in the second century.

115. The possible allusion to Acts 8:18–19 in AcVer 23 (the Simon episode), treated below, and a possible reference to Rom 16:25 at the end of AcVer 24.

116. For a typology of the uses of gospel materials in the Apocryphal Acts, see François Bovon, "The Synoptic Gospels and the Noncanonical Acts of the Apostles," *HTR* 81 (1988) 19–36. Bovon identifies five usages: selection, elimination, citation, adaptation, and imitation.

117. Reference to Acts 4:10, 12 can also be found in chap. 17; Acts 4:12 is cited in *AcPaul* 7 (Julian V. Hills, "The Acts of the Apostles in the *Acts of Paul*," in *Society of Biblical Literature Seminar Papers* [Atlanta: Scholars Press, 1994] 24–54, esp. 47–48).

118. Vouaux suggests that *procuratio* may be a translation of οἰκονομία, meaning the divine economy of salvation (*Actes de Pierre*, 272 n.1 ad loc.).

119. Reading *uolens omne scandalum et omnem ign‹o›rantiam* [MS ignarantiam] *et omnem inergaemam diaboli, initia et uires infirm‹are›* [MS infirmes] *quibus pr‹ae›ualebat* [MS proualebat] *olim* (Lipsius 53.19–30). The sentence is corrupt. Lipsius suggests this reading, or *uires infirmes dissoluere*, since the *uolens* is best completed by an infinitive. Usener suggests reading *dolens* (cited in Lipsius). Turner reads *uolens tollere*, which yields a good sense ("Latin Acts," 123). I prefer to follow Lipsius, since, at many other points in the manuscript, the scribe mistakenly substitutes a related word in the incorrect part of speech (53.19–30).

120. MS reads *ambulaui*, "I walked." Although the episode of Peter walking on the water is recounted at length later (chap. 10), the emphasis in this passage is on Christ's miraculous deeds, so the third person is more likely.

121. Chapter 7 would seem to be a wholesale interpolation: Peter is addressing those who have believed in Christ in the speech, yet the frame narrative mentions that he is surrounded merely by a large crowd in Rome; Peter begins speaking in chapter 7, and is only informed in chapter 8 of the true situation at Rome (the Ariston episode in chapter 6 performs this function, but it, too, is an interpolation); Peter has two speeches in quick succession; the introductory phrase for the chapter is repeated at the beginning of the next. The beginning of chapter 8 reads *paenitentes autem fratres rogabant Petrum, ut expugnaret Simonem* (Lipsius 54.31–32); the beginning of chapter 9, *rogabant autem fratres Petrum ut conmitteret se cum Simonem* (Lipsius 56.20–21).

122. Lipsius transposes this sentence to the end of the chapter, thinking that it was mistakenly copied in the wrong spot. He attributes the sentence to Simon as direct speech and substitutes *praestabo* for *praestare*. Vouaux (*Actes de Pierre*, 368–69, n. 4 ad loc.) and Turner ("Latin Acts,"129) independently argue that this phrase is in fact found in the LXX of Isa 7:13 and should stand in its place; Vouaux suggests that it was probably included here by the author, not because it made any particular sense in the argument, but because it referred to an ἀγών.

123. At least in the case of the *Actus Vercellenses*, one would need to revise the statement of François Bovon and Éric Junod that most of the Apocryphal Acts, including "perhaps" the *Acts of Peter*, refer to no external literary corpus, in contrast to the rest of Christian literature, which they view as a literature of reference ("Reading the Apocryphal Acts of the Apostles," *Semeia* 38 [1986] 161–71, see esp. 171); in this speech, the reference to prophetic writings is explicit. They are some of the same specific citations that one finds in the synoptic gospels, and they appear at an early level of the *Acts of Peter*.

124. Psalm 118:2 in Mark 12:10–11 and parallels; Dan 7:13 in Mark 13:26, 14:62, and parallels.

125. *de profeticas scribturas et quae dominus noster Iesus Christus egisset et verbo et factis* (Lipsius 61.8–10).

126. See Stoops, "Departing."

127. This would, incidentally, cohere well with the external attestation of the Acts of the Apostles in other sources. It begins to be cited with frequency by Clement of Alexandria, Irenaeus, and Tertullian. See ad loc. in Centre d'Analyse et de Documentation Patristiques, *Biblia patristica: Index de citations et allusions bibliques dans la littérature patristique* (Paris: Éditions du Centre National de la Recherche Scientifique, 1986) vol. 1.

128. Elsewhere in the *Actus Vercellenses*, Peter himself is a Jew, as is Simon Magos (chaps. 6, Lipsius 51.27; and chap. 22, Lipsius 70.1).

129. *uidetis enim . . . eum exfugasse a Iudaea propter inposturas quas fecit Eubulae, honestae feminae et simplicissim‹a›e* [Vouaux; MS *simplicissime*], *magica arte faciens. unde effugatus a me hu{n}c venit, putans quoniam posset latere inter uos: et ecce stat in comminus. dic Simon, non tu Hierosolymis procidisti ad pedes mihi et Paulo, uidens per manus nostras remedia quae facta sunt, dicens: "Rogo uos, accipite a me mercedem quantum uultis, ut possim manum inponere et tales uirtutes facere"* (Lipsius 71.9–17).

130. As noted above, the "Syriac History of Peter" reads, "Did you not fall at my feet and at those of the other apostles in Jerusalem?"

131. As noted by Stoops, "Departing."

132. Christopher R. Matthews, "The *Acts of Peter* and Luke's Intertextual Heritage," *Semeia* 80 (1997 [1999]) 207–22. See also an earlier version of the argument in idem, "Philip and Simon, Luke and Peter: A Lukan Sequel and Its Intertextual Success," in Eugene H. Lovering Jr., ed., *Society of Biblical Literature 1992 Seminar Papers* (Atlanta: Scholars Press, 1992) 133–45.

133. See Chapter Three.

134. Matthews, "Heritage," 208–14.

135. Simon, in the *Apophasis Megale* cited in Hippolytos (*Refutatio* 6.9–18) is said to have called himself merely the "Great Power." This text is, however, neither a particularly early nor direct source on Simon Magos. Josef Frickel's investigation has shown that Hippolytos was not quoting the *Apophasis Megale* itself, but rather a paraphrase, a Simonian work that philosophizes the contents of the document it paraphrases (*Die Apophasis Megale in Hippolyt's Refutatio [VI, 9–18]: Eine Paraphrase zur Apophasis Simons* [Orientalia Christiana analecta 182; Rome: Pont. institutum orientalium studiorum, 1968]).

136. Matthews, "Philip and Simon," 136.

137. Matthews, "Heritage," 214–19.

138. The *Didascalia Apostolorum* also locate Simon in Jerusalem, not Samaria (6.7–9). This work knows of Simon's trip to Rome and his failed attempt to fly over the city.

139. A "multiform" is one of the variant versions resulting from multiple oral performances of a narrative. It is described and employed in Albert Lord, *The Singer of Tales* (Harvard Studies in Comparative Literature 24; Cambridge: Harvard University Press, 1960) passim.

140. Poupon, "Remaniement," 4370.

141. καὶ γάρ τινας τῶν πρὸς χεῖρα αὐτοῦ ὁ Πέτρος μαθητεύσας ἀποστῆναι αὐτοὺς ἐποίησεν . . . ἐζήτει γὰρ πάντας τοὺς ὑπὸ τοῦ Πέτρου μαθητευθέντας ἀδελφοὺς ἀπολέσαι (Lipsius 100.18–102.1).

142. ΠΡΑΞΕΙΣ ΠΑΥΛΟΥ: *Acta Pauli nach dem Papyrus der Hamburger Staats- und Universitäts-Bibliothek* (Glückstadt/Hamburg: Augustin, 1936).

143. On the ramifications of the manuscript, see Carl Schmidt, "Zur Datierung der alten Petrusakten," *Zeitschrift für die neutestamentliche Wissenschaft* 29 (1930) 150–55.

144. Text in Schmidt, ΠΡΑΞΕΙΣ ΠΑΥΛΟΥ, 50–55.

145. In the Hamburg papyrus, Jesus' statement that he is to be crucified anew, and Paul's response to it, do not even appear in the text, but are written at the bottom of the page; their

point of insertion is indicated in the text by a P (Schmidt, *ΠΡΑΞΕΙΣ ΠΑΥΛΟΥ*, 54.39-40). These lines clearly appeared in the ancient *Acts of Paul*–they are not a later insertion–for Origen knew them, and the scribal error is easy to explain; but it is interesting to note that, with these two lines absent, nothing whatsoever in the remaining account is reminiscent of the *quo vadis* scene in the *Actus Vercellenses*.

146. Dennis R. MacDonald, "Which Came First? Intertextual Relationships Among the Apocryphal Acts of the Apostles," *Semeia* 80 (1997 [1999]) 11-41, esp. 13-24. See also idem, "*The Acts of Paul* and *The Acts of Peter*: Which Came First?" in Eugene H. Lovering Jr., ed., *Society of Biblical Literature 1992 Seminar Papers* (Atlanta: Scholars Press, 1992) 214-24. MacDonald also presents the martyrdom account as evidence of the dependent relationship. He is right that the martyrdom account and first three chapters of the *Acts of Peter* depend on the *Acts of Paul*: the introduction of Nero in *AcVer* 41 is especially suspect. But if chapters 1-3 and 41 are secondary additions to the *Acts of Peter*, this cannot be evidence for the relationship between the rest of the *Acts of Peter* and the *Acts of Paul*. MacDonald also argues that the attribution of Peter's death to the jilted husbands Agrippa and Albinus is a secondary motif borrowed from elsewhere in the *Acts of Paul* to avoid the anti-Roman sentiment of attributing Peter's death to Nero. But this ignores the fact that Nero's appearance in the *Acts of Peter* ruptures its chronology and is thus secondary; and the fact that Agrippa and Albinus are based on first-century characters and are thus early elements in the development of the narrative. See Chapter Three below.

147. "Intertextual Relationships," 14-18.

148. "Intertextual Relationships," 17.

149. And elsewhere. See Christian Grappe, "Du témoin pleutre de la Passion au martyr: images de Pierre aux deux premiers siècles," *Cahiers de Biblia Patristica* 3 (1991) 53-106; idem, *Images de Pierre aux deux premiers siècles* (Études d'histoire et de philosophie religieuses 75; Paris: Presses universitaires de France, 1995) 49-81.

150. As noted in Thomas, "Acts of Peter" 121-22, see esp. n. 6; idem, "The 'Prehistory' of the *Acts of Peter*," in Bovon, *Apocryphal Acts* 39-62, esp. 60. Robert Stoops makes the same point without citing these earlier sources but additionally notes that Peter's attitude in the *quo vadis* scene forms a good parallel with the attitude of Polycarp in the *Martyrdom of Polycarp* ("Intertextual Context," 79).

151. I have treated MacDonald's arguments briefly here to avoid a lengthy detour. For a more thorough treatment, see Stoops ("Intertextual Context," 73-81), who responds concisely and judiciously to MacDonald. Stoops also rightly emphasizes the great difference in the relationship of the *Acts of Paul* and the *Acts of Peter* to the surrounding "text" of the culture: the *Acts of Peter* are accommodationist, the *Acts of Paul* confrontative (81-83). See also Willy Rordorf, who finds MacDonald's arguments about the priority of the *quo vadis* account in the *Acts of Paul* convincing, but does not believe they settle the issue of the interdependence of the two texts because of the presence of oral tradition and because of the subsequent redaction of the *Acts of Peter* ("The Relation Between the *Acts of Peter* and the *Acts of Paul*: State of the Question," in Bremmer, *Acts of Peter*, 178-91).

Chapter 3

1. The *Acts of Peter* also underwent a similar development in Syriac tradition; since these two corpora developed independently of one another, the Syriac texts have not been included in the present study. See J. Flamion, "Les actes apocryphes de Pierre," *Revue d'histoire ecclésiastique* 12 (1911) 209-30, 437-50, esp. 215-21. The texts are edited in the first volume of Paulus Bedjan, *Acta martyrum et sanctorum Syriace* (1890-97; 7 vols.; Hildesheim: G. Olms, 1968) 1.30-33. See also F. Nau, "La version syriaque inédite des martyres de S. Pierre, S. Paul, et S.

Luc d'après un manuscrit du dixième siècle," *Revue de l'orient chrétien* 13 (1898) 39–57, 151–67, esp. 43–50.

2. Hypothesis put forth by Richard Adelbert Lipsius (*Die apokryphen Apostelgeschichten und Apostellegenden: Ein Beitrag zur altchristlichen Literaturgeschichte* [3 parts in 2 vols.; Braunschweig: C. A. Schwetschke und Sohn, 1883–87] 2.1.109–35), but universally rejected by later scholars.

3. Flamion argues that Linus depends on Pseudo-Hegesippos, which requires at least a very late-fourth-century date for the former ("Actes de Pierre [1910]," 18–28). Gérard Poupon rejects this, postulating a common source ("La Passion de S. Pierre Apôtre," Magister diss., Université de Genève, 1975, 5–7). His chief reason for so doing is that Pseudo-Hegesippos seems to be an epitome.

4. Flamion provides a thorough investigation of these texts into the early middle ages in the east and west. His study comprises both narrative reworkings and patristic citations and is chiefly church-political in orientation, showing which parts of the narrative were being used as normative texts in which locations and times ("Les actes apocryphes de Pierre," *Revue d'histoire ecclésiastique* 11 [1910] 5–28, 223–56, 447–70, 675–92; 12 [1911] 209–30, 437–50). Jean-Daniel Kaestli and Éric Junod provide a similar study for the Acts of John (*L'histoire des Actes apocryphes des apôtres du IIIe au IXe siècle: le cas des Actes de Jean* [Cahiers de la Revue de théologie et de philosophie 7; Geneva/ Lausanne/ Neuchâtel: La Concorde, 1982]).

5. See Christian Grappe, *Images de Pierre aux deux premiers siècles* (Études d'histoire et de philosophie religieuses 75; Paris: Presses universitaires de France, 1995); also Oscar Cullmann, *Peter: Disciple, Apostle, Martyr: A Historical and Theological Study* (2d ed.; Philadelphia: Westminster, 1962) 79–131. Daniel O'Connor combines the literary and archaeological record (*Peter in Rome, the Literary, Liturgical and Archaeological Evidence* [New York: Columbia University Press, 1969]).

6. For an overview of scholarship on the question, see F. Stanley Jones, "The Pseudo-Clementines: A History of Research," *The Second Century* 2 (1982) 1–33, 63–96.

7. See Wilhelm Schneemelcher, ed., *New Testament Apocrypha* (5th German ed.; 1989; ed. R. McL. Wilson; Louisville, Ky.: John Knox, 1992) 2.20–21. More extensive in idem, *New Testament Apocrypha* (3d ed.; ed. R. McL. Wilson; Philadelphia: Westminster, 1965) 2.45–50.

8. Text in Richard Adalbert Lipsius, ed., *Acta Apostolorum Apocrypha* (Leipzig: Hermann Mendelssohn, 1891) 1.1–22; and also in A. H. Salonius, "Martyrium beati Petri Apostoli a Lino episcopo conscriptum," in *Commentationes Humanarum Litterarum* (Helsinki: Societas Scientiarum Fennica; Leipzig: Harrasowitz, 1922-27) 1.22-58; and Gérard Poupon, "La Passion de S. Pierre Apôtre," Magister diss., Université de Genève, 1975. Except where noted, I cite Lipsius's text because it is the most widely available. Although the text does not often present serious problems, I have noted the occasional passages where Salonius or Poupon improves on Lipsius.

9. On this and other issues, see Lipsius, *Apostelgeschichten* 2.1.109–42.

10. Argued by Poupon, "Passion," 4–5.

11. Lipsius, *Apostelgeschichten*, 117.

12. Poupon, "Passion," 9–10, 25–32.

13. Poupon believes that this episode is a later interpolation ("Passion," v–vi).

14. Text in Vincent Ussani, *Hegesippi qui dicitur historiae libri V* (CSEL 66; Vienna/ Leipzig: Hoelder-Pichler-Tempsky/ Akademische Verlagsgesellschaft, 1932) 1.183–87.

15. This version is published as πράξεις τῶν ἁγίων ἀποστόλων Πέτρου καὶ Παύλου, Lipsius, *Acta*, 1.178–222. Gaudomelete probably refers to an island more generally known as Gaudos, Kaudos, or Klauda, a treeless island due south of southwest Crete with no true harbor. It was inhabited from post-Minoan times throughout antiquity, and was a bishopric in the middle ages. Paul lands on this island (Κλαῦδα) in Acts 27:16–17 when he is blown off course from Crete on his way to Rome (νησίον δέ τι ὑποδραμόντες καλούμενον Κλαῦδα; some MSS read

Καῦδα), and this explains why he arrives at Rome from that location in the Byzantine Greek Marcellus tradition.

16. Text in Lipsius, *Acta*, 1.118–77, as Μαρτύριον τῶν ἁγίων ἀποστόλων Πέτρου καὶ Παύλου / *Passio sanctorum apostolorum Petri et Pauli*.

17. The continence motif does appear in the Marcellus text: Peter convinces Livia and Agrippina to abstain from sexual relations with their husbands (*Marcellus* 10). But this is not the motive for Peter's martyrdom, as it is in the *Actus Vercellenses*.

18. Text in Hans Achelis, *Acta SS. Nerei et Achillei: Text und Untersuchung* (TU 11.2; Leipzig: J. C. Hinrichs, 1893).

19. *Comes* is a title, "count."

20. Cf. Boris Ejxenbaum, "The Theory of the Formal Method," in Ladislav Matejka and Krystyna Pomorska, eds., *Readings in Russian Poetics: Formalist and Structuralist Views* (Cambridge, Mass.: MIT Press, 1971) 3–37, esp. 20–21.

21. I am using these terms as they are generally used in literary-critical handbooks and dictionaries, cf. Gerald Prince, *A Dictionary of Narratology* (Lincoln: University of Nebraska Press, 1987), *s.v.* "fabula," "sjuzhet," 30, 87.

22. Mieke Bal adds this third category of "text" to the two already described by the Russian Formalists (*Narratology: Introduction to the Theory of Narrative*, trans. Christine van Boheemen [Toronto: University of Toronto Press, 1985] 5–8 for basic distinctions among the three categories, 119–150 on the topic of "text").

23. "Narrative Strategies and Synoptic Quandaries: A Response to Dennis MacDonald's Reading of *Acts of Paul* and *Acts of Peter*," in Eugene H. Lovering Jr., ed., *Society of Biblical Literature 1992 Seminar Papers* (Atlanta: Scholars Press, 1992) 234–39.

24. On Peter's martyrdom, see *Scorpiace* 15. Tertullian shows knowledge of the *Acts of Paul* in *de baptismo* 17.

25. The parallelism of Marcellus to Peter is emphasized throughout the *AcVer*. Marcellus works his miracle immediately after Peter causes a dog to speak and drives a demon out of a man; Marcellus' vision in chap. 22 follows Peter's vision of the contest in chap. 16. Although chap. 10 most likely belongs to the late-second-century redaction, the motif of shaky faith seems to have been a theme in the *Acts of Peter* even before the controversy about lapsed Christians (*pace* Gérard Poupon). The famous *quo vadis* narrative (*AcVer* 35), which has a variant version in the *Acts of Paul*, illustrates precisely this; Peter begins to flee the persecution that awaits him at Rome, following the advice of his Christian friends, but Jesus meets him on his way out of the city and incites him to turn back. See Christian Grappe, *Images de Pierre aux deux premiers siècles* (Études d'histoire et de philosophie religieuses 75; Paris: Presses universitaires de France, 1995) 49–81.

26. *te autem Petrum hic Simon infidelem dixit, in aquas dubitantem. . . . ergo si uos quibus et manus inposuit, quos et elegit, cum quibus et mirabilia fecit, dubitabatis, habens ergo hoc testimonium paeniteor, et ad praeces tuas confugio. suscipias animam meam* (Lipsius 58.3–4, 6–9).

27. This image manages to be racist, sexist, and classist all at once: the woman is said to "look like an Ethiopian, not an Egyptian, completely black" (*in aspectu Ethiopiss{im}am, neque Aegyptiam, sed totam negram*) and to be "wrapped in filthy rags" (*sordidis* [MS *sordibus*] *pannis inuolutam, AcVer* 22; Lipsius 70.8–11).

28. The reading is corrupt here. The text reads *omnes uiri Simoni et dei ipsius haec est*, which makes no sense. Lipsius suggests *omnes vires*, "all the powers of Simon" or *omnis virtus*, "all of Simon's excellence." Léon Vouaux reads the latter (*Les Actes de Pierre* [Paris: Letouzey et Ané, 1922] 358 ad loc.). I find it equally easy, on paleographic grounds, to read *omnis vis Simoni*, "all of Simon's power," as a reference to Simon's traditional title δύναμις μεγάλη. If this reading holds, it would be one instance in which the *AcVer* are not dependent on Luke's Acts for their designation of Simon. Christopher Matthews has argued that, in other locations, the appella-

tion of Simon as the "great power of God" is dependent upon Luke, who added "of God" to the traditional title, "great power" ("Philip and Simon, Luke and Peter: A Lukan Sequel and Its Intertextual Success," in Eugene H. Lovering Jr., ed., *Society of Biblical Literature 1992 Seminar Papers* [Atlanta: Scholars Press, 1992] 133–45, esp. 135–37; "The Acts of Peter and Luke's Intertextual Heritage," *Semeia* 80 [1997 (1999)] 207–22, esp. 210–12). Perhaps this older title was misunderstood by the scribe of the *AcVer*, thus giving rise to the corrupt reading in this passage.

29. *Tanta‹m› substantia‹m› inpendi tanto tempore, superuacuo credens in d‹e›i notitiam me erogare!* (Lipsius 55.14–16).

30. *si enim ille uersatus non fuisset, nec nos remoti fuissemus a sancta fide* (Lipsius 55.12–13).

31. Gerhard Ficker, *Die Petrusakten: Beiträge zu ihrem Verständnis* (Leipzig: Barth, 1903) 38–39, 43–44. On M. Granius Marcellus, see *Prosopographia Imperii Romani*[2] G 211. Marcellus was proconsular governor of Bithynia in 14–15 C.E.

32. Translation modified from Michael Grant, ed., *Tacitus: The Annals of Imperial Rome*, rev. ed. (New York: Penguin, 1971) 74–75.

33. *Nec multo post Granium Marcellum praetorem Bithyniae quaestor ipsius Cäepio Crispinus maiestatis postulavit subscribente Romanio Hispone. . . . Marcellum insimulabat sinistros de Tiberio sermones habuisse, inevitabile crimen. . . . addidit Hispo statuam Marcelli altius quam Caesarum sitam, et alia in statua amputato capite Augusti effigiem Tiberii inditam. . . . [Tiberius]. . . . tulit absolvi reum criminibus maiestatis. de pecuniis repetundis ad reciperatores itum est.* Text in Heinrich Heubner, ed., *P. Cornelii Taciti libri qui supersunt* (Stuttgart: Teubner, 1983) 1.43–44.

34. *cui imperator dixit: 'Ab omni officio te abstineo, ne prouincias expolians Christianis conferas.' cui Marcellus respondit: 'Et mea omnia tua sunt.' cui dixit Caesar: 'Mea essent, si mihi ea{m} custodires; nunc autem, {quia} non sunt mea, ‹quia› cui uis ea dona‹s›* [Lipsius; MS dona] *et hoc nescio quibus infimis'* (Lipsius 55.5–10). Turner suggests the transposition of *quia*, which yields a better sense ("The Latin Acts of Peter," *Journal of Theological Studies* 32 [1931] 119–33; see esp. 124). The other reading leads to a more "Christianized" understanding, which unfortunately misses the point of this *chreia*: "because they are not mine, you give them to whomever you please."

35. In ancient rhetorical theory, this dialogue would be categorized as a *chreia*, a pithy saying encased within a short narrative or dialogue. See Ronald F. Hock and Edward N. O'Neil, eds., *The Chreia in Ancient Rhetoric. Volume 1: The Progymnasmata*, Society of Biblical Literature Texts and Translations 27 (Atlanta: Scholars Press, 1986) 3–9, 23–47.

36. Noted also by Vouaux, *Actes de Pierre*, 108–9.

37. The crowning insult is that Marcellus's house, which was once a Christian refuge, is now offered to Simon as part of the relationship of ξενία between them.

38. *erat enim statua Caesaris* (Lipsius 59.9). See a similar account in the biography of Apollonius of Tyana (4.20) by Philostratos the sophist (Flavius [b. ca. 170], to be distinguished from Philostratos Lemnius [b. ca. 191], his son-in-law, perhaps author of the first Εἰκόνες, and Philostratos the Younger, grandson of Lemnius, author of the second Εἰκόνες).

39. The *curiosi* were intelligence officals of the Roman emperor, *agentes in rebus*. After 359 C.E., they reported directly to the emperor and became feared as spies. See Chapter Two.

40. *si enim hoc innotuerit Caesari per aliquem de curiosis, magnis poenis nos adfliget* (Lipsius 59.11–12).

41. In Tacitus, the Marcellus episode takes place six years after Varus's defeat in the Teutoburg forest (9 C.E.; *Annals* 1.62).

42. Jack Goody and Ian Watt, "The Consequences of Literacy," in Jack Goody, ed., *Literacy in Traditional Societies* (Cambridge: Cambridge University Press, 1968) 27–68, esp. 28–34.

43. Recognized by William M. Ramsay, *The Church in the Roman Empire before A.D. 170* (London: Hodder and Stoughton, 1893) 382–89; see Dennis Ronald MacDonald, *The Legend*

*and the Apostle: The Battle for Paul in Story and Canon* (Philadelphia: Westminster, 1983) 20–21. Ramsay provides a useful collection of the historical evidence, though he downplays the divergences between this and the presentation in the *Acts of Paul*. See more recently David Magie, *Roman Rule in Asia Minor to the End of the Third Century*, 2 vols. (Princeton: Princeton University Press, 1950) 1.513, 2.1368 n. 51.

44. See *Prosopographia Imperii Romani*[2] A 900.

45. *Prosopographia Imperii Romani*[2] B 199. If this person is the same as the one mentioned in chapter 3, the *Actus Vercellenses* is mistaken in calling him an *eques*, since he would have to be of senatorial rank to hold this office.

46. . . . *qui [Simon] me tantum suasit ut statuam illi ponerem, suscribtion‹e›* [Lipsius; MS *suscribtioni*] *tali: 'Simoni iuueni deo'* (Lipsius 57.24–25).

47. *Inscriptiones Latinae Selectae* 3474. See Carl Erbes, "Petrus nicht in Rom, sondern in Jerusalem gestorben," *Zeitschrift für Kirchengeschichte* 22 (1901) 1–47, 161–224, see esp. 12.

48. Erbes describes the absence of early Roman traditions about Peter's activity in Rome ("Petrus," 1–47).

49. Fragment cited by Clement of Alexandria, *Stromateis* 6.5.43.

50. Cited in Eusebios, *Ecclesiastical History* 5.18.14. Jerome (*de viris illustribus* 40) relates that Tertullian added a seventh book to his already published (lost) work in six books, "On Ecstasy," in which he refutes the work written by Apollonios. The first version of "On Ecstasy" probably dates to around 207–8 C.E., so Tertullian must have read the work of Apollonios shortly thereafter.

51. Eusebios also believes that Peter came to Rome under Claudius, to combat Simon (*Ecclesiastical History* 2.14.6).

52. The first three chapters of the *Actus Vercellenses*, which tell of Paul's departure to Spain from Rome before Peter's arrival, are probably a later addition, as has been argued in Chapter Two. These three chapters assume that Paul is to return within a year, to be martyred shortly after his return to Rome. He, too, is expected to die under the reign of Nero: *‹urgebant› autem fratres Paulum . . . ut annum plus non abesset. . . . Et cum diu lacrimantes rogarent eum, sonus de caelis factus est . . . dicens: Paulus . . . inter manus Neronis hominis impii et iniqui sub oculis uestris consummabitur* (AcVer 1; Lipsius 46.1–9; MS reads *lucebant*).

53. Ὁ δὲ Νέρων γνοὺς ὕστερον τὸν Πέτρον ἀπηλλαγμένον τοῦ βίου, ἐμέμψατο τῷ πραιφέκτῳ Ἀγρίππᾳ, ὅτι μὴ μετὰ γνώμης αὐτοῦ ἀνῃρέθη. ἐβούλετο γὰρ αὐτὸν περισσοτέρᾳ κολάσει καὶ μεῖζον τιμωρήσασθαι (Lipsius 100.15–18).

*Imperator uero postquam scibit Petrum mortuum, arguit Agrippam praefectum quod sine consilio suo fecisset. uolebat enim Petrum uariis cruciatibus perdere* (Lipsius 101.9–11).

54. *Scorpiace* 15.

55. Μετὰ δὲ ταῦτα ὤφθη ὁ κύριος τῷ ἀποστόλῳ Πέτρῳ ἐν ὁράματι λέγων· Νέρων καὶ Σίμων πλήρεις δαιμόνων ὑπάρχοντες κατὰ σοῦ μελετῶσιν (Achelis 13.22–24).

56. *querebatur enim se ipsius praestigiis desolatum Symone suae salutis praesule, et dolebat pro tanti amici casu qui sibi et reipublicae* (Linus 17; Lipsius 22.1–3).

57. *Domine, quo uis abscede, quia imperatorem oblitum tui iam credimus. sed iste iniquissimus Agrippa pelicum amore et intemperantia suae libidinis inflammatus perdere te festinat* (Lipsius 6.22–24).

58. AcVer 22: *Senator sum generis mag‹n›i* (MS *magi*; Lipsius 70.14); see also AcVer 8.

59. *Marcello . . . Marci praefecti filio* (Linus 3; Lipsius 4.20–21).

60. The *Actus Vercellenses* describe him as *clarissimus vir*, that is, of senatorial class (AcVer 34; Lipsius 87.1–2); the Linus text escalates his social standing to *Caesaris amicissimus* (Linus 3; Lipsius 4.1).

61. The office that is indicated for Agrippa in the *AcVer* is that of *praefectus urbis*, the official in charge of public order in the city of Rome, who, during the high empire, had the authority to try civil and criminal cases and could execute criminals guilty of public disturbance or

capital crimes. This is the role played by Agrippa: the prefect supervises the public competition between Simon Magos and Peter in the *Forum Iulium* (*AcVer* 25, 29) and is the person before whom Peter's case, involving charges of civic disorder, is heard (*AcVer* 36). The Linus text specifies that Agrippa is the *praefectus urbis* (*Linus* 8; Lipsius 9.10) and notes that he was accompanied by lictors (*Linus* 8), which is accurate: this official had six at his disposal. The office was usually held by a senator who had been consul, for an unspecified period of time that was at the discretion of the emperor. See E. Sachers, "Praefectus urbis," in *Pauly's Real-Encyclopädie der classischen Altertumswissenschaft* 22 (1953) 2502-34.

62. Τί οὖν περιμένεις, Ἀγρίππα; εὕρωμεν αὐτὸν, καὶ ὡς περίεργον ἄνδρα ἀνέλωμεν ὅπως ἔξωμεν ἡμῶν τὰς γυναῖκας, ἵνα κἀκείνους ἐκδικήσωμεν τοὺς μὴ δυναμένους αὐτὸν ἀνελεῖν, ὧν καὶ αὐτῶν ἀπέστησεν τὰς γυναῖκας (Lipsius 86.16-19).

63. *Unde factum est ut . . . consiliaretur quatinus una cum Agrippae manu uelut auem laqueo Petrum caperet et ut maleficum pessumdaret* (Lipsius 4.13-18).

64. This is an important allusion to the trial of Socrates, whose Apology formed a generic model for second-century apologetic and martyrological texts.

65. Τίς σοι ἐπέτρεψεν τοιοῦτον πρᾶγμα ποιῆσαι δεινόν; (Lipsius 166.18-19).

66. κινάρας σιδηρᾶς or *cardis ferreis*. The phrase is quizzical. The primary meaning of κινάρα is "artichokes." Lampe recognizes that this could not be the correct translation in this passage and suggests "rod" (G. W. H. Lampe, *A Patristic Greek Lexicon*, 5 vols. [Oxford: Clarendon, 1961-68] *s.v.* "κινάρα"). This cannot be correct, however, for the meaning is not derived from any of the root meanings of the word; since Lampe cites only the passages in the Marcellus text, he is probably devising something to suit the context. The Latin translation offers a clue: "thistle, nettle" is a primary meaning of *cardus*. Greek literature attests ἄκανθα κυνάρα and κύναρος ἄκανθα (LSJ, *s.v.* κινάρα). Since ἄκανθα means "thistle, thorny plant" it is likely that a κινάρα could be a spiky plant that resembles an artichoke in its many points. The Latin text understood—with good justification—κινάρα to mean "nettle," so what is probably meant are iron devices with sharp points to tear the flesh.

67. Ἱερώτατε βασιλεῦ, οὐχ ἁρμόζει εἰς τούτους ὃ ἐκέλευσας, ἐπειδὴ ὁ Παῦλος ἀθῷος φαίνεται παρὰ τὸν Πέτρον. . . . δίκαιόν ἐστιν ἀποτμηθῆναι τοῦ Παύλου τὴν κεφαλήν, τὸν δὲ Πέτρον ἐπὶ σταυροῦ ἀρθῆναι ὡς αἴτιον τοῦ φόνου (Lipsius 168.9-14).

68. Nero's wives were actually Octavia, Poppaea Sabina, and Statilia Messalina (the latter mentioned in *Annals* 15.68, though Tacitus's account breaks off before her wedding to Nero; also found in Suetonius, *Nero* 35 and on coins).

69. ὥστε καὶ περιελεῖν ἑαυτὰς ἀπὸ τῆς τῶν ἰδίων ἀνδρῶν πλευρᾶς.

70. *Nero . . . dolens tanti casu amici . . . indignatus quarere coepit causas, quibus Petrum occideret* (Lipsius 128.16-18).

71. *Nereus and Achilleus* do not narrate the arrest and execution.

72. This location is mentioned in *AcVer* 15 (Lipsius 62.8).

73. *Quid dicis, Petre? ecce puer mortuus iacet, quem et imperator libenter habet, et non illi peperci. utique habebam alios conplures iuuenes; sed confidens in te et in dominum tuum quem predicas, si uere certi et ueri estis: ideo hunc uolui mori* (Lipsius 73.21-25). The Greek vellum fragment (P. Oxy. 849) covers this part of the text, but has a lacuna, so I do not reproduce it here.

74. When Agrippa I died in 44 C.E., Claudius brought Judea under the direct control of Rome through a series of procurators.

75. E.g., Tacitus, *Annals* 12.23, 13.7.

76. E.g., Miriam T. Griffin, *Nero: The End of a Dynasty* (London: B. T. Batsford, 1984) 101.

77. Ἰδὼν δὲ ὅτι ἀρεστόν ἐστιν τοῖς Ἰουδαίοις, προσέθετο συλλαβεῖν καὶ Πέτρον, —ἦσαν δὲ ἡμέραι τῶν ἀζύμων—ὃν καὶ πιάσας ἔθετο εἰς φυλακὴν παραδοὺς τέσσαρσιν τετραδίοις στρατιωτῶν φυλάσσειν αὐτόν, βουλόμενος μετὰ τὸ πάσχα ἀναγαγεῖν αὐτὸν τῷ λαῷ.

78. The *Actus Vercellenses* have a lacuna at this point.

79. *ut praefectura carens priuatus et contemptus domo propria degeret* (*Linus* 17; Lipsius 22.5–6). Here I am preferring Lipsius's reading to that of Salonius and Poupon, who follow other mss in reading *privatus et contentus domo propria degeret*; the context of being deprived of office does not seem to indicate happy contentment.

80. As noted by Erbes, "Petrus," 187.

81. Erbes cites them as evidence that Peter died in Jerusalem ("Petrus," 185–88), but he also bases his case on other data, as well as on the lack of strong early traditions about Peter in Roman authors.

82. Tacitus, *Annals* 2.58.2–3, 2.59.1. For his career, see Hans-Georg Pflaum, *Les Carrières procuratoriennes équestres sous les Haut-Empire romain*, 4 vols. (Paris: Paul Geuthner, 1960), vol. 1, no. 33.

83. Erbes, "Petrus," 183–86.

84. Lipsius 1.177.

85. *Marcello nihilominus, Marci praefecti filio, qui postquam Symonis magi pestiferam doctrinam auerterat, apostolo fideliter et utiliter in cunctis adhaeserat . . . innotuit* (Lipsius 4.20–5.2).

86. Καὶ αὐτοὶ ἅμα Μαρκέλλῳ ἀνδρὶ ἰλλυστρίῳ, ὅστις καὶ πεπίστευκε Πέτρῳ καταλιπὼν τὸν Σίμωνα, ἦραν τὸ σῶμα αὐτοῦ (Lipsius 172.10–12).

87. Hans Achelis notes that this is a Byzantine touch; the poem of Damasus mentioning them designates them as Praetorian guards (Achelis, *Acta SS. Nerei et Achillei: Text und Untersuchung* [TU 11.2; Leipzig: J. C. Hinrichs, 1893] 44). As Achelis demonstrates, *Nereus and Achilleus* shows a detailed knowledge of Roman topography and was doubtless written there.

88. Καὶ τίς ἐστιν ὁ τοῦτον μὴ γινώσκων. . .Ὁ τοιούτῳ προσώπῳ μὴ πιστεύων μέγας ἄφρων τυγχάνει.

89. ἐν ᾧ τόπῳ ὁ Σίμων τῷ Πέτρῳ διεμάχετο.

90. See Achelis, *Acta*, 66–68.

91. The sarcophagus has been lost since the sixteenth century, but the inscription was recorded: *Aur. Petronillae filiae dulcissimae* (*Corpus Inscriptionum Latinarum* VI 13367). See Achelis, *Acta*, 40–42.

92. Parts of this section were presented as a conference paper on 29 December 1994 at the American Philological Association Annual Meeting: "Renegotiating the Past: Fixity and Fluidity in the *Acts of Peter*."

93. πολλαὶ δὲ καὶ ἄλλαι γυναῖκες τοῦ λόγου τῆς ἁγνείας ἐρασθεῖσαι τῶν ἀνδρῶν ἐχωρίζοντο, καὶ ἄνδρες τῶν ἰδίων γυναικῶν τὰς κοίτας ἐχώριζον . . . θορύβου οὖν μεγίστου ὄντος ἐν τῇ Ῥώμῃ (Lipsius 86.8–12).

*multae autem conplures et aliae honestae feminae, audientes uerbum de castitate, recedebant a uiris suis, et uiri a mulieribus . . . tumultu autem non minimo concitato* (Lipsius 87.7–10).

94. *Prosopographia Imperii Romani*[2] L 327. For some comments on this account, see Robert M. Grant, "A Woman of Rome: The Matron in Justin, 2 *Apology* 2.1–9," *Church History* 54 (1985) 461–72. Eusebios cites Justin's account verbatim (*Ecclesiastical History*, 4.17.1–13).

95. It is unclear whether this was actually the case, but the comments of Celsus (*apud* Origen, *Contra Celsum*, 3.55) show that this was the perception in the mid-second century: Celsus claims that children and ignorant women were the target audience of the Christians. In cases where husbands converted, and their wives did not, one would wonder whether the women would be legally or socially likely to prosecute their husbands.

96. Stevan Davies provides a perceptive analysis of the standpoint of the Apocryphal Acts on the role of women and the value of sexual continence, illustrating vividly how it would have come into conflict against the male-dominated ideology of the orthodox. It was, as he portrays it, a revolt of the orders of widows and virgins against the male church hierarchy (*The Revolt of the*

*Widows: The Social World of the Apocryphal Acts* [Carbondale, Ill.: Southern Illinois University Press, 1980] 110–29).

97. On the emphasis on patronage, see Robert F. Stoops, "Patronage in the *Acts of Peter*," *Semeia* 38 (1986) 91–100. In an important article, David Konstan demonstrates that it is not the purpose of the apostles in the Apocryphal Acts to sunder husband-wife relations, but to strengthen them, so long as the couple remain celibate. The Apocryphal Acts are not destroying social bonds as much as placing them in a different context ("Acts of Love: A Narrative Pattern in the Apocryphal Acts," *Journal of Early Christian Studies* 6 [1998] 15–36).

98. *surrexerunt quidam ex senatoribus in conuentu senatus et dixerunt: Suggerimus amplitudini uestrae, nobiles uiri, quod ad peruersionem urbis aeternae Petrus conubia diuortiis mancipat, uxores nostras a nobis disiungit et nescimus quam nobis nouam et inauditam legem inducit* (Lipsius 5.2–7).

99. ὕστερον δὲ εὑρέθη μετὰ Νέρωνος τοῦ καίσαρος . . . . Πονηρὸς δὲ ὁ Νέρων τυγχάνων πονηρὸν φίλον τῇ ἑαυτοῦ φιλίᾳ συνέζευξεν (Achelis 13.18–21).

100. *cui adiumentum uictoriae, subiectiones gentium, uitae longaeuitatem, salutis custodiam feralibus artibus pollicebatur* (Ussani 183.24–184.1).

101. The term points to a provincial origin for the *Acts of Peter*, rather than the city of Rome, since it is frequent in imperial letters to provincial governors and other high officials (Jan Bremmer, "Aspects of the *Acts of Peter*: Women, Magic, Place, and Date," in idem, ed., *The Apocryphal Acts of Peter: Magic, Miracles, and Gnosticism* [Leuven: Peeters, 1998] 1–20, esp. 6).

102. ἐκεῖνος οὖν μαινόμενος καὶ ἐρῶν τῆς Ξαντίππης καὶ θαυμάζων ὅτι οὐδὲ ἐπ᾽ αὐτῆς τῆς κλίνης καθεύδει ἅμα αὐτῷ, ὡς θηρίον ἠγριαίνετο, βουλόμενος τὸν Πέτρον διαχειρίσασθαι (Lipsius 86.4–7).

*ipse autem furiens et amans eam mirabatur, quoniam neque in eodem lecto maneret, et tamquam bestiius* [Lipsius; MS *besteus*] *furiabatur ad eam, quaerens quomodo Petrum perderet* (Lipsius 87.4–7).

103. Virginia Burrus, *Chastity as Autonomy: Women in the Stories of the Apocryphal Acts* (Lewiston, N.Y.: E. Mellen, 1987). The units she examines concern the concubines of Agrippa, and Xanthippe, wife of Albinus, in the *Acts of Peter*; Maximilla in the *Acts of Andrew*; Drusiana in the *Acts of John*; Thekla in the *Acts of Paul and Thekla*; Artemilla and Eubula in the Hamburg Papyrus of the *Acts of Paul*; the bride in the first chapter of the *Acts of Thomas*; and Mygdonia and Tertia in the *Acts of Thomas*.

104. See Stoops, "Patronage," and idem, "Christ as Patron in the *Acts of Peter*," *Semeia* 56 (1991) 143–57.

105. *[Simon] accessit ad lectum defuncti, incantare atque immurmurare dira carmina coepit. uisus est agitare caput qui mortuus erat. Clamor ingens gentilium quod iam uiueret, quod loqueretur cum Simone. . . . tunc sanctus apostolus poposcit silentium et ait: 'si uiuit defunctus, loquatur; si resuscitatus est, surgat, ambulet, fabuletur.'*

106. Τότε ὁ Σίμων τοὺς δαίμονας ἐπικαλεσάμενος τῇ μαγικῇ αὐτοῦ τέχνῃ ἤρξατο ποιεῖσθαι σαλεύεσθαι τοῦ τεθνεῶτος τὸ σῶμα, ὅπερ οἱ ὄχλοι θεασάμενοι ἤρξαντο κράζειν ἐπαίνους τῷ Σίμωνι προσάγοντες, τῷ δὲ Πέτρῳ ἀπώλειαν καταψηφιζόμενοι. Τότε Πέτρος μετὰ βίας ποιήσας αὐτοὺς σιγῆσαι εἶπεν πρὸς τὸν λαόν· Ἐὰν ζῇ, λαλησάτω, περιπατησάτω, μεταλάβῃ τροφῆς καὶ ἀποστραφήτω εἰς τὸν οἶκον αὐτοῦ (Achelis 11.27–12.1).

107. See Christine M. Thomas, "Revivifying Resurrection Accounts: Techniques of Composition and Rewriting in the *Acts of Peter* cc. 25–28," in Jan N. Bremmer, ed., *The Apocryphal Acts of Peter: Magic, Miracles, and Gnosticism* (Leuven: Peeters, 1998) 65–83. I argue that these stories are examples of the elaboration of an elastic base narrative composed of fixed and fluid elements that is developed according to context and redactional interests, arguing for a "fluid conceptualization of intertextual relationships" (82). See also Robert F. Stoops, "The Acts of

*Peter* in Intertextual Context," *Semeia* 80 (1997 [1999]) 57-86, esp. 59-63. Stoops argues similarly to me that the three accounts are literary variations on a base theme conditioned by techniques of expansion and elaboration common in rhetorical composition, but seems to be unaware of my 1998 article, which appeared a year before the Semeia volume (this appeared in fall 1999 despite the printed publication date). He is similarly unaware of my 1995 thesis, in which these three resurrection scenes are described as multiforms, that is, variant compositional elaborations of a base narrative (Christine M. Thomas, "The *Acts of Peter*, the Ancient Novel, and Early Christian History," [Ph.D. diss., Harvard University, 1995] 158-60). He also fails to cite my use of rhetorical elaboration of the *chreia* as an explanation for this multiformity on a written level (Thomas, "Acts of Peter," 113-15). Stoops instead accuses me of being unaware of the very compositional techniques I detail in these earlier studies, while at the same time following my arguments about these compositional techniques closely and without attribution (Stoops, "Intertextual Context," 63 n. 2). This is all the more interesting given the fact that Stoops responded at the 1996 national meeting of the *Society of Biblical Literature* to the paper on which my 1998 article was based (see the note of thanks in Thomas, "Revivifying," 83 n. 34).

108. *Praesentis scripturae intuere et proba tibi gesta. Cum hortulanus quidam habuerit filiam uirginem quae cum una esset patri, petiit orari pro illa ad Petro; qui cum petierit, apostolus rursus ei dicit praestiturum dominum quod aptum esset animae eius. Statim puella iacuit mortua. O digna lucra et deo semper apta effugire carnis audatiam ac mortificare sanguinis gloriam. Sed ille senes diffidus et nesciens quantum sit coelestis gratia, ignorans scilicet beneficia diuina, rogauit Petrum suscitari sibi unicam filiam. Ut autem suscitaretur, non post multos denique dies sicut hodie, inruit homo uinctus fidelis in domum eius senes conmorari perdiditque puellam et ambo nusquam comparuerunt.* Latin text in D. De Bruyne, "Nouveaux fragments des Actes de Pierre, de Paul, de Jean, d'André et de l'Apocalypse d'Élie," *Revue Bénédictine* 25 (1908) 149-60, esp. 151-53; translation modified from Schneemelcher, *Apocrypha*, 2.287.

109. Even Chariton's Kallirhoe seems to be based on a nameless daughter of the Syracusan general Hermokrates, known from Plutarch and Diodorus; see below. Robert Stoops also notes that the identification of the girl as Peter's daughter is probably secondary ("Miracle Stories and Vision Reports in the Acts of Peter," Ph.D. diss., Harvard, 1983, 85). He thinks that the episode of the temporary healing of Peter's daughter is the author's creation, noting the lack of an independent, self-contained story, and the lack of distinctive elements assignable to earlier tradition. He believes that the story of Peter's vision after his daughter's birth and her paralysis on the night of her abduction was traditional, and the episode of her temporary healing was developed in connection to this tradition ("Miracle Stories," 59-60).

110. αὔριον γὰρ ἐγὼ καταλιπὼν ὑμᾶς ἀθεοτάτους καὶ ἀσεβεστάτους, ἀναπτήξομαι πρὸς τὸν θεόν, οὗ ἡ δύναμις ἐγὼ εἰμι ἀσθενήσασα (Lipsius 80.35-36).

*sed crastina die volabo ad dominum cuius ego uirtutem ‹me› noui* (Lipsius 81.31-83.1).

111. Dennis MacDonald similarly argues that two stories listed separately may be different performances of a single story ("From Audita to Legenda: Oral and Written Miracle Stories," *Foundations and Facets Forum* 2 [1986] 15-26, esp. 17-18). The example he has in mind are the stories about Thekla in Antioch and Thekla in Ikonion in the *Acts of Paul*, in both of which Thekla is accused by rejected suitors and faces death at the hands of a Roman official.

112. On the influence of narrative context on multiforms, see Thomas, "Revivifying," 75-83.

113. On the basis of oral traditional techniques, Dennis MacDonald also differentiates between stable and variable features. The stable features, he argues, may be story patterns, motifs, type scenes, themes, and sets of characters; variability results from expansion, elaboration, truncation, pacing, thematic, rhetorical, or formal transformations. Names of people and places may vary from one telling to another ("Audita," 17). In my analysis, however, I recognize that, within some narrative trajectories, certain names do not change and that, though story patterns are fairly stable, causes and motivations are strikingly fluid.

114. John Miles Foley, "*Guslar* and *Aiodos*: What South Slavic Oral Epic Can—and Cannot—Tell Us about Homer," *Abstracts* for the American Philological Association Annual Meeting (Atlanta: Scholars Press, 1995); published without this statement in idem, "*Guslar* and *Aoidos*: Traditional Register in South Slavic and Homeric Epic," *Transactions of the American Philological Association* 126 (1996) 11–41.

### Chapter Four

1. See Otto Bardenhewer, *Geschichte der Altkirchlichen Litteratur*, 5 vols. (Freiburg im Breisgau: Herder, 1902–32) 1.428–32.

2. F. Stanley Jones, "The Pseudo-Clementines: A History of Research," 2 (1982) 1–33, 63–96, esp. 8–14.

3. Parts of this chapter were presented as a conference paper, "Where Is the Text in This Text? Fluidity in the Alexander Romance and the Apocryphal Acts," 24 November 1992, Society of Biblical Literature Annual Meeting, San Francisco.

4. Of the Greek novels, the most papyri have been found for Achilles Tatius: six total, three on scrolls and three on codices, all from the late second through the fourth century. See William H. Willis, "The Robinson-Cologne Papyrus of Achilles Tatius," *Greek, Roman, and Byzantine Studies* 31.1 (1990) 73–102; see esp. 75–76.

5. See Willis, "Achilles Tatius." 79.

6. Ken Dowden, "Pseudo-Callisthenes: The Alexander Romance," in Reardon, ed., *Ancient Greek Novels* (1989) 650–735, esp. 650.

7. A: Wilhelm Kroll, ed., *Historia Alexandri Magni* (Berlin: Weidman, 1926); β: Leif Bergson, ed., *Der griechische Alexanderroman: Rezension β* (Stockholm: Almqvist & Wiksell, 1965); Helmut van Thiel, ed., *Leben und Taten Alexanders von Makedonien: Der griechische Alexanderroman nach der Handschrift L* (Darmstadt: Wissenschaftliche Buchgesellschaft, 1974); λ: Helmut van Thiel, ed., *Die Rezension λ des Pseudo-Kallisthenes* (Bonn: R. Habelt, 1959); ε: Jürgen Trumpf, ed., *Vita Alexandri regis Macedonum* (Stuttgart: Teubner, 1974); γ: *Der griechische Alexanderroman: Rezension γ*, vol. 1: Ursula von Lauenstein, ed., *Buch I* (Meisenheim am Glan: Anton Hain, 1962); vol. 2: Helmut Engelmann, ed., *Buch II* (Meisenheim am Glan: Anton Hain, 1963); vol. 3: Franz Parthe, ed., *Buch III* (Meisenheim am Glan: Anton Hain, 1968).

8. Reinhold Merkelbach and Jürgen Trumpf, "Die Überlieferung," in Reinhold Merkelbach, *Die Quellen des griechischen Alexanderromans*, 2d ed. (Munich: C. H. Beck, 1977) 93–108, esp. 94.

9. Significant in this context is the presence of a textual instability in Codex D of the New Testament of such a degree that the variants introduce completely new information into the text at various points: that is, they are not merely stylistic variations. This degree of wildness appears only in the Acts of the Apostles, the most "novelistic" text in the New Testament canon. See Eldon Jay Epp, *The Theological Tendency of Codex Bezae Cantabrigiensis in Acts* (Cambridge: Cambridge University Press, 1966) 1–40.

10. Merkelbach and Trumpf, "Überlieferung," 103–6. See also the comments in Richard Stoneman, "Introduction," in idem, ed., *The Greek Alexander Romance* (London: Penguin, 1991) 1–27; and idem, "The Alexander Romance: From History to Fiction," in J. R. Morgan and Richard Stoneman, eds., *Greek Fiction: The Greek Novel in Context* (London/ New York: Routledge, 1994) 117–29. The situation is analogous to the conundrum of New Testament textual criticism. For the Alexander romance, one could speak of families of manuscripts, as B. F. Westcott and F. J. Hort have in their various editions of *The New Testament in the Original Greek* published by Macmillan.

11. The New Testament text is, again, the best analogous example of this degree of textual corruption; one cannot set up stemmata of New Testament manuscripts for the same reason,

the continual collation. Merkelbach and Trumpf claim that, even in antiquity, ancient authors citing other sources would often collate their own manuscripts against another copy or, failing that, against another work in which their source was cited ("Überlieferung," 104); Strabo complains that bad copyists do not collate (ἀντιβάλλω, 13.1.54). For some introductory remarks, see L. D. Reynolds and N. G. Wilson, *Scribes and Scholars: A Guide to the Transmission of Greek and Latin Literature* (Oxford: Clarendon, 1968) 1–25.

12. Merkelbach, *Quellen*, 75–77, 164–92, 149–53.

13. Merkelbach, *Quellen*, 193–98.

14. Merkelbach's demonstration of this point is short and convincing (*Quellen*, 11–19).

15. There are two letters to Poros from Alexander, clearly the same letter in two different versions. One is contained in the Alexander Romance (3.2), and the other is in *P. Hamb.* 129 (1st c. C.E.).

16. So, with some frustration, claim Merkelbach and Trumpf, "Überlieferung," 94. Valerius was consul in 338 C.E.; see Richard Stoneman, "The Metamorphoses of the Alexander Romance," in Gareth Schmeling, ed., *The Novel in the Ancient World* (Leiden: E. J. Brill, 1996) 601–12 (esp. 601), which also presents a lucid overview of the various reworkings of the romance.

17. Plutarch, *Alexander* 43; Curtius Rufus 5.13.24–25. Curtius Rufus also suggests that Alexander may have arrived while Darius was still breathing.

18. Diodorus Siculus 17.73.4.

19. See Adolf Ausfeld, *Der griechische Alexanderroman*, ed. Wilhelm Kroll (Leipzig: Teubner, 1907) 164–65.

20. Jan Bremmer, "The Novel and the Apocryphal Acts: Place, Time, and Readership," in H. Hofmann and M. Zimmerman, eds., *Groningen Colloquia on the Novel: Volume IX* (Groningen: Egbert Forsten, 1998) 157–80, esp. 160.

21. Gareth Schmeling, "*Historia Apollonii Regis Tyri*," in idem, *The Novel in the Ancient World* (Leiden: E. J. Brill, 1996) 517–51; see esp. 527–28. Schmeling's edition prints three recensions consecutively, instead of presenting them as a synopsis, with the laudable goal of directing attention to the text and its interpretation (*Historia Apollonii Regis Tyri* [Leipzig: Teubner, 1988]).

22. Gerald N. Sandy, "The History of Apollonius King of Tyre," in B. P. Reardon, *Collected Ancient Greek Novels* (Berkeley: University of California Press, 1989) 736–72, esp. 738; Georgius Kortekaas, *Historia Apollonii Regis Tyri: Prolegomena, Textual Edition of the Two Principal Latin Recensions, Bibliography, Indices, and Appendices* (Groeningen: Bouma's Boekhus 1984) 130. Schmeling argues, on the other hand, that the textual allusions in the work are all from Latin authors, and that the metals, coins, and measures are all in Latin ("*Historia*," 530). Although these are important considerations, a translator could easily have "updated" such details in a text as unstable as the *Historia*. Unlike the other Latin novels, the *Historia* is not an ego-narrative, but in third person narration similar to the Greek novels. Stephens and Winkler raise the possibility that the novel of Apollonius may be attested in two Greek fragments, though they are not extensive enough to provide certainty (Susan A. Stephens and John J. Winkler, *Ancient Greek Novels: The Fragments: Introduction, Text, Translation, and Commentary* [Princeton: Princeton University Press, 1996] 391–99).

23. For the information on the textual traditions of Daniel and Esther, I am indebted to Prof. Lawrence M. Wills, who allowed me to see his manuscript in advance of publication while I was working on the first draft of this book (*The Jewish Novel in the Ancient World* [Ithaca: Cornell, 1995]).

24. Lawrence M. Wills, "The Jewish Novellas," in J. R. Morgan and Richard Stoneman, eds., *Greek Fiction: The Greek Novel in Context* (London: Routledge, 1994) 223–38, esp. 225–28.

25. Wills, *Novel*, 104–5.

26. Wills, *Novel*, 105–8.

27. The two main indicators of the older source document are the preponderance of converted verbs and the use of pronominal suffixes on finite verbs. See Lawrence Wills, *The Jew in the Court of the Foreign King: Ancient Jewish Court Legends* (Harvard Dissertations in Religion; Minneapolis: Fortress, 1990) 157–70.

28. See Wills, *Novel*, 107–8.

29. Estimates of the date, and even the provenience, of this work vary wildly. The majority of scholars consider it a Jewish work and date it to the first century B.C.E. or the first century C.E. (Christoph Burchard, "Zum Text von 'Joseph und Aseneth," *Journal for the Study of Judaism* 1 [1970] 3–34, now conveniently republished in idem, *Gesammelte Studien zu Joseph und Aseneth*, Studia in Veteris Testamenti Pseudepigrapha 13 [Leiden: E. J. Brill, 1996] 3–34; Marc Philonenko, *Joseph et Aséneth: Introduction, text critique, traduction et notes* [Leiden: Brill, 1968] 108–109 [the first decades of the second century C.E.]; Angela Standhartinger, *Das Frauenbild im Judentum der hellenistischen Zeit: Ein Beitrag anhand von "Joseph und Aseneth"* [Leiden: Brill, 1995] 14–20). Gideon Bohak considers its authors to be supporters of the Oniad temple in Heliopolis, and the text to date to the Ptolemaic period (*Joseph and Aseneth and the Jewish Temple in Heliopolis* [Early Judaism and Its Literature 10; Scholars Press: Atlanta, 1996] 81–100). Ross Kraemer, on the other hand, argues that the document is a product of late antiquity, from around the third century (*When Aseneth Met Joseph: A Late Antique Tale of the Biblical Patriarch and His Egyptian Wife, Reconsidered* [New York: Oxford, 1998] 225–39). She suggests that the work is not necessarily Jewish, but may instead be Christian; it bears close affinities to Neoplatonist (*Aseneth*, 167–79) and Hekhalot literature (*Aseneth*, 110–38).

30. Christoph Burchard gives a concise overview of the textual history in "Joseph and Aseneth," in James H. Charlesworth, ed., *The Old Testament Pseudepigrapha* (Garden City, N.Y.: Doubleday, 1983–85) 2.178–81. The edition of Philonenko (*Joseph et Aséneth*) essentially follows the *d* text, which Burchard considers to be an epitome. See the extended argument in Burchard, "Zum Text von 'Joseph und Aseneth.'" Burchard has published his text in idem, "Ein vorläufiger griechischer Text von Joseph und Aseneth," *Dielheimer Blätter zum Alten Testament* 14 (1979) 2–53, now available in idem, *Gesammelte Studien*, 161–209. Standhartiger (*Frauenbild*, 219–25) and Kraemer (*Aseneth*, 225–39) argue with Philonenko that the shorter text (*d*) is the original, and the longer text (*b*) a later elaboration. Bohak (*Joseph and Aseneth*, 105–9) supports Burchard in believing the *b* text to be the original, and the shorter version to be an epitome.

31. Both quotations from Burchard, "Joseph and Aseneth," 180.

32. Some scholars, however, have argued that chaps. 22–29 of *Joseph and Aseneth* are a later addition.

33. All of them would then be styling themselves as historians, imitators of Xenophon of Athens. The *Cypriaka* of Xenophon of Cyprus sets about the novelization of just such local heroic and mythological figures as one would expect to appear in a local history; its characters are Kinyras, Myrrha, and Adonis. See Ben Edwin Perry, *The Ancient Romances: A Literary-Historical Account of Their Origins*, Sather Classical Lectures 37 (Berkeley: University of California Press, 1967) 167–69.

34. First in Karl Bürger, "Zu Xenophon von Ephesus," *Hermes* 27 (1892) 36–67; for arguments that Xenophon is not an epitome, see Tomas Hägg, "Die Ephesiaka des Xenophon Ephesios—Original oder Epitome?" *Classica et Mediaevalia* 27 (1966) 118–61. Supporting the hypothesis of epitomization, see also Hans Gärtner, "Xenophon von Ephesos," *Pauly's Real-Encyclopädie der classischen Altertumswissenschaft* 2.18 (1967) 2055–89, esp. 2070–72; and also more recently, David Konstan, "Xenophon of Ephesus: Eros and Narrative in the Novel," in Morgan and Stoneman, *Greek Fiction*, 49–63.

35. Philostratos, in one of his epistles (*Ep.* 66), criticizes a writer named Chariton, probably the novelist. See Chapter One.

36. On papyrus codices, see Eric G. Turner, *The Typology of the Early Codex* (Philadelphia: University of Pennsylvania Press, 1977) 35–42, 89–97.

37. Dennis R. MacDonald, *Christianizing Homer: The Odyssey, Plato, and the Acts of Andrew* (Oxford: Oxford University Press, 1994) 290–91; idem, "Is There a Privileged Reader? A Case from the Apocryphal Acts," *Semeia* 71 (1995) 29–43.

38. In contrast to the approach taken in my study, MacDonald views the later redactions as misreadings that objectify the account and obscure its fictive nature (*Christianizing Homer*, 292).

39. At issue is also the proper understanding of scribal habits, for it was presumably the same scribes who were transmitting both the more fixed texts and elaborating the more fluid ones.

40. Carl Schmidt, ed., *Acta Pauli aus der Heidelberger koptischen Papyrushandschrift* (Leipzig: J. C. Hinrichs, 1905). See Chapter Two.

41. See the introductory remarks in Éric Junod and Jean-Daniel Kaestli, eds., *Acta Iohannis*, Corpus Christianorum: Series Apocrypha 1–2 (Turnhout: Brepols, 1983).

42. Harold W. Attridge, "The Original Language of the *Acts of Thomas*," in idem et al., eds., *Of Scribes and Scrolls: Studies on the Hebrew Bible, Intertestamental Judaism, and Christian Origins* (Lanham, Md.: University Press of America, 1990) 241–45.

43. Yves Tissot, "Les Actes de Thomas: exemple de recueil composite," in Bovon, ed., *Actes apocryphes* (1981) 223–32.

44. See Helmut Koester, "History and Development of Mark's Gospel (From Mark to *Secret Mark* and 'Canonical' Mark)," in Bruce Corley, ed., *Colloquy on New Testament Studies: A Time for Reappraisal and Fresh Approaches* (Macon: Mercer University Press, 1983) 35–57. See also the treatment in idem, *Ancient Christian Gospels: Their History and Development* (Philadelphia: Trinity Press, 1990) 295–303. See also Philip Sellew, "Secret Mark and the History of Canonical Mark," in Birger Pearson, et al., eds., *The Future of Early Christianity: Essays in Honor of Helmut Koester* (Minneapolis: Fortress, 1991) 242–57. The *editio princeps* of the manuscript is Morton Smith, *Clement of Alexandria and a Secret Gospel of Mark* (Cambridge, MA: Harvard University, 1973). See Charles W. Hedrick with Nikolaos Olympiou, "Secret Mark: New Photographs, New Witnesses," *The Fourth R: An Advocate for Religious Literacy* 13.5 (2000) 3–11 for new photographs and an account of the recent history of the manuscript.

45. Robert Kysar, "The Fourth Gospel: A Report on Recent Research," *Aufstieg und Niedergang der römischen Welt* 2.25.3 (1985) 2389–480, see esp. 2391–411.

46. Paul J. Achtemeier, "Toward the Isolation of Pre-Markan Miracle Catenae," *Journal of Biblical Literature* 89 (1970) 265–91.

47. Eldon Jay Epp, *The Theological Tendency of Codex Bezae Cantabrigiensis in Acts* (Cambridge: Cambridge University Press, 1966).

48. Bart Ehrman, *The Orthodox Corruption of Scripture* (New York: Oxford, 1993) 279–80.

49. Variations in the citation of Homer in antiquity are primarily limited to those textual variants noted already by the Alexandrian critics; see Stanley, Christopher D., "Paul and Homer: Greco-Roman Citation Practice in the First Century C.E.," *Novum Testament* 32 (1990) 48–78; also idem, *Paul and the Language of Scripture: Citation Technique in the Pauline Epistles and Contemporary Literature*, Society of New Testament Studies Manuscript Series 69 (Cambridge: Cambridge University Press, 1992) 267–91.

50. See Merkelbach, *Quellen*, 33–34, 76, 164–92. The text is very interested in Perdikkas and makes him the main ruler after Alexander's death, though Perdikkas himself died in 321 B.C.E. More recently see Richard Stoneman, "The Metamorphoses of the Alexander Romance," in Gareth Schmeling, ed., *The Novel in the Ancient World* (Leiden: E. J. Brill, 1996) 601–12, and idem, *The Greek Alexander Romance* (Harmondsworth: Penguin, 1991) on the composition of something akin to the A version in Alexandria in the second or even third century B.C.E.

51. See Rosalind Thomas, *Literacy and Orality in Ancient Greece* (Cambridge: Cambridge University Press, 1992) 108–13.

52. See Jack Goody and Ian Watt, "The Consequences of Literacy," in Jack R. Goody, ed., *Literacy in Traditional Societies* (Cambridge: Cambridge University Press, 1968) 27–68, see esp. 28–34.

53. Goody and Watt, "Consequences," 32.

54. Briefly on this, see M. T. Clanchy, "Remembering the Past and the Good Old Law," *History* 55 (1970) 165–76. At greater length, M. T. Clanchy, *From Memory to Written Record: England 1066–1307*, 2d ed. (Oxford: Blackwell, 1993), and Mary Carruthers, *The Book of Memory: A Study of Memory in Medieval Culture* (Cambridge: Cambridge University Press, 1990).

55. William Harris is conservative in his estimate of literacy and yet still paints a picture of a society permeated by literacy throughout its upper reaches (*Ancient Literacy* [Cambridge, Mass.: Harvard University Press, 1989]). On literacy in the early Christian communities, see Harry Y. Gamble, *Books and Readers in the Early Church: A History of Early Christian Texts* (New Haven: Yale University Press, 1995) 2–10. Harris estimates that literacy ran about five or ten percent for the western provinces. More specific studies of the provinces suggest considerable variation within this range, and a higher rate overall than Harris predicts. Leonard Curchin has shown that illiteracy is higher in less-Romanized central Spain than in the more Romanized coastal settlements, but that the central region is still permeated with inscriptions. Moreover, Curchin found no evidence that illiteracy was higher in rural regions than in the urban centers, suggesting that high degrees of administrative and economic contact with Rome spread literacy in a fairly uniform fashion ("Literacy in the Roman Provinces: Qualitative and Quantitative Data from Central Spain," *American Journal of Philology* 116 [1995] 461–76). Curchin's findings match those of Thomas Drew-Bear and myself in rural Phrygia. Although this province is overwhelmingly rural, lacking any cities at all, the peasants and shepherds nevertheless set up hundreds of votive offerings bearing inscriptions, most produced by folk artists, not professional workshops; of these, only three or four were the work of illiterate or semi-literate workmen. Phrygia was thoroughly Hellenized and had been under the influence of a literate culture for centuries (Thomas Drew-Bear, Christine M. Thomas, Melek Yıldızturan, *Phrygian Votive Steles* [Ankara: Museum of Anatolian Civilizations; Paris: de Boccard, 1999] 43–44).

56. Walter J. Ong, *Orality and Literacy: The Technologizing of the Word* (London: Methuen, 1982) 78–93. See also Gamble on the continuous interaction between oral and literate culture in early Christianity (*Books and Readers*, 28–32).

57. Josef Balogh, "'Voces paginarum': Beiträge zur Geschichte des lauten Lesens und Schreibens," *Philologus* 82 (1926–27) 84–109, 202–40. For an important critique, which limits Balogh's claims but does not impinge on his argument proper, see Bernard M. W. Knox, "Silent Reading in Antiquity," *Greek, Roman, and Byzantine Studies* 9 (1968) 421–35. For religious texts in antiquity, see Paul J. Achtemeier, "*Omne verbum sonat*: The New Testament and the Oral Environment of Late Western Antiquity," *Journal of Biblical Literature* 109 (1990) 3–27. Frank D. Gilliard limits Achtemeier's claims as Knox did Balogh's, demonstrating that silent reading was common from the fifth century B.C.E. onward, but nevertheless granting Achtemeier's basic point: that ancient Christian culture had a high degree of residual orality, which must condition the manner in which modern scholars read their texts ("More Silent Reading in Antiquity: *Non Omne Verbum Sonabat*," *Journal of Biblical Literature* 112 [1993] 689–96).

58. Herodotos is the first said to have done this, for which Thukydides criticizes him indirectly (1.22). In the Hellenistic and Roman periods, public reading usually preceded or accompanied the dissemination of written copies. See Arnaldo Momigliano, "The Historians of the Classical World and Their Audiences," *American Scholar* 47 (1977–78) 193–204. In view of the broad dissemination of "high" literature in public readings, Tomas Hägg's argument that the novel was intended for a broader readership than standard literary projects is flawed ("Orality, Literacy, and the 'Read-

ership' of the Early Greek Novel," in Roy Eriksen, ed., *Contexts of Pre-Novel Narrative: the European Tradition* [Berlin: de Gruyter, 1994] 47–81). Hägg argues that compositional features in the novels make them especially suited for oral delivery to audiences that included non-literate "listeners" (rather than "readers"). As Hägg himself notes, however, these features are widely evident even in "high" literature; the argument depends on whether the degree to which these features appear in the novels is significantly greater than elsewhere in Greek literature, and also, I believe, on whether these features tell us anything about the literary level of the real or intended audiences, rather than merely reflecting that of the authors. E. L. Bowie's critical assessment also points out that many of these "oral" features are equally helpful for "silent" readers who are reading from cumbersome scrolls ("The Ancient Readers of the Greek Novel," in Schmeling, ed., *The Novel*, 87–106). Additionally, Bowie points out that, whatever the "intended" readership of the novel, the evidence of the papyri, ostraca, allusions to novels in other literature, and references to novels in art points to the same audiences who read "high" literature, the educated elite.

59. See Thomas, *Literacy and Orality*, 15–28.

60. Chariton comes the closest to having any explicit relationship to world history, in that Kallirhoe, the female lead, is the daughter of a Syracusan general Hermokrates mentioned in Thukydides. See Chapter One and the discussion in Chapter Five below.

61. Martin Braun, *History and Romance in Graeco-Oriental Literature* (Oxford: Blackwell, 1938) 34–35, referring to the Alexander romance, the *Testament of the Twelve Patriarchs*, and the Sesostris stories.

62. Peter Schäfer and Gershom Scholem disagree on this point; the latter postulates that the devotee ascends to heaven, the former that an angel is adjured to descend. See Peter Schäfer, "The Aim and Purpose of Early Jewish Mysticism," in idem, ed., *Hekhalot-Studien* (Tübingen: J. C. B. Mohr [Paul Siebeck], 1988) 277–95.

63. Schäfer, *Hekhalot-Studien*, 8–10, 12.

64. *Synopse zur Hekhalot-Literatur* (Tübingen: Mohr, 1981).

65. "Research into Rabbinic Literature: An Attempt to Define the Status Quaestionis," *Journal of Jewish Studies* 37 (1986) 139–52, see esp. 149.

66. Peter Schäfer, "Once Again the Status Quaestionis of Research into Rabbinic Literature: An Answer to Chaim Milikowsky," *Journal of Jewish Studies* 40 (1989) 89–94, see esp. 90.

67. Schäfer, "Research," 150. This raises the interesting question of why fluid texts eventually become fixed; it seems to be either a case of extreme neglect of a text, as Schäfer suggests, or of extreme interest in it, as in the case of canonization.

68. Schäfer, "Research," 151.

69. Daniel Harrington and Anthony Saldarini, eds., *Targum Jonathan of the Former Prophets*, The Aramaic Bible 10 (Wilmington, Del.: M. Glazier, 1987) 2.

70. Rebecca Lesses, *Ritual Practices to Gain Power: Angels, Incantations, and Revelation in Early Jewish Mysticism* (Harrisburg, Pa.: Trinity, 1998) 242.

71. The Orphic gold tablets offer a further example of religious texts that, though closely related, display a degree of fluidity, with shorter and longer versions of the same text (M. L. West offers a stemma in "Zum neuen Goldplättchen aus Hipponion," *Zeitschrift für Papyrologie und Epigraphik* 18 [1975] 229–36). Again, the fluidity may ultimately stem from their nature as performed texts. They are perhaps physical objects intended as an *aide-mémoire* for performance of the text by the deceased in the afterlife. See R. Janko, "Forgetfulness in the Golden Tablets of Memory," *Classical Quarterly* n.s. 34 (1984) 89–100; and Charles Segal, "Dionysus and the Gold Tablets from Pelinna," *Greek, Roman, and Byzantine Studies* 31 (1990) 411–19. I thank Albert Henrichs for this example.

72. On the influence of performance on the oral and written aspects of texts, see also Gregory Nagy, *Poetry and Performance: Homer and Beyond* (Cambridge: Cambridge University Press, 1996).

73. Translation from Ronald F. Hock and Edward N. O'Neil, eds., *The Chreia in Ancient Rhetoric: Volume 1: The Progymnasmata*, Society of Biblical Literature Texts and Translations 27 (Atlanta: Scholars Press, 1986) 100–3.

74. Codex Vatopedi begins with the words, μηνι 'Ιουνίῳ κθ μαρτύριον τοῦ ἁγίου ἀποστόλου Πέτρου.

75. See Esther 9:20–32 in the Hebrew version employed in the Jewish and Protestant canons for the account of the institution of Purim by Queen Esther herself. Although these paragraphs do not detail the ritual reading or performance of the text of Esther, they specify that the events recorded in it are to be remembered and commemorated, which indicates a ritual response.

76. William A. Graham, *Beyond the Written Word: Oral Aspects of Scripture in the History of Religion* (Cambridge: Cambridge University Press, 1987) 76–77, who relies on the study by Philip Lutgendorf.

*Chapter 5*

1. Hermokrates enters the story at numerous points, first at 4.58.

2. Plutarch, *Dion* 3; Diodorus Siculus, 13.96.3 (her marriage), 13.112.4 (the attack), 14.44.5 (her death). See Ben Edwin Perry, "Chariton and His Romance from a Literary-Historical Point of View," *American Journal of Philology* 51 (1930) 93–134.

3. See Chapter One above.

4. English translation by Gerald N. Sandy, "Metiochus and Parthenope," in B. P. Reardon, *Collected Ancient Greek Novels* (Berkeley: University of California Press, 1989) 813–15. Complete text in H. Maehler, "Der Metiochos-Parthenope-Roman," *Zeitschrift für Papyrologie und Epigraphik* 23 (1976) 1–20, and in Susan A. Stephens and John J. Winkler, *Ancient Greek Novels: The Fragments: Introduction, Text, Translation, and Commentary* (Princeton: Princeton University Press, 1996) 72–100.

5. See Stephens, "Fragments of Lost Novels," in Gareth Schmeling, ed., *The Novel in the Ancient World* (Leiden: E. J. Brill, 1996) 655–83, esp. 662–69. See also Perry, *Ancient Romances*, 137–40, 164–66.

6. See Martin Braun, *History and Romance in Graeco-Oriental Literature* (Oxford: Blackwell, 1938) 6–13.

7. Complete text in Stephens and Winkler, *Fragments*, 23–71. English translation by Gerald N. Sandy, "Ninus," in Reardon, ed., *Ancient Greek Novels* (1989) 803–8.

8. Jack Goody and Ian Watt, "The Consequences of Literacy," in Jack R. Goody, ed., *Literacy in Traditional Societies* (Cambridge: Cambridge University Press, 1968) 27–68, esp. 32.

9. L. A. Bohannan, cited in Rosalind Thomas, *Literacy and Orality in Ancient Greece* (Cambridge: Cambridge University Press, 1992) 109.

10. Braun, *History and Romance*.

11. Walter J. Ong calls these "heavy" heroic figures; this manner of characterization is a mnemonic device in oral tradition (*Orality and Literacy: The Technologizing of the Word* [London: Methuen, 1982] 69–71).

12. Speech acts are utterances in front of an audience which accomplish some end in their very expression, e.g. , "I promise." This manner of analyzing language puts heavy emphasis on performative context. See J. L. Austin, *How to Do Things with Words*, 2d ed. (Cambridge, Mass.: Harvard University Press, 1975).

13. Alexander romance 1.14. Translation by Ken Dowden, "Pseudo-Callisthenes: The Alexander Romance," in Reardon, ed., *Ancient Greek Novels* (1989) 650–735, esp. 663.

14. Her name was Mandane; Herodotos 1.107–108.

15. Herodotos 3.2.

16. Tzvetan Todorov, *The Fantastic: A Structuralist Approach to a Literary Genre*, trans. R. Howard (Ithaca: Cornell University, 1975) 21-22.

17. Michel Foucault, "What Is an Author?" in Josué V. Harari, ed., *Textual Strategies* (Ithaca, N.Y.: Cornell University Press, 1979) 141-60.

18. Similarly, Robert M. Price argues that, if genre is more a matter of reader expectation than authorial intentionality, genres do evolve according to changes in their audience. The main argument of his article, that the Apocryphal Acts of the Apostles were written after, and in response to, an allegorized Christian readings of the erotic novels, fails on chronological grounds: the Apocryphal Acts and the erotic novels are coeval. His suggestions about Christianized allegorization of the erotic novels, however, are fascinating and offer an explanation of their undeniable popularity among Christian audiences throughout the Byzantine period ("Implied Reader Response and the Evolution of Genres: Transitional Stages Between the Ancient Novels and the Apocryphal Acts," *Hervormde Teologiese Studies* 53.4 [1997] 909-38).

19. Glen Bowersock, *Fiction as History: Nero to Julian*, Sather Classical Lectures 58 (Berkeley: University of California Press, 1994); see esp. the first lecture, "Truth in Lying," 1-27, and the sixth, "Polytheism and Scripture," 121-43.

20. For example, Bowersock, *Fiction*, 139, n. 43.

21. Bowersock de-emphasizes the early Jewish or fragmentary novels, dismissing them on a single page (*Fiction*, 21). He mentions *Ninos* and *Joseph and Aseneth* as "romantic narratives about famous legendary characters" and views them as "perhaps even" antecedents of the fictional production of the Roman empire—a hair too cautious.

22. See Bowersock, *Fiction*, again the sixth chapter for cannibalism and the fifth chapter, "Resurrection," 99-119.

23. Bowersock is, at least, far ahead of many scholars of early Christianity in finding no dividing line between canonical and apocryphal Christian narratives: all these literary products are essentially fictitious in his analysis.

24. The Clementine literature is mentioned in Bowersock, *Fiction*, 140-41.

25. Tomas Hägg, "The Beginnings of the Historical Novel," in Roderick Beaton, ed., *The Greek Novel A. D. 1-1985* (London: Croom Helm, 1988) 169-81, esp. 171. See also idem, "Callirhoe and Parthenope: The Beginnings of the Historical Novel," *Classical Antiquity* 6.2 (1987) 184-204, a longer version of the former.

26. See Hägg, "Beginnings," 176; and Richard I. Pervo, "What Should a Well-Dressed Emperor Wear?: An Early Christian Reading of *The Alexander Romance*," *American Philological Association Annual Meeting* (Atlanta, Ga.: 1994) 31.

27. Since the main events of *Kallirhoe* are already found in historical accounts, one wonders whether even this example is truly fictitious in the sense Hägg wants it to be; he recognizes the problem ("Callirhoe," 195 n. 63).

28. Rosa Söder, *Die apokryphen Apostelgeschichten und die romanhafte Literatur der Antike* (1932; Stuttgart: Kohlhammer, 1969) 188-215.

29. *The Novel in Antiquity* (Berkeley: University of California Press, 1983) 125.

30. This is closer to Richard I. Pervo's understanding of the term "historical novel" (*Profit with Delight: The Literary Genre of the Acts of the Apostles* [Philadelphia: Fortress, 1987] 115-35).

31. See Quintilian 2.4.2. See the treatment of the rhetoricians in D. C. Feeney, "Towards an Account of the Ancient World's Concepts of Fictive Belief," in Christopher Gill and T. P. Wiseman, eds., *Lies and Fiction in the Ancient World* (Austin, Tex.: University of Texas Press, 1993) 230-44.

32. πλάσμα δε [ἔκθεσις] πραγμάτων μὴ γενομένων μὲν ὁμοίως δὲ τοῖς γενομένοις λεγομένων, ὡς αἱ κωμικαὶ ὑποθέσεις καὶ οἱ μῖμοι.

33. David Konstan, "The Invention of Fiction," in Ronald F. Hock, J. Bradley Chance, et al., eds., *Ancient Fiction and Early Christian Literature* (Atlanta: Scholars Press, 1998) 3-17, esp. 6.

34. See Reinhold Merkelbach, *Die Quellen des griechischen Alexanderromans*, 2d ed. (Munich: C. H. Beck, 1977) 33–34, 76, 164–92. In the Alexander romance (3.32), Perdikkas becomes the main ruler and marries Roxanna, although he himself died in 321 B.C.E. Another episode recounts that Perdikkas, suspecting that Ptolemy would be Alexander's successor since they were half-brothers through Philip, makes Ptolemy swear an oath that if either of them inherited the realm, the one would split it with the other. Ptolemy agreed, not knowing his advantage. The story justifies Ptolemy's armed resistance against the attempts of Perdikkas to centralize rule.

35. For a careful and thorough treatment, see above all Richard A. Burridge, *What Are the Gospels? A Comparison with Graeco-Roman Biography*, Society for New Testament Study Manuscript Series 70 (Cambridge: Cambridge University Press, 1992).

36. Charles H. Talbert, *What Is A Gospel? The Genre of the Canonical Gospels* (Philadelphia: Fortress, 1977). David Pao, "The Genre of the *Acts of Andrew*," *Apocrypha* 6 (1995) 179–202; see the reservations of Éric Junod, "Les Vies de philosophes et les Actes apocryphes poursuivent-elles un dessein similaire?" in Bovon, ed., *Actes apocryphes* (1981) 209–19, who answers negatively the question posed in his title.

37. The biography of Apollonios of Tyana is more likely to have been influenced by the Gospels and Apocryphal Acts than them by it, since it is a third-century work. One could just as well classify it as a gospel itself, since the genre already existed.

38. See the remarks by Pao, "Genre," 197–99.

39. Lawrence Wills, *The Quest of the Historical Gospel: Mark, John, and the Origins of the Gospel Genre* (London: Routledge, 1997) 16–17.

40. Charles William Fornara, *The Nature of History in Ancient Greece and Rome* (Berkeley: University of California Press, 1983) 34–36.

41. Pao also notes that presentation of character, even if the subject is presented as a "finished product," is nevertheless constitutive of the genre of biography ("Genre," 184, 194).

42. "Acts of Love: A Narrative Pattern in the Apocryphal Acts," *Journal of Early Christian Studies* 6 (1998) 15–36, esp. 34.

43. Mary Ann Tolbert, *Sowing the Gospel: Mark's World in Literary-Historical Perspective* (Minneapolis: Fortress, 1989) 48–79. Marius Reiser compares the Greek style of Mark with that of the Alexander romance ("Der Alexanderroman und das Markusevangelium," in Hubert Cancik, ed., *Markus-Philologie* [Wissenschaftliche Untersuchungen zum Neuen Testament 33; Tübingen: Mohr-Siebeck, 1984] 131–63).

44. Tolbert, *Sowing*, 65–66.

45. Wills, *Quest*, 12.

46. There is a long history of understanding the Gospels as being sui generis, a unique literary form created according to the dictates of Christian theology.

47. Richard Reitzenstein treats this passage at length in *Hellenistische Wundererzählungen* (Leipzig: Teubner, 1906) 84–99, 152–69.

48. Sallust, writing between 44 and 40 B.C.E., downplays Cicero's role in the disclosure and prosecution of the conspiracy of Catiline. The two antithetical speeches in the Senate which Sallust presents are, instead, by Caesar and Marcus Portius Cato. Perhaps Cicero was still too controversial a figure to mention by this time, or perhaps Cicero exaggerates his own role, which would not be surprising for this individual.

49. None of which are now extant.

50. Sallust ends instead with the death of Lucius Catiline, the antihero of his narrative.

51. Translation from W. Glynn Williams, ed., *Cicero: The Letters to His Friends*, Loeb Classical Library (Cambridge, Mass.: Harvard University Press, 1965) 1.365–79, esp. 371–73.

52. Hägg, "Beginnings," 173–74.

53. Martin Hengel, *Acts and the History of Earliest Christianity* (Philadelphia: Fortress, 1980) 13–14, 36–37.

54. Adela Yarbro Collins, *The Beginning of the Gospel: Probings of Mark in Context* (Minneapolis: Fortress, 1992) 26–28.

55. Hayden White, "The Historical Text as Literary Artifact," in idem, ed., *Tropics of Discourse: Essays in Cultural Criticism* (1978; Baltimore: Johns Hopkins University Press, 1982) 81–100.

56. Konstan of course admits that all texts, even fiction, refer to the outside world in fundamental ways: geography, psychology, moral truths, culturally shared values, and the like. What he means might be described as *narrative* reference ("Invention," 6–7).

57. Konstan, "Invention," 5.

58. "Make-Believe and Make Believe: The Fictionality of the Greek Novels," in Gill and Wiseman, eds., *Lies and Fiction*, 175–229; see esp. 176.

59. James A. Francis, for example, considers the *Life of Apollonius of Tyana* to be a novel that uses fictional techniques to embellish its topic, such as the self-authenticating feature of the discovery of the tablets of Damis that form the putative source of Philostratus's work. Francis ultimately concludes that the work may not in fact be fiction because it is too verisimilar, which seems to construe the relationship between *plasma* and verisimilitude in a manner exactly the opposite of what an ancient reader would have done ("Truthful Fiction: New Questions to Old Answers on Philostratus' *Life of Apollonius,*" *American Journal of Philology* 119 [1998] 419–41). Stefan Merkle is closer to ancient sensibilities in describing Dictys and Dares as "fictions in *the form* of history" (my emphasis), because they were constructed around "characters and events which antiquity regarded as historical" ("The Truth and Nothing but the Truth: Dictys and Dares," in Gareth Schmeling, ed., *The Novel in the Ancient World* [Leiden: E. J. Brill, 1996] 563–580, esp. 579).

60. Harry Gamble notes that the generic evaluation of Christian literature is hampered by the lacunose preservation and lack of scholarly study of nonelite literary works such as medical or scientific texts. Thus the literary scene in the Roman world was likely far more variegated (*Books and Readers in the Early Church: A History of Early Christian Texts* [New Haven: Yale University Press, 1995] 17–20).

61. This factual prose is identified by Lars Rydbeck and described as *Fachprosa*, professional writing with no literary aspirations (*Fachprosa, vermeintliche Volkssprache und Neues Testament: Zur Beurteilung der sprachlichen Niveauunterschiede im nachklasischen Griechisch* [Stockholm: Almqvist & Wiksell, 1967]). Loveday Alexander has extended Rydbeck's study with an investigation of Luke's prefaces for his gospel and the Acts of the Apostles that demonstrates their close similarity to prefaces in these types of scientific or informational works (*The Preface to Luke's Gospel: Literary Convention and Social Context in Luke 1:1–4 and Acts 1:1*, Society for New Testament Study Manuscript Series 78 [Cambridge: Cambridge University Press, 1993]). See discussion of both in Gamble, *Books and Readers*, 32–40.

62. Konstan, "Invention," 8.

63. As he notes, the point of common reference for the community of readers of the novel was the novel itself ("Invention," 15).

64. The term is Konstan's ("Invention," 17).

*Appendix Three*

1. Poupon; Lipsius, Salonius *frequentare illum*

2. Poupon and Salonius; Lipsius *molestabantur esse*

3. Poupon and Salonius correct to *eisdem,* but the reading is an orthographic variant.

4. I reject Usener's emendation *adinueniendo* as creating a grammatical infelicity.

5. Lipsius. Poupon and Salonius follow other MSS in reading *proripere,* but the attestation of *prorumpere* is better, and the reading makes sense: the women are "breaking out" to see Peter.

# Bibliography

Achelis, Hans. *Acta SS. Nerei et Achillei: Text und Untersuchung.* Texte und Untersuchungen 11.2. Leipzig: J. C. Hinrichs, 1893.

Achtemeier, Paul J. "Toward the Isolation of Pre-Markan Miracle Catenae." *Journal of Biblical Literature* 89 (1970) 265–91.

Achtemeier, Paul J. "Jesus and the Disciples as Miracle Workers in the Apocryphal New Testament." In *Aspects of Religious Propaganda in Judaism and Early Christianity*, ed. Elisabeth Schüssler-Fiorenza, 149–86. Notre Dame: University of Notre Dame, 1976.

———. "*Omne verbum sonat:* The New Testament and the Oral Environment of Late Western Antiquity." *Journal of Biblical Literature* 109 (1990) 3–27.

Adamik, Tamás. "The Language and Style of the *Acts of Peter.*" In *Estudios de Lingüística Latina: Actas del IX Coloquio Internacional de Lingüística Latina*, ed. Benjamín García-Hernandez, 1063–72. Madrid: Ediciones Clásicas, 1998.

Alexander, Loveday. *The Preface to Luke's Gospel: Literary Convention and Social Context in Luke 1:1–4 and Acts 1:1.* Society for New Testament Study Manuscript Series 78. Cambridge: Cambridge University Press, 1993.

Anderson, Graham. *Ancient Fiction: The Novel in the Graeco-Roman World.* London: Croom Helm and Totowa; N.J.: Barnes and Noble, 1984.

———. *The Second Sophistic: A Cultural Phenomenon in the Roman Empire.* London: Routledge, 1993.

Attridge, Harold W. "The Original Language of the *Acts of Thomas.*" In *Of Scribes and Scrolls: Studies on the Hebrew Bible, Intertestamental Judaism, and Christian Origins*, ed. idem et al., 241–45. Lanham, Md.: University Press of America, 1990.

Aune, David. *The New Testament in Its Literary Environment.* Philadelphia: Westminster, 1987.

Ausfeld, Adolf. *Der griechische Alexanderroman.* Leipzig: Teubner, 1907.

Austin, J. L. *How to Do Things with Words.* 2d ed. Cambridge, Mass.: Harvard University Press, 1975.

Bakhtin, M. M. "Epic and Novel." Trans. idem and Caryl Emerson. In *The Dialogic Imagination*, ed. Michael Holquist, 3–40. Austin: University of Texas Press, 1981.

Bal, Mieke. *Narratology: Introduction to the Theory of Narrative.* Trans. Christine van Boheemen. Toronto: University of Toronto Press, 1985.

Balogh, Josef. "'Voces paginarum': Beiträge zur Geschichte des lauten Lesens und Schreibens." *Philologus* 82 (1927) 84–109, 202–40.

Bardenhewer, Otto. *Geschichte der altkirchlichen Litteratur*. 5 vols. Freiburg im Breisgau: Herder, 1902-32.

Barnikol, Ernst. "Die Eintragung des Paulus in die Grundschrift der Petrusakten." *Theologische Jahrbücher (Halle)* 2 (1934) 153-57.

——. "Marcellus in den Petrus-Akten (U und V)." *Theologische Jahrbücher (Halle)* 2 (1934) 158-64.

——. "Petrus vor dem Caesar?" *Theologische Jahrbücher (Halle)* 2 (1934) 115-22.

——. "Spanienreise und Römerbrief des Paulus in den Petrus-Akten." *Theologische Jahrbücher (Halle)* 2 (1934) 1-12.

Bartsch, Shadi. *Decoding the Ancient Novel: The Reader and the Role of Description in Heliodorus and Achilles Tatius*. Princeton: Princeton University Press, 1989.

Bäuml, Franz H. "Varieties and Consequences of Medieval Literacy and Illiteracy." *Speculum* 55 (1980) 237-65.

Bedjan, Paulus. *Acta martyrum et sanctorum Syriace*. 1890-97. Reprint Hildesheim: G. Olms, 1968.

Ben-Amos, Dan. "Analytical Categories and Ethnic Genres." In *Folklore Genres*, ed. Dan Ben-Amos, 215-42. Austin: University of Texas Press, 1976.

Berger, Klaus. "Hellenistische Gattungen im Neuen Testament." *Aufstieg und Niedergang der römischen Welt* 2.25/2 (1984) 1031-432, 1831-85 (index).

Bergmeier, Roland. "Die Gestalt des Simon Magus in Act 8 und in der simonianischen Gnosis—Aporien einer Gesamtdarstellung." *Zeitschrift für die neutestamentliche Wissenschaft* 77 (1986) 267-75.

Bergson, Leif, ed. *Der griechische Alexanderroman: Rezension β*. Stockholm: Almqvist and Wiksell, 1965.

Biebuyck, Daniel, and Kahombo C. Mateene, eds. *The Mwindo Epic from the Banyanga (Congo Republic)*. Berkeley: University of California, 1969.

Blumenthal, Martin. *Formen und Motive in den apokryphen Apostelgeschichten*. Texte und Untersuchungen 48/1. Leipzig: J. C. Hinrichs, 1933.

Bohak, Gideon. *Joseph and Aseneth and the Jewish Temple in Heliopolis*. Early Judaism and Its Literature 10. Scholars Press: Atlanta, 1996.

Bovon, François. "La vie des apôtres: Traditions bibliques et narrations apocryphe." In *Actes apocryphes*, ed. idem et al., 141-58.

——. "The Synoptic Gospels and the Noncanonical Acts of the Apostles." *Harvard Theological Review* 81 (1988) 19-36.

——. "Le discours missionaire de Jésus: Réception patristique et narration apocryphe." *Études théologiques et religieuses* 68 (1993-94) 481-97.

——. "Jesus' Missionary Speech as Interpreted in the Patristic Commentaries and the Apocryphal Narratives." In *Texts and Contexts: Biblical Texts in Their Textual and Situational Contexts*, ed. Tord Fornberg and David Hellholm, 871-86. Oslo: Scandinavian University Press, 1995.

Bovon, François, et al., eds. *Les Actes apocryphes des apôtres: Christianisme et monde païen*. Publications de la Faculté de Théologie de l'Université de Genève 4. Geneva: Labor et Fides, 1981.

Bovon, François, Ann Graham Brock, and Christopher R. Matthews, eds. *The Apocryphal Acts of the Apostles: Harvard Divinity School Studies*. Cambridge, Mass.: Harvard, 1999.

Bovon, François, and Éric Junod. "Reading the Apocryphal Acts of the Apostles." *Semeia* 38 (1986) 161-71.

Bowersock, Glen. *Greek Sophists in the Roman Empire*. Oxford: Clarendon, 1969.

——. *Fiction as History: Nero to Julian*. Sather Classical Lectures 58. Berkeley: University of California Press, 1994.

Bowie, E. L. "The Novels and the Real World." In *Erotica Antiqua*, ed. B. P. Reardon, 91-96. Bangor, Wales: [s. n.], 1977.

———. "The Greek Novel." In *The Hellenistic Period and the Empire*, ed. P. E. Easterling and B. M. W. Knox, 23-39. Cambridge History of Classical Literature 1.4. Cambridge: Cambridge University Press, 1985.

———. "The Readership of Greek Novels in the Ancient World." In *Search*, ed. Tatum, 435-59.

———. "The Ancient Readers of the Greek Novel." In *The Novel*, ed. Schmeling, 87-106.

Bowie, Ewen L., and S. J. Harrison. "The Romance of the Novel." *Journal of Roman Studies* 83 (1993) 159-78.

Brashler, James, and Douglas M. Parrott. "The Act of Peter." In *Nag Hammadi Codices V, 2-5 and VI with Papyrus Berolinensis 8502, 1 and 4*, ed. Douglas M. Parrott, 473-93. Nag Hammadi Studies 11; Coptic Gnostic Library. Leiden: Brill, 1979.

Braun, Martin. *History and Romance in Graeco-Oriental Literature*. Oxford: Blackwell, 1938.

Bremmer, Jan, ed. *The Acts of Peter: Magic, Miracles, and Gnosticism*. Leuven: Peeters, 1998.

———. "Aspects of the *Acts of Peter*: Women, Magic, Place, and Date." In *Acts of Peter*, ed. Bremmer, 1-20.

———. "The Novel and the Apocryphal Acts: Place, Time, and Readership." In *Groningen Colloquia on the Novel: Volume IX*, ed. H. Hofmann and M. Zimmerman, 157-80. Groningen: Egbert Forsten, 1998.

Burchard, Christoph. "Zum Text von 'Joseph und Aseneth.'" *Journal for the Study of Judaism* 1 (1970) 3-34.

———. "Ein vorläufiger griechischer Text von Joseph und Aseneth." *Dielheimer Blätter zum Alten Testament* 14 (1979) 2-53.

———. "Joseph and Aseneth." In *Pseudepigrapha*, ed. Charlesworth, 2: 177-247.

———. *Gesammelte Studien zu Joseph und Aseneth*. Studia in Veteris Testamenti Pseudepigrapha 13. Leiden: E. J. Brill, 1996.

Bürger, Karl. "Zu Xenophon von Ephesus." *Hermes* 27 (1892) 36-67.

Burridge, Richard A. *What are the Gospels? A Comparison with Graeco-Roman Biography*. Society for New Testament Studies Manuscript Series 70. Cambridge: Cambridge University Press, 1992.

Burrus, Virginia. *Chastity as Autonomy: Women in the Stories of the Apocryphal Acts*. Lewiston, N.Y.: E. Mellen, 1987.

———. "Chastity as Autonomy." *Semeia* 38 (1986) 101-17.

Cambe, M. "La Prédication de Pierre." *Apocrypha* 4 (1993) 177-95.

Cameron, Averil. "Stories People Want." In *Christianity and the Rhetoric of Empire*, ed. eadem, 89-119. Sather Classical Lectures 55. Berkeley: University of California Press, 1991.

Cancik, Hubert. "Die Gattung Evangelium: Das Evangelium des Markus im Rahmen der antiken Historiographie." In *Markus-Philologie*, ed. idem, 85-113. Wissenschaftliche Untersuchungen zum Neuen Testament 33. Tübingen: Mohr-Siebeck, 1984.

Carruthers, Mary. *The Book of Memory: A Study of Memory in Medieval Culture*. Cambridge: Cambridge University Press, 1990.

Cartlidge, David R. "Transfigurations of Metamorphosis Traditions in the Acts of John, Thomas, and Peter." *Semeia* 38 (1986) 53-66.

———. "Combien d'unités avez-vous de trois à quatre? What Do We Mean by Intertextuality in Early Church Studies?" In *Society of Biblical Literature 1990 Seminar Papers*, ed. David J. Lull, 400-11. Atlanta: Scholars Press, 1990.

Castellani, Victor. "Clio vs. Melpomene; or, Why So Little Historical Drama from Classical Athens?" In *Historical Drama*, 1-16. Cambridge: Cambridge University Press, 1986.

Centre d'Analyse et de Documentation Patristiques. *Biblia patristica: Index de citations et allusions bibliques dans la littérature patristique*. Paris: Éditions du Centre National de la Recherche Scientifique, 1986.

Cerro, G. del. "Los Hechos apócrifos de los Apóstolos: su género literario." *Estudios Bíblicos* 51 (1993) 207-32.

Chalk, H. H. O. "Mystery Cults and the Romance." *Classical Review* 13 (1963) 161-63.

Charlesworth, James H., ed. *The Old Testament Pseudepigrapha.* 2 vols. Garden City, N.Y.: Doubleday, 1983-85.

Clanchy, M. T. "Remembering the Past and the Good Old Law." *History* 55 (1970) 165-76.

——. *From Memory to Written Record: England 1066-1307.* 2d ed. Oxford: Blackwell, 1993.

Conzelmann, Hans. "Zu Mythos, Mythologie und Formgeschichte, geprüft an der dritten Praxis der Thomas-Akten." *Zeitschrift für die neutestamentliche Wissenschaft* 67 (1976) 111-22.

Cullmann, Oscar. *Peter: Disciple, Apostle, Martyr: A Historical and Theological Study.* 2d ed. Philadelphia: Westminster, 1962.

Curchin, Leonard. "Literacy in the Roman Provinces: Qualitative and Quantitative Data from Central Spain." *American Journal of Philology* 116 (1995) 461-76.

Davies, Stevan L. *The Revolt of the Widows: The Social World of the Apocryphal Acts.* Carbondale: Southern Illinois University Press, 1980.

De Bruyne, D. "Nouveaux fragments des Actes de Pierre, de Paul, de Jean, d'André et de l'Apocalypse d'Élie." *Revue Bénédictine* 25 (1908) 149-60, esp. 151-53.

Dégh, Linda, and Andrew Vázsonyi. "Legend and Belief." In *Folklore Genres*, ed. Dan Ben-Amos, 93-123. Austin: University of Texas Press, 1976.

Delehaye, Hippolyte. *The Legends of the Saints.* Notre Dame: University of Notre Dame Press, 1961.

Demoen, Kristoffel. "S. Pierre se régalant de lupins; à propos de quelques traces d'apocryphes concernant Pierre dans l'œuvre de Grégoire de Nazianze." *Sacris Erudiri (Steenbrugge)* 32 (1991) 95-106.

Dihle, Albrecht."Zur Datierung des Metiochos-Romans." *Würzburger Jahrbücher für die Altertumswissenschaft* n. s. 4 (1978) 47-55.

Dobschütz, Ernst von. "Der Roman in der altchristlichen Literatur." *Deutsche Rundschau* 111 (1902) 87-106.

Dowden, Ken. "Pseudo-Callisthenes: The Alexander Romance." In *Ancient Greek Novels*, ed. Reardon, 650-735.

Drew-Bear, Thomas, Christine M. Thomas, and Melek Yıldızturan. *Phrygian Votive Steles.* Ankara: Museum of Anatolian Civilizations; Paris: de Boccard, 1999.

Edwards, M. J. "The *Clementina*: A Christian Response to the Pagan Novel." *Classical Quarterly* 42 (1992) 459-74.

Ehrmann, Bart. *The Orthodox Corruption of Scripture.* New York: Oxford University Press, 1993.

Ejxenbaum, Boris. "The Theory of the Formal Method." In *Readings in Russian Poetics: Formalist and Structuralist Views*, ed. Ladislav Matejka and Krystyna Pomorska, 3-37. Cambridge, Mass.: MIT Press, 1971.

Elliott, J. K. "The Acts of Peter." In *The Apocryphal New Testament*, ed. idem, 390-96. Oxford: Clarendon Press, 1993.

Engelmann, Helmut, ed. *Der griechische Alexanderroman: Rezension γ, Buch II.* Meisenheim am Glan: Anton Hain, 1963.

——. "Ephesos und die Johannesakten." *Zeitschrift für Papyrologie und Epigraphik* 103 (1994) 297-302.

Epp, Eldon Jay. *The Theological Tendency of Codex Bezae Cantabrigiensis in Acts.* Cambridge: Cambridge University Press, 1966.

Erbes, Carl. "Petrus nicht in Rom, sondern in Jerusalem gestorben." *Zeitschrift für Kirchengeschichte* 22 (1901) 1-47, 161-224.

——. "Ursprung und Umfang der Petrusakten." *Zeitschrift für Kirchengeschichte* 32 (1911) 161-85, 353-77, 497-530.

Feeney, D. C. "Towards an Account of the Ancient World's Concepts of Fictive Belief." In *Lies and Fiction*, ed. Gill and Wiseman, 230–44.

Festugière, A. J. "Aspects de la religion populaire grecque." *Revue de théologie et de philosophie* 11 (1961) 19–31.

———. "Pensée grecque et pensée chrétienne." *Revue de théologie et de philosophie* 11 (1961) 113–22.

Ficker, Gerhard. *Die Petrusakten: Beiträge zu ihrem Verständnis*. Leipzig: Barth, 1903.

———. "Petrusakten." In *Handbuch zu den neutestamentlichen Apokryphen*, ed. Edgar Hennecke. 395–491. Tübingen: Mohr/Siebeck, 1904.

Flamion, J. "Les actes apocryphes de Pierre." *Revue d'histoire ecclésiastique* 9 (1908) 233–54, 465–90.

———. "Les actes apocryphes de Pierre." *Revue d'histoire ecclésiastique* 10 (1909) 5–29, 245–77.

———. "Les actes apocryphes de Pierre." *Revue d'histoire ecclésiastique* 11 (1910) 5–28, 223–56, 447–70, 675–92.

———. "Les actes apocryphes de Pierre." *Revue d'histoire ecclésiastique* 12 (1911) 209–30, 437–50.

Foley, John Miles. "*Guslar* and *Aiodos*: What South Slavic Oral Epic Can—and Cannot—Tell Us about Homer." In *Abstracts for the American Philological Association Annual Meeting*. Atlanta: Scholars Press, 1995.

———. "*Guslar and Aoidos*: Traditional Register in South Slavic and Homeric Epic." *Transactions of the American Philological Association* 126 (1996) 11–41.

Fornara, Charles William. *The Nature of History in Ancient Greece and Rome*. Berkeley: University of California Press, 1983.

Foucault, Michel. "What Is an Author?" In *Textual Strategies*, ed. Josué V. Harari, 141–60. Ithaca, N.Y.: Cornell University Press, 1979.

Francis, James A. "Truthful Fiction: New Question to Old Answers on Philostratus' *Life of Apollonius*." *American Journal of Philology* 119 (1998) 419–41.

Frickel, Josef. *Die Apophasis Megale in Hippolyts Refutatio (VI, 9–18): Eine Paraphrase zur Apophasis Simons*. Orientalia Christiana analecta 182. Rome: Pont. institutum orientalium studiorum, 1968.

Gamble, Harry Y. *Books and Readers in the Early Church: A History of Early Christian Texts*. New Haven, Conn.: Yale University Press, 1995.

Gärtner, Hans. "Xenophon von Ephesos." *Pauly's Real-Encyclopädie der classischen Altertumswissenschaft* 2.18 (1967) 2055–89.

Geerard, Maurice. *Clavis apocryphorum Novi Testamenti*. Corpus Christianorum. Turnhout: Brepols, 1992.

Gero, S. "The Legend of Alexander the Great in the Christian Orient." *Bulletin of the John Rylands University Library* 75 (1993) 3–9.

Gill, Christopher, and T. P. Wiseman, ed. *Lies and Fiction in the Ancient World*. Austin: University of Texas Press, 1993.

Gilliard, Frank D. "More Silent Reading in Antiquity: *Non Omne Verbum Sonabat*." *Journal of Biblical Literature* 112 (1993) 689–96.

Goody, Jack, and Ian Watt. "The Consequences of Literacy." In *Literacy in Traditional Societies*, ed. Jack R. Goody, 27–68. Cambridge: Cambridge University Press, 1968.

Graham, William A. *Beyond the Written Word: Oral Aspects of Scripture in the History of Religion*. Cambridge: Cambridge University Press, 1987.

Grant, Michael, ed. *Tacitus: The Annals of Imperial Rome*. Rev. ed. New York: Penguin, 1971.

Grant, Robert M. "A Woman of Rome: The Matron in Justin, 2 *Apology* 2.1–9." *Church History* 54 (1985) 461–72.

Grappe, Christian. "Du témoin pleutre de la Passion au martyr: images de Pierre aux deux premiers siècles." *Cahiers de Biblia Patristica* 3 (1991) 53–106.

Grappe, Christian. *Images de Pierre aux deux premiers siècles*. Études d'histoire et de philosophie religieuses 75. Paris: Presses universitaires de France, 1995.

Grenfell, Bernard P., and Arthur S. Hunt, ed. *The Oxyrhynchus Papyri*. London: Egypt Exploration Fund, 1908.

Griffin, Miriam T. *Nero: The End of a Dynasty*. London: B. T. Batsford, 1984.

Gronewald, M. "Ein neues Fragment zu einem Roman." *Zeitschrift für Papyrologie und Epigraphik* 35 (1979) 15-20.

Gutschmid, A. von. "Die Königsnamen in den apokryphen Apostelgeschichten." *Rheinisches Museum für Philologie* 19 (1864) 161-83, 380-401.

Hadas, Moses. *Three Greek Romances*. Indianapolis: Bobbs-Merrill, 1953.

Haenchen, Ernst. "Simon Magus in der Apostelgeschichte." In *Gnosis und Neues Testament: Studien aus Religionswissenschaft und Theologie*, ed. Karl-Wolfgang Tröger, 267-79. Gütersloh: Mohn, 1973.

Hägg, Tomas. "Die Ephesiaka des Xenophon Ephesios—Original oder Epitome?" *Classica et Mediaevalia* 27 (1966) 118-61.

———. *The Novel in Antiquity*. Berkeley: University of California Press, 1983.

———. "Callirhoe and Parthenope: The Beginnings of the Historical Novel." *Classical Antiquity* 6.2 (1987) 184-204.

———. "The Beginnings of the Historical Novel." In *The Greek Novel A. D. 1-1985*, ed. Roderick Beaton, 169-81. London: Croom Helm, 1988.

———. "Orality, Literacy, and the 'Readership' of the Early Greek Novel." In *Contexts of Pre-Novel Narrative: the European Tradition*, ed. Roy Eriksen, 47-81. Berlin: de Gruyter, 1994.

Hammond, N. G. L. *Three Historians of Alexander the Great: The So-Called Vulgate Authors, Diodorus, Justin, and Curtius*. Cambridge: Cambridge University Press, 1983.

———. *Sources for Alexander the Great: An Analysis of Plutarch's Life and Arrian's Anabasis Alexandrou*. Cambridge: Cambridge University Press, 1993.

Handler, Richard, and Jocelyn Linnekin. "Tradition, Genuine or Spurious." *Journal of American Folklore* 97 (1984) 273-90.

Harrington, Daniel, and Anthony Saldarini, ed. *Targum Jonathan of the Former Prophets*. Aramaic Bible 10. Wilmington, Del.: M. Glazier, 1987.

Harris, William V. *Ancient Literacy*. Cambridge, Mass.: Harvard University Press, 1989.

Havelock, Eric A. *The Literate Revolution in Greece and Its Cultural Consequences*. Princeton, N.J.: Princeton University Press, 1982.

———. *The Muse Learns to Write: Reflections on Orality and Literacy from Antiquity to the Present*. New Haven, Conn.: Yale University Press, 1986.

Hedrick, Charles W. with Nikolaos Olympiou. "Secret Mark: New Photographs, New Witnesses." *The Fourth R: An Advocate for Religious Literacy* 13.5 (2000) 3-11.

Henderson, I. H. "*Didache* and Orality in Synoptic Comparison." *Journal of Biblical Literature* 111 (1992) 283-306.

Hengel, Martin. *Acts and the History of Earliest Christianity*. Philadelphia: Fortress, 1980.

Henrichs, Albert. *Die Phoinikika des Lollianos: Fragmente eines neuen griechischen Romans. Papyrologische Texte und Abhandlungen 14*. Bonn: R. Habelt, 1972.

———. "Changing Dionysiac Identities." In *Jewish and Christian Self-Definition*, ed. Ben F. Meyer and E. P. Sanders, 3.137-60, 213-36. London: SCM, 1982-83.

Heubner, Heinrich, ed. *P. Cornelii Taciti libri qui supersunt*. Stuttgart: Teubner, 1983.

Hilgenfeld, Adolf. "Die alten Actus Petri." *Zeitschrift für wissenschaftliche Theologie* 46 (1903) 321-41.

Hills, Julian V. "The Acts of the Apostles in the *Acts of Paul*." In *Society of Biblical Literature Seminar Papers*, 24-54. Atlanta: Scholars Press, 1994.

Hock, Ronald F., and Edward N. O'Neil, ed. *The Chreia in Ancient Rhetoric: Volume 1: The Progymnasmata*. Society of Biblical Literature Texts and Translations 27. Atlanta: Scholars Press, 1986.

Hofmann, J. "Linus – erster Bischof von Rom und Heiliger der orthodoxen Kirche." Ostkirchliche Studien 46 (1997) 105–41.

Holl, Karl. "Die schriftstellerische Form des griechischen Heiligenlebens." In *Gesammelte Aufsätze zur Kirchengeschichte*, ed. idem, 2. 249–69. Tübingen: J. C. B. Mohr/Paul Siebeck, 1928.

Holzberg, Niklas. *The Ancient Novel: An Introduction*. London: Routledge: 1995.

——. "The Genre: Novels Proper and the Fringe." In *The Novel*, ed. Gareth Schmeling, 11–28.

Jacoby, F. "Hekataios." *Pauly's Real-Encyclopädie der classischen Altertumswissenschaft* 7 (1912) 2666–769.

Jakob-Sonnabend, W. *Untersuchungen zum Nero-Bild der Spätantike*. Hildesheim: Olms, 1990.

Janko, R. "Forgetfulness in the Golden Tablets of Memory." *Classical Quarterly* n.s. 34 (1984) 89–100.

Jones, A. H. M. *The Later Roman Empire*. Oxford: Oxford University Press, 1964.

Jones, F. Stanley. "The Pseudo-Clementines: A History of Research." *The Second Century* 2 (1982) 1–33, 63–96.

——. "Principal Orientations on the Relations between the Apocryphal Acts." In *Society of Biblical Literature 1993 Seminar Papers*, ed. Eugene H. Lovering Jr., 485–505. Atlanta: Scholars Press, 1993.

Junod, Éric. "Les Vies de philosophes et les Actes apocryphes poursuivent-elles un dessein similaire?" In *Actes apocryphes*, ed. Bovon et al., 209–19.

——. "Créations romanesques et traditions ecclésiastiques dans les Actes apocryphes des Apôtres: l'alternative fiction romanesque–vérité historique: une impasse." *Augustinianum (Rome)* 23 (1983) 271–85.

Junod, Éric, and Jean-Daniel Kaestli. "Les traits charactéristiques de la théologie des 'Actes de Jean'." *Revue de théologie et de philosophie* 26 (1976) 125–45.

——. *L'histoire des Actes apocryphes des apôtres du IIIe au IXe siècle: le cas des Actes de Jean*. Cahiers de la Revue de théologie et de philosophie 7. Geneva: La Concorde, 1982.

——, eds. *Acta Iohannis*. Corpus Christianorum: Series Apocrypha 1–2. Turnhout: Brepols, 1983.

Kaestli, Jean-Daniel. "Les principales orientations de la recherche sur les Actes apocryphes des apôtres." In *Actes apocryphes*, ed. Bovon et al., 49–67.

——. "Le rôle des textes bibliques dans la genèse et le dévelopment des légends apocryphes: le cas du sort final de l'apôtre Jean." *Augustinianum* 23 (1983) 319–36.

——. "Mémoire et pseudépigraphie dans le christianisme de l'âge post-apostolique." *Revue de Théologie et de Philosophie* 125 (1993) 41–63.

Kee, Howard C. "Aretalogy and Gospel." *Journal of Biblical Literature* 92 (1973) 402–22.

Kerényi, Karl. *Die griechisch-orientalische Romanliteratur in religionsgeschichtlicher Beleuchtung: Ein Versuch*. Tübingen: J. C. B. Mohr (Paul Siebeck), 1927.

——. "Rosa Söder, *Die apokryphen Apostelgeschichten*. . . ." *Gnomon* 10 (1934) 301–9.

Knoch, O. B. "Gab es eine Petrusschule in Rom? Überlegungen zu einer bedeutsamen Frage." *Studien zum Neuen Testament und seiner Umwelt* 16 (1991) 105–26.

Knox, Bernard M. W. "Silent Reading in Antiquity." *Greek, Roman, and Byzantine Studies* 9 (1968) 421–35.

Koester, Helmut. *Introduction to the New Testament*. 2 vols. Philadelphia: Fortress, 1982.

——. "History and Development of Mark's Gospel (From Mark to Secret Mark and 'Canonical' Mark)." In *Colloquy on New Testament Studies: A Time for Reappraisal and Fresh Approaches*, ed. Bruce Corley, 35–57. Macon, Ga.: Mercer University Press, 1983.

———. *Ancient Christian Gospels: Their History and Development.* Philadelphia: Trinity Press, 1990.

———. "Written Gospels or Oral Tradition?" *Journal of Biblical Literature* 113 (1994) 293-97.

Konstan, David. "Xenophon of Ephesus: Eros and Narrative in the Novel." In *Greek Fiction*, ed. Morgan and Stoneman, 49-63.

———. "Acts of Love: A Narrative Pattern in the Apocryphal Acts." *Journal of Early Christian Studies* 6 (1998) 15-36.

———. "The Invention of Fiction." In *Ancient Fiction and Early Christian Narrative*, eds. Hock, et al., 3-17. Atlanta: Scholars Press, 1998.

Kortekaas, Georgius. *Historia Apollonii Regis Tyri: Prolegomena, Textual Edition of the Two Principal Latin Recensions, Bibliography, Indices, and Appendices.* Groeningen: Bouma's Boekhus, 1984.

Kraemer, Ross. *When Aseneth Met Joseph: A Late Antique Tale of the Biblical Patriarch and His Egyptian Wife, Reconsidered.* New York: Oxford, 1998.

Kroll, Wilhelm, ed. *Historia Alexandri Magni.* Berlin: Weidman, 1926.

Kysar, Robert. "The Fourth Gospel: A Report on Recent Research." *Aufstieg und Niedergang der römischen Welt* 2.25.3 (1985) 2389-480.

Lampe, G. W. H. *A Patristic Greek Lexicon.* 5 vols. Oxford: Clarendon, 1961-68.

Lefkowitz, Mary R. "Did Ancient Women Write Novels?" In *"Women Like This": New Perspectives on Jewish Women in the Greco-Roman World*, ed. Amy-Jill Levine, 199-219. Atlanta: Scholars Press, 1991.

Lesses, Rebecca. *Ritual Practices to Gain Power: Angels, Incantations, and Revelation in Early Jewish Mysticism.* Harrisburg, Pa.: Trinity, 1998.

Lipsius, Richard Adelbert. *Die apokryphen Apostelgeschichten und Apostellegenden: Ein Beitrag zur altchristlichen Literaturgeschichte.* 3 parts in 2 vols. Braunschweig: C. A. Schwetschke und Sohn, 1883-87.

Lipsius, Richard Adalbert, and Maximillian Bonnet, eds. *Acta Apostolorum Apocrypha.* 3 parts in 2 vols. Leipzig: Hermann Mendelssohn, 1891.

Ljungvik, H. *Studien zur Sprache der apokryphen Apostelgeschichten.* Uppsala Universitet Aarsskrift 8. Uppsala: 1926.

Lord, Albert. *The Singer of Tales. Harvard Studies in Comparative Literature 24.* Cambridge, Mass.: Harvard University Press, 1960.

———. "The Gospels as Oral Traditional Literature." In *The Relationships among the Gospels: An Interdisciplinary Dialogue*, ed. William O. Walker Jr., 33-91. San Antonio, Tex.: Trinity University, 1978.

———. "The Merging of Two Worlds: Oral and Written Poetry as Carriers of Ancient Values." In *Oral Tradition in Literature: Interpretation in Context*, ed. John Miles Foley, 19-64. Columbia: University of Missouri Press, 1986.

Luttikhuizen, Gerard. "Simon Magus as a Narrative Figure in the *Acts of Peter*." In *Acts of Peter*, ed. Bremmer, 39-51.

MacDonald, Dennis. *The Legend and the Apostle: The Battle for Paul in Story and Canon.* Philadelphia: Westminster, 1983.

———. "From Audita to Legenda: Oral and Written Miracle Stories." *Foundations and Facets Forum* 2 (1986) 15-26.

———, ed. *The Acts of Andrew and the Acts of Andrew and Matthias in the City of the Cannibals.* Atlanta: Scholars Press, 1991.

———. "*The Acts of Paul* and *The Acts of Peter*: Which Came First?" In *Society of Biblical Literature 1992 Seminar Papers*, ed. Eugene H. Lovering Jr., 214-24. Atlanta: Scholars Press, 1992.

———. "*The Acts of Paul* and the *Acts of John*: Which Came First?" In *Society of Biblical Literature 1993 Seminar Papers*, ed. Eugene H. Lovering Jr., 506-10. Atlanta: Scholars Press, 1993.

———. "*The Acts of Peter* and the *Acts of John*: Which Came First?" In *Society of Biblical Literature 1993 Seminar Papers*, ed. Eugene H. Lovering Jr., 623-26. Atlanta: Scholars Press, 1993.

———. *Christianizing Homer: The Odyssey, Plato, and the Acts of Andrew.* Oxford: Oxford University Press, 1994.

———. "Is There a Privileged Reader? A Case from the Apocryphal Acts." *Semeia* 71 (1995) 29–43.

———. "Which Came First? Intertextual Relationships among the Apocryphal Acts of the Apostles." *Semeia* 80 (1997 [1999]) 11–41.

Maehler, H. "Der Metiochos-Parthenope-Roman." *Zeitschrift für Papyrologie und Epigraphik* 23 (1976) 1–20.

Magie, David. *Roman Rule in Asia Minor to the End of the Third Century.* 2 vols. Princeton: Princeton University Press, 1950.

Matthews, Christopher R. "Philip and Simon, Luke and Peter: A Lukan Sequel and Its Intertextual Success." In *Society of Biblical Literature 1992 Seminar Papers,* ed. Eugene H. Lovering Jr., 133–45. Atlanta: Scholars Press, 1992.

———. "The *Acts of Peter* and Luke's Intertextual Heritage." *Semeia* 80 (1997 [1999]) 207–22.

McNeil, Brian. "A Liturgical Source in *Acts of Peter* 38." *Vigilae Christianae* 33 (1979) 342–46.

Meeks, Wayne. "Simon Magus in Recent Research." *Religious Studies Review* 3 (1977) 137–42.

Merkelbach, Reinhold. *Roman und Mysterium in der Antike.* Munich: Beck, 1962.

———. *Die Quellen des griechischen Alexanderromans.* 2d ed. Munich: C. H. Beck, 1977.

———. "Novel and Aretalogy." In *Search,* ed. Tatum, 283–95.

Merkelbach, Reinhold, and Jürgen Trumpf. "Die Überlieferung." In *Quellen,* ed. Merkelbach, 93–107.

Merkle, Stefan. "Telling the True Story of the Trojan War: The Eyewitness Account of Dictys of Crete." In *Search,* ed. Tatum, 183–96.

———. "The Truth and Nothing but the Truth: Dictys and Dares." In *The Novel,* ed. Schmeling, 563–80.

Miller, R. H. "Liturgical Materials in the *Acts of John.*" *Studia Patristica* 13 (1975) 375–81.

Molinari, Andrea. "Augustine, *Contra Adimantum, Pseudo-Titus,* BG 8502.4 and the *Acts of Peter*: Attacking Carl Schmidt's Theory of an Original Unity Between the *Act of Peter* and the *Acts of Peter.*" In *Society of Biblical Literature Seminar Papers,* 426–27. Atlanta: Scholars Press, 1999.

———. *"I Never Knew the Man": The Coptic Act of Peter (Papyrus Berolinensis 8502.4): Its Independence from the Apocryphal Acts of Peter, Genre and Legendary Origins.* Laval: University of Laval, 2000.

Momigliano, Arnaldo. "The Historians of the Classical World and Their Audiences." *American Scholar* 47 (1977–78) 193–204.

———. *The Development of Greek Biography.* Carl Newell Jackson Lectures. Cambridge, Mass.: Harvard University Press, 1993.

Morard, F. "Souffrance et Martyre dans les Actes apocryphes des apôtres." In *Actes apocryphes,* ed. Bovon et al., 95–108.

Morgan, J. R. "History, Romance, and Realism in the *Aithiopika* of Heliodoros." *Classical Antiquity* 1 (1982) 221–65.

———. "Make-Believe and Make Believe: The Fictionality of the Greek Novels." In *Lies and Fiction,* ed. Gill and Wiseman, 175–229.

Morgan, J. R., and Richard Stoneman, ed. *Greek Fiction: The Greek Novel in Context.* London: Routledge, 1994.

Müller, C. W. "Chariton von Aphrodisias und die Theorie des Romans in der Antike." *Antike und Abendland* 22 (1976) 115–36.

Nagel, Peter. "Die apokryphen Apostelakten des 2. und 3. Jahrhunderts in der manichäischen Literatur." In *Gnosis und Neues Testament: Studien aus Religionswissenschaft und Theologie,* ed. Karl-Wolfgang Tröger, 149–82. Gütersloh: Mohn, 1973.

Nagy, Gregory. *Poetry and Performance: Homer and Beyond.* Cambridge: Cambridge University Press, 1996.

Nau, F. "La version syriaque inédite des martyres de S. Pierre, S. Paul, et S. Luc d'après un manuscrit du dixième siècle." *Revue de l'orient chrétien* 13 (1898) 39–57, 151–67.

——. "Fragment syriaque des 'Voyages' de Saint Pierre." *Revue de l'orient chrétien* 2d series, 14 (1909) 131–31.

Norelli, E. "Situation des apocryphes Pétriniens." *Apocrypha* 2 (1991) 31–83.

O'Connor, Daniel. *Peter in Rome, the Literary, Liturgical and Archaeological Evidence.* New York: Columbia University Press, 1969.

——. "Peter in Rome: A Review and Position." In *Christianity, Judaism, and Other Greco-Roman Cults: Studies for Morton Smith at Sixty,* ed. Jacob Neusner, 2.146–60. 2 vols. SJLA 12. Leiden: Brill, 1975.

Ong, Walter J. *Orality and Literacy: The Technologizing of the Word.* New Accents. London: Methuen, 1982.

——. "Text as Interpretation: Mark and After." In *Oral Tradition in Literature: Interpretation in Context,* ed. John Miles Foley, 147–69. Columbia: University of Missouri Press, 1986.

Pao, David. "The Genre of the *Acts of Andrew.*" *Apocrypha* 6 (1995) 179–202.

Parthe, Franz, ed. *Der griechische Alexanderroman: Rezension γ, Buch III.* Meisenheim am Glan: Anton Hain, 1968.

Perkins, Judith. "The Apocryphal Acts of Peter: A Roman à Thèse." *Arethusa* 25 (1992) 445–57.

Perkins, Judith. "The *Acts of Peter* as Intertext: Response to Dennis MacDonald." In *Society of Biblical Literature 1993 Seminar Papers,* ed. Eugene H. Lovering Jr., 627–33. Atlanta: Scholars Press, 1993.

——. "The Social World of the *Acts of Peter.*" In *Search,* ed. Tatum, 296–307.

Perry, Ben Edwin. "Chariton and His Romance from a Literary-Historical Point of View." *American Journal of Philology* 51 (1930) 93–134.

——. *The Ancient Romances: A Literary-Historical Account of Their Origins.* Sather Classical Lectures 37. Berkeley: University of California Press, 1967.

Pervo, Richard. *Profit with Delight: The Literary Genre of the Acts of the Apostles.* Philadelphia: Fortress, 1987.

——. "Early Christian Fiction." In *Greek Fiction,* ed. Morgan and Stoneman, 239–54.

——. "Romancing an Oft Rejected Stone: The Pastoral Epistles and the Epistolary Novel." *Journal of Higher Criticism* 1 (1994) 25–48.

——. "What Should a Well-Dressed Emperor Wear?: An Early Christian Reading of the Alexander Romance." *American Philological Association Annual Meeting.* Atlanta, 1994.

——. "The Ancient Novel Becomes Christian." In *The Novel,* ed. Gareth Schmeling, 685–711.

——. "Juggling Acts: Orientations and Principles or: Egging on the Chickens." *Semeia* 80 (1997 [1999]) 43–56.

Pflaum, Hans-Georg. *Les carrières procuratoriennes équestres sous les Haut-Empire romain.* 4 vols. Paris: Paul Geuthner, 1960.

Philonenko, Marc. *Joseph et Aséneth: Introduction, text critique, traduction et notes.* Leiden: Brill, 1968.

Plümacher, Eckhard. "Apokryphe Apostelakten." *Supplement* to *Pauly's Real-Encyclopädie der classischen Altertumswissenschaft* 15 (1978) 11–70.

Poupon, Gérard. "La Passion de S. Pierre Apôtre." Magister dissertation, Université de Genève, 1975.

——. "Les 'Actes de Pierre' et leur remaniement." *Aufstieg und Niedergang der römischen Welt* 2.25/6 (1988) 4363–83.

——. "L'Origine africaine des *Actus Vercellenses.*" In *Acts of Peter,* ed. Bremmer, 192–99.

Price, Robert M. "Implied Reader Response and the Evolution of Genres: Transitional Stages Between the Ancient Novels and the Apocryphal Acts." *Hervormde Teologiese Studies* 53.4 (1997) 909–38.

Prieur, Jean-Marc. *Acta Andreae. Corpus Christianorum, Series Apocryphorum 5–6.* 2 vols. Turnhout: Brepols, 1989.

Prince, Gerald. *A Dictionary of Narratology.* Lincoln: University of Nebraska Press, 1987.

Ramsay, William M. *The Church in the Roman Empire before A.D. 170.* London: Hodder and Stoughton, 1893.

Reardon, Bryan P. "The Greek Novel." *Phoenix* 23 (1969) 291–310.

———. "The Second Sophistic and the Novel." In *Approaches to the Second Sophistic*, ed. G. W. Bowersock, 23–29. University Park, Pa.: APA, 1974.

———. "Aspects of the Greek Novel." *Greece and Rome* 23 (1976) 118–31.

———. "The Form of Ancient Greek Romance." In *The Greek Novel A. D. 1–1985*, ed. Roderick Beaton, 205–16. London: Croom Helm, 1988.

———. *Collected Ancient Greek Novels.* Berkeley: University of California Press, 1989.

———. *The Form of Greek Romance.* Princeton: Princeton University Press, 1991.

Reiser, Marius. "Der Alexanderroman und das Markusevangelium." In *Markus-Philologie*, ed. Hubert Cancik, 131–63. Wissenschaftliche Untersuchungen zum Neuen Testament 33. Tübingen: Mohr-Siebeck, 1984.

Reitzenstein, Richard. *Hellenistische Wundererzählungen.* Leipzig: Teubner, 1906.

Reynolds, L. D., and N. G. Wilson. *Scribes and Scholars: A Guide to the Transmission of Greek and Latin Literature.* Oxford: Clarendon, 1968.

Ricoeur, Paul. "The Narrative Function." Trans. John B. Thompson. In *Hermeneutics and the Human Sciences: Essays on Language, Action, and Interpretation*, ed. idem, 274–96. Cambridge: Cambridge University Press, 1988.

Robert, Louis. *Opera Minora Selecta.* Vol. 5. Amsterdam: A. M. Hakkert, 1989.

Rohde, Erwin. *Der griechische Roman und seine Vorläufer.* 1876. 2d ed. Leipzig: Breitkopf und Hartel, 1900.

Rordorf, Willy. "Die neronische Christenverfolgung im Speigel der apokryphen Paulusakten." *New Testament Studies* 28 (1982) 365–74.

———. "Tradition and Composition in the Acts of Thecla: The State of the Question." *Semeia* 38 (1986) 43–52.

———. "In welchem Verhältnis stehen die apokryphen Paulusakten zur kanonischen Apostelgeschichte und zu den Pastoralbriefen?" In *Text and Testimony: Essays on New Testament and Apocryphal Literature in Honor of A. F. J. Klijn*, ed. Tjitze Baarda, 225–41. Kampen: Kok, 1988.

———. "The Relation between the *Acts of Peter* and the *Acts of Paul*: State of the Question." In Bremmer, *Acts of Peter*, 178–91.

Rydbeck, Lars. *Fachprosa, vermeintliche Volkssprache und Neues Testament: Zur Beurteilung der sprachlichen Niveauunterschiede im nachklasischen Griechisch.* Stockholm: Almqvist & Wiksell, 1967.

Salonius, A. H. "Martyrium beati Petri Apostoli a Lino episcopo conscriptum." In *Commentationes Humanarum Litterarum*, 1.22–58. Helsinki: Societas Scientiarum Fennica; Leipzig: Harrasowitz, 1922–27.

Sandy, Gerald N. "The History of Apollonius King of Tyre." In *Ancient Greek Novels*, ed. Reardon, 736–72.

———. "Metiochus and Parthenope." In *Ancient Greek Novels*, ed. Reardon, 813–15.

———. "Ninus." In *Ancient Greek Novels*, ed. Reardon, 803–8.

Schaeffer, Susan E. "The Gospel of Peter, the Canonical Gospels, and Oral Tradition." Ph.D. dissertation, Union Theological Seminary, 1991.

Schäfer, Peter. *Synopse zur Hekhalot-Literatur*. Tübingen: Mohr, 1981.

——. "Research into Rabbinic Literature: An Attempt to Define the Status Quaestionis." *Journal of Jewish Studies* 37 (1986) 139–52.

——. "The Aim and Purpose of Early Jewish Mysticism." In *Hekhalot-Studien*, ed. idem, 277–95.

——. *Hekhalot-Studien*. Tübingen: J. C. B. Mohr [Paul Siebeck], 1988.

——. "Once Again the Status Quaestionis of Research into Rabbinic Literature: An Answer to Chaim Milikowsky." *Journal of Jewish Studies* 40 (1989) 89–94.

Schäferdiek, Knut. "Herkunft und Interesse der alten Johannesakten." *Zeitschrift für die neutestamentliche Wissenschaft* 74 (1983) 247–67.

——. "Die Leukios Charinos zugeschriebene manichäische Sammlung apokrypher Apostelgeschichten." In *Apokryphen*, ed. Schneemelcher, 2.81–93.

Schmeling, Gareth. *Historia Apollonii Regis Tyri*. Leipzig: Teubner, 1988.

——. *The Novel in the Ancient World*. Leiden: Brill, 1996.

——. "*Historia Apollonii Regis Tyre*." In *The Novel*, ed. idem, 517–51.

Schmidt, Carl. *Die alten Petrusakten im Zusammenhang der apokryphen Apostelliteratur nebst einem neuentdeckten Fragment*. Texte und Untersuchungen n. s. 9.1. Leipzig: J. Hinrichs, 1903.

——. *Acta Pauli aus der Heidelberger koptischen Papyrushandschrift*. Leipzig: J. C. Hinrichs, 1905.

——. "Studien zu den alten Petrusakten." *Zeitschrift für Kirchengeschichte* 43 (1924) 321–48.

——. "Studien zu den alten Petrusakten: II. Die Komposition." *Zeitschrift für Kirchengeschichte* 45 (1926) 481–513.

——. "Zur Datierung der alten Petrusakten." *Zeitschrift für die neutestamentliche Wissenschaft* 29 (1930) 150–55.

——. *ΠΡΑΞΕΙΣ ΠΑΥΛΟΥ: Acta Pauli nach dem Papyrus der Hamburger Staats- und Universitäts-Bibliothek*. Glückstadt/Hamburg: Augustin, 1936.

Schneemelcher, Wilhelm, ed. *New Testament Apocrypha*. 3d ed. 2 vols. Philadelphia: Westminster, 1965.

——. *New Testament Apocrypha*. 5th German ed. 2 vols. 1989. Louisville, Ky.: John Knox, 1992.

Schott, Rüdiger. "Das Geschichtsbewusstsein schriftloser Völker." *Archiv für Begriffsgeschichte* 12 (1968) 166–205.

Schwartz, Eduard. *Fünf Vorträge über den griechischen Roman*. Berlin: Georg Reimer, 1896.

Segal, Charles. "Dionysus and the Gold Tablets from Pelinna." *Greek, Roman, and Byzantine Studies* 31 (1990) 411–19.

Selden, Daniel L. "Genre of Genre." In *Search*, ed. Tatum, 39–64.

Sellew, Philip. "Composition of Didactic Scenes in Mark's Gospel." *Journal of Biblical Literature* 108 (1989) 613–34.

——. "Oral and Written Sources in Mark 4, 1–34." *New Testament Studies* 36 (1990) 234–67.

——. "Secret Mark and the History of Canonical Mark." In *The Future of Early Christianity: Essays in Honor of Helmut Koester*, eds. Birger Pearson et al., 242–57. Minneapolis: Fortress, 1991.

——. "*Laodiceans* and the Phillippians Fragment Hypothesis." *Harvard Theological Review* 87 (1994) 17–28.

Smith, Morton. "Reinhold Merkelbach, *Roman und Mysterium in der Antike*." *Classical World* 27 (1964) 378.

——. *Clement of Alexandria and a Secret Gospel of Mark*. Cambridge, MA: Harvard University, 1973.

Söder, Rosa. *Die apokryphen Apostelgeschichten und die romanhafte Literatur der Antike*. Stuttgart: Kohlhammer, 1932.

Standhartinger, Angela. *Das Frauenbild im Judentum der hellenistischen Zeit: Ein Beitrag anhand von "Joseph und Aseneth."* Leiden: Brill, 1995.

Stanley, Christopher D. "Paul and Homer: Greco-Roman Citation Practice in the First Century C.E." *Novum Testament* 32 (1990) 48-78.

———. *Paul and the Language of Scripture: Citation Technique in the Pauline Epistles and Contemporary Literature.* Society for New Testament Studies Manuscript Series 69. Cambridge: Cambridge University Press, 1992.

Stephens, Susan A. "Who Read Ancient Novels?" In *Search*, ed. Tatum, 405-18.

———. "Fragments of Lost Novels." In *The Novel*, ed. Schmeling, 655-83.

Stephens, Susan A., and John J. Winkler. *Ancient Greek Novels: The Fragments: Introduction, Text, Translation, and Commentary.* Princeton: Princeton University Press, 1996.

Stoneman, Richard. *The Greek Alexander Romance.* ed. London: Penguin, 1991.

———. "The Alexander Romance: From History to Fiction." In *Greek Fiction*, ed. Morgan and Stoneman, 117-29.

———. "The Metamorphoses of the Alexander Romance." In *The Novel*, ed. Schmeling, 601-12.

Stoops, Robert. "Miracle Stories and Vision Reports in the Acts of Peter." Ph.D. dissertation, Harvard University, 1983.

———. "Patronage in the *Acts of Peter*." *Semeia* 38 (1986) 91-100.

———. "Christ as Patron in the *Acts of Peter*." *Semeia* 56 (1991) 143-57.

———. "Peter, Paul, and Priority in the Apocryphal Acts." In *Society of Biblical Literature 1992 Seminar Papers*, ed. Eugene H. Lovering Jr., 225-33. Atlanta: Scholars Press, 1992.

———. "Apostolic Apocrypha: Where Do We Stand with Schneemelcher's Fifth Edition?" In *Society of Biblical Literature 1993 Seminar Papers*, ed. Eugene H. Lovering Jr., 634-41. Atlanta, Scholars Press, 1993.

———. "Departing to Another Place: The *Acts of Peter* and the Canonical Acts of the Apostles." In *Society of Biblical Literature Seminar Papers*, 390-404. Atlanta: Scholars Press, 1994.

———. "Text as Tool: The Acts of Peter in its Social Context." *American Philological Association Annual Meeting.* Atlanta, 1994.

———. "The Acts of Peter in Intertextual Context." *Semeia* 80 (1997 [1999]) 57-86.

———. "Acts of Peter." In *New Testament Apocrypha*. Sonoma, Calif.: Polebridge, forthcoming.

Szepessy, Tibor. "Les actes d'apôtres apocryphes et le roman antique." *Acta Antiqua (Budapest)* 36 (1995) 133-61.

Talbert, Charles H. *What Is A Gospel? The Genre of the Canonical Gospels.* Philadelphia: Fortress, 1977.

———. "Oral and Independent or Literary and Interdependent? A Response to Albert B. Lord." In *The Relationships among the Gospels: An Interdisciplinary Dialogue*, ed. William O. Walker Jr., 93-102. San Antonio, Tex.: Trinity University, 1978.

———. "Luke-Acts." In *The New Testament and Its Modern Interpreters*, ed. Eldon Jay Epp and Goerge W. MacRae, 297-320. Philadelphia: Fortress, 1989.

———. "*What Are the Gospels? . . .* by Richard A. Burridge." *Journal of Biblical Literature* 112 (1993) 714-15.

Tatum, James. *The Search for the Ancient Novel.* Baltimore, Md.: Johns Hopkins University Press, 1994.

Thomas, Christine M. "Word and Deed: The *Acts of Peter* and Orality." *Apocrypha* 3 (1992) 125-64.

———. "The *Acts of Peter*, the Ancient Novel, and Early Christian History." Ph.D. dissertation, Harvard University, 1995.

———. "Canon and Antitype: The Relationship between the *Acts of Peter* and the New Testament." *Semeia* 80 (1997 [1999]) 185-205.

———. "Revivifying Resurrection Accounts: Techniques of Composition and Rewriting in the *Acts of Peter* cc. 25-28." In *Acts of Peter*, ed. Bremmer, 65-83.

———. "The 'Prehistory' of the *Acts of Peter*." In *Apocryphal Acts*, ed. Bovon, et al., 39-62.

Thomas, Rosalind. *Literacy and Orality in Ancient Greece.* Cambridge: Cambridge University Press, 1992.

Tissot, Yves. "Les Actes de Thomas: exemple de recueil composite." In *Actes apocryphes,* ed. Bovon, et al., 223–32.

Todorov, Tzvetan. *The Fantastic: A Structuralist Approach to a Literary Genre.* Trans. R. Howard. Ithaca: Cornell University, 1975.

Tolbert, Mary Ann. *Sowing the Gospel: Mark's World in Literary-Historical Perspective.* Minneapolis, Minn.: Fortress, 1989.

Trumpf, Jürgen, ed. *Vita Alexandri regis Macedonum.* Stuttgart: Teubner, 1974.

Tsantsanoglu, K., and G. M. Parássoglu. "Two Gold Lamellae from Thessaly." *Hellenika* 38 (1987) 3–16.

Turner, C. H. "The Latin Acts of Peter." *Journal of Theological Studies* 32 (1931) 119–33.

Turner, Eric G. *The Typology of the Early Codex.* Philadelphia: University of Pennsylvania Press, 1977.

Ussani, Vincent. *Hegesippi qui dicitur historiae libri V.* Corpus Scriptorum Ecclesiasticorum Latinorum 66. Vienna: Hoelder-Pichler-Tempsky and Leipzig: Akademische Verlagsgesellschaft, 1932.

Valantasis, Richard. "Narrative Strategies and Synoptic Quandaries: A Response to Dennis MacDonald's Reading of *Acts of Paul* and *Acts of Peter*." In *Society of Biblical Literature 1992 Seminar Papers,* ed. Eugene H. Lovering Jr., 234–39. Atlanta: Scholars Press, 1992.

van Bekkum, W. J. *A Hebrew Alexander Romance According to MS London, Jews' College no. 145.* Leuven: Peeters, 1992.

van Seters, John. *In Search of History: Historiography in the Ancient World and the Origins of Biblical History.* New Haven, Conn.: Yale University Press, 1983.

van Thiel, Helmut, ed. *Die Rezension λ des Pseudo-Kallisthenes.* Bonn: R. Habelt, 1959.

——, ed. *Leben und Taten Alexanders von Makedonien: Der griechische Alexanderroman nach der Handschrift L.* Darmstadt: Wissenschaftliche Buchgesellschaft, 1974.

Vielhauer, Philip. *Geschichte der urchristlichen Literatur.* Berlin: de Gruyter, 1975.

von Lauenstein, Ursula, ed. *Der griechische Alexanderroman: Rezension γ, Buch I.* Meisenheim am Glan: Anton Hain, 1962.

Vouaux, Léon. *Les Actes de Pierre.* Paris: Letouzey et Ané, 1922.

Warren, David H. "The Greek Language of the Apocryphal Acts of the Apostles." In *Apocryphal Acts,* ed. Bovon, et al, 101–24.

Wehnert, Jürgen. "Literarkritik und Sprachanalyse: Kritische Anmerkungen zum gegenwärtigen Stand der Pseudoklementinen-Forschung." *Zeitschrift für die neutestamentliche Wissenschaft* 74 (1983) 268–301.

Wesseling, Berber. "The Audience of the Ancient Novels." In *Groningen Colloquia on the Novel,* ed. H. Hofmann, 1. 67–79. Groningen: Egbert Forsten, 1988.

West, M. L. "Zum neuen Goldplättchen aus Hipponion." *Zeitschrift für Papyrologie und Epigraphik* 18 (1975) 229–36.

Westra, Liuwe. "*Regula fidei* and Other Credal Formulations in the *Acts of Peter*." In *Acts of Peter,* ed. Bremmer, 134–47.

White, Hayden. "The Historical Text as Literary Artifact." In *Tropics of Discourse: Essays in Cultural Criticism,* ed. idem, 81–100. 1978. Baltimore: Johns Hopkins University Press, 1982.

Williams, W. Glynn, ed. *Cicero: The Letters to his Friends.* 3 vols. Loeb Classical Library. Cambridge, Mass.: Harvard University Press, 1965.

Willis, William H. "The Robinson-Cologne Papyrus of Achilles Tatius." *Greek, Roman, and Byzantine Studies* 31.1 (1990) 73–102.

Wills, Lawrence. *The Jew in the Court of the Foreign King: Ancient Jewish Court Legends.* Harvard Dissertations in Religion. Minneapolis, Minn.: Fortress, 1990.

——. *The Jewish Novel in the Ancient World.* Ithaca N.Y.: Cornell, 1995.

——. *The Quest of the Historical Gospel: Mark, John, and the Origins of the Gospel Genre.* London: Routledge, 1997.

——. "The Jewish Novellas." In *Greek Fiction*, ed. Morgan and Stoneman, 223–38.

Winkler, John J. "The Invention of Romance." In *Search*, ed. Tatum, 23–38.

Xyngopoulos, Andreas. *Hai mikrographiai tou Mythistorematos tou M. Alexandrou eis ton kodika tou Hellenikou Institoutou tes Venetias. Vivliotheke tou Hellenikou Institoutou Venetias Vyzantinon kai Metavyzantinon Spoudon.* Athens: Hellenic Institute of Venice, 1966.

Yarbro Collins, Adela. *The Beginning of the Gospel: Probings of Mark in Context.* Minneapolis, Minn.: Fortress, 1992.

Zachariades-Holmberg, Evie. "Philological Aspects of the Apocryphal Acts of the Apostles." In *Apocryphal Acts*, ed. Bovon, et al., 125–42.

Zandee, J. "Der apokryphe Brief des Jakobus (NHC I,2) und die Akte des Petrus (Pap. Berol. 4)." *Bibliotheca Orientalis* 47 (1990) 277–89.

Zuntz, Günther. *The Text of the Epistles: A Disquisition upon the Corpus Paulinum.* London: British Academy, 1953.

Zycha, Joseph, ed. *Sancti Aureli Augustini. . . .* Corpus Scriptorum Ecclesiasticorum Latinorum 25.1. Vienna: F. Tempsky and G. Freytag, 1891.

# Index of Ancient Texts

The italic page number references contain the passage in question in its original language. In parentheses after it are the page number and line number of the Lipsius edition.

# Subject Index